Best wishes,

Pete Waldmeir

Ever the shameless panderer to people in power, Author Waldmeir grovels before President Richard Nixon during a reception in the East Room of the White House. And yes, that is Bowie Kuhn standing beside Nixon. Advised Waldmeir: "Deny everything, Dick. It always works for me." To which the prez responded, "Real funny, kid. You ought to be a writer."

"Pete's always been my kind of writer. Fair, accurate –
an entertaining story teller. His style bridges generations."
Ernie Harwell, Sportscaster

"Pete Waldmeir's column is the first thing I read in The News.
He tells it like it is. He's his own master."
Joey Nederlander, Fisher Theatre Impressario

"Nobody can poke holes in an ego or paint a word picture like Pete.
His sports stuff, particularly, still is some of the best I've ever read."
Don Canham, University of Michigan

"Pete who?"
John Engler, MSU '70

LITTLE BEADS OF BLOOD

Pete Waldmeir

GOLD LEAF PRESS

Editorial Director
Anne Abate

Research & Typing
Betty Shannon

Layout & Design
Michael J. Sklarski, Midnite Oil

Cover Design
Lisa Sabo, SMZ Advertising

Published by
Gold Leaf Press
33 Crocker Blvd.
Mt. Clemens, MI 48043

Library of Congress Catalog Card Number: 95-08108

ISBN: 1-886769-04-4
$15.95 Hardcover

For Marilyn, Lindsey and Christopher, Patti and Pete,
for their love and friendship, patience and sacrifice.
And for Mom, who worked so hard and always understood.

•

*Special thanks to Lisa and Mike, Anne and Rebecca,
who did so much to turn this turkey into a peacock,
and to Detroit News Editor Bob Giles for the permission
to reprint all this stuff.*

FOREWORD

A lot of years ago, when I was a grunt reporter trying to make a living covering any assignment that The Detroit News' sports editor of the moment wanted me to cover, I asked the late Doc Greene what it was like to write a daily newspaper column.

Doc thought a moment and then responded, "Kid, it's like being married to a sex maniac. It's fun for the first six months. But after that it's the same old routine, day after day, day after day."

Back then, it should be noted here, Doc and I both were working seven days a week the year around – jumping from baseball to football to hockey to basketball, then back again. Fun, right? A barrel of laughs. Five towns in five days was never unusual. Maybe Christmas off. Maybe not.

Wife? Family? Who were they? Whadaya want? A job and a life, too? Get real.

Words churned out of ancient, loud, clacking typewriters were handed over to Western Union operators who – and, with God as my witness, this is true – sometimes even sent them by Morse code (you know, dot dot dot, dash dash dash dash) back to the office in Detroit. Thousands of words. Millions of words. So many words I can't even hope to remember even a small number of them.

So when it came time to pull together this representative selection of my most recent 23 years of columns, I had to laugh.

"Give us the best of Pete Waldmeir," they said. "Take a couple of days and dig through your files and come up with 100 or so examples of your most provocative, humorous, spiteful (etc.) works from the pages of The Detroit News and we'll put them into a book and your fans will snap them up."

Well, now, even I know that last part's baloney. But so's the first.

For one thing, there is no "Best of Pete Waldmeir." And even if there were, I'd be the worst judge of which columns to include.

This book, my friends, contains a collection – a sampling, if you will; a small number of columns that I found interesting or entertaining, and figured that you might find them interesting or entertaining, too. Some to make you laugh, some to make you cry. Some to make you think, if only for a few moments, about what our existence here is all about.

I must admit here that I was forced to struggle mightily to resist the urge to make this a collection which might be titled, "Pete Waldmeir Does Hizonner." I think I succeeded. There are the obligatory slams, digs and humorous and remorseful musings concerning former Detroit Mayor Coleman Alexander Young's 20-year reign.

But there is life after Coleman, you know. And we'd probably all be better off to get on with it.

There are those who will tell you that I would have been nothing – just another nothing, at that – if I hadn't happened along at the time when Hizonner landed on the Detroit political scene with both feet, kicking and swearing. There's probably a germ of truth to that.

He sure did make the job a lot easier for a lot of years. But there were others, too, who deserve at least an equal share of credit for helping my career along – folks big and folks small. Victims of crime and abuse. Pompous judges, dishonest politicians, murderers, robbers, mobsters, hookers. Dogs, kids.

Life is a huge allegorical mural. Each time I write, I snip out a tiny piece and try to explain why it's there.

And about the title. For that and for a million other pleasant memories, I owe a debt of gratitude to the late Walter Wellesley "Red" Smith, sports columnist extraordinaire, who once labored for the old New York Herald-Tribune and later The New York Times and was one of the finest writers of his or any other generation.

One day our conversation turned to the technique of writing a daily newspaper column. I allowed as to how I like to arrange my notes in order, on numbered pages, fanned out around the keyboard so that I might find the highlights more easily. And I blabbed on endlessly about how I customarily try this lede, then that lede, then another and another before I finally find just the right one and am able to get into the meat of my work.

"So much for me," I said at length. "What's your system?"

"Well," Red responded, smiling, "I generally lock myself in my room, put a blank sheet of paper in the typewriter and wring my hands until little beads of blood appear on my forehead."

Little beads of blood, I thought.

A great title for a book.

Pete Waldmeir

November, 1995

CONTENTS

PART I

1972 - 1982

Pages 11 - 132

PART II

1983 - 1995

Pages 133 - 224

PART I

It's a new ball game

May 1, 1972

Observing that I had switched this dodge from one page to another, a newspapering friend interrupted the nursing of his fire-brewed libation long enough to insert a gentle needle.

"Welcome," he said, "to the real world."

The inference, of course, was as plain as the egg on Edmund Muskie's face. Having spent the better part of the last 20 years watching grown men play children's games for money, I supposedly now have been liberated.

Funny. It doesn't feel much different at all.

Oh, there are likely to be some "pointy headed intellectuals" to be heard expounding their theories on everything from constitutional reform to the joys and benefits of acupuncture. But the only real difference between these actors and Joe Schmidt, I suspect, is that no one is required to pay $7.50 to watch them perform in public.

My interest, however, goes beyond these visible and sometimes very loud characters. There must be more to life than social extremists and football coaches.

It has been a long and affectionate relationship, my love affair with the sports department of this newspaper – one which I am certain will never entirely be severed.

No need, really, to sever it.

At this point I shall resist the temptation to deliver "Game of Life" sermon No. 42 because it's a lot of baloney. Life's no game for a lot of people. Too many are sick and jobless and oppressed and without hope.

That is not to say, however, that there can be no humor amid the travail of our day-to-day existence; that the sad clown with his tired long face cannot be the most entertaining performer in this perpetual three-ringed circus.

The last few days a lot of well-intentioned friends have asked what sort of column I'm planning to write and who am I intending to write about? There appears to be no simple answer.

Those of you who have been subjected to this daily nonsense for the last few years have me pretty well pegged by now. My thing generally has been people. And there is little reason to change now.

Events and discoveries, after all, are merely reflected in the lives of those who experience them. Industry, politics, education, labor, sports – it makes little difference. They all require human resources.

Frankly, I figure that the occupants of and movers in the so-called "real world" will be hard-pressed to measure up – for pure entertainment – to some of the oddballs with whom I've been fencing for the last 20 years.

Suffice to say that I'll be happier than Tom Adams in a riverfront stadium if Roman Gribbs and Frank Ditto turn out to be half as entertaining and challenging as, say, Denny McLain and Muhammad Ali have been in the past.

But of course Gribbs and Ditto aren't in the entertainment business. And I'm interested in whatever business it is they're in.

Detroit is my town. I was born, raised, schooled and otherwise turned out here. I've seen the first home I can remember – an apartment house at Fourth and Ferry – turn into a slum tenement and then into a parking lot.

Every time I remember that neighborhood I think of golfer Lee Trevino's crack about being raised in a Mexican-American ghetto in Texas. "My family was so poor," Trevino said dourly, "that we couldn't afford a mother. The lady next door had me."

We were infinitely more fortunate. We could afford a mother and we had a good one. She was 70 yesterday and some day I'll tell you about her, if you're nice.

There are other people and places and events that deserve more than a glancing shot and as time passes we'll linger together over some of them.

From time to time I'll even dig out the old felt hat with the press card in the band and slip into a sports story. If the hat still fits.

And so, as Mickey Lolich sinks slowly in the west, we bid adieu to the Toy Department and dive headlong into the mail sack. What's this? A letter from Lou Gordon?

"Dear Pete," it begins. "Welcome to the 'straight' world."

To which I can only answer, "Lou, baby, if you're in the 'straight' world, I wonder what the curved one looks like?"

The tribulations of a smut store

June 20, 1972

Y ou don't get service with a smile in Curly Hakim's cozy little bookstore out Jefferson on Detroit's far east side.

"This," says Hakim, "is a serious business. We don't want the customers to think we're laughing at them.

"Actually, the joint's real quiet all the time. Like a library."

The marquee that juts out over the narrow sidewalk proclaims the establishment as the "Moulin Book Shoppe." There is, however, nothing Dickensian about the racks that line the walls inside.

It's porn, baby. Hard-core pornography.

Curly stationed himself behind a counter that sits on a riser along one wall of the long, narrow room. The room is divided into two sections.

The front one-third is used to display the usual newsstand wares – newspapers, racing forms, paperback novels and a wide assortment of magazines.

The back two-thirds, however, is where the action is. To gain entry, you must pass between Curly's checkpoint and a wall partition and you are supposed to leave a 75-cent deposit, which can be credited against any purchase you might make.

"Shoplifters," said Curly, scowling. "That's to discourage the lifters in the back. There for a while they were killing me. I caught one guy one day with 40 magazines tucked into his shirt front.

"He was working with another guy and a broad. The broad would engage the clerk in conversation and the other two would boost the material from the shelves.

"I couldn't figure out where all that stuff was going. You know, you lose 40 books at $5 a pop, that's a lot of money. Good looking bunch of people, too. But that's not unusual. We get a lot of high-class dudes in here."

The smut business in Detroit is only about three years old. The Moulin Book Shoppe was one of the first. It underwent all of the growing pains (neighbors picketing, throwing bricks, etc.) and remains in business on a virtual day-to-day basis, its shatter proof plexiglas windows shuttered at night.

There are 26 to 28 similar book stores operating in Detroit and its environs today. Church groups, irate citizens and the law keep trying to close them down. But somehow they stay.

"We get a real mixed clientele," says Curly. "But it's not all factory guys. I'd say the bulk of my customers have money.

"Most shops only get 5 to 10 percent women. We get 25 percent."

The Moulin Book Shoppe is located only a couple of miles from the Grosse Pointe Park city limits.

"We're far enough into Detroit so that the people from up there will shop here," Curly explained.

"If it was closer to the suburbs, the suburban people wouldn't come in because they'd be afraid of being seen.

"People are funny. That's what I mean about smiling or laughing when they're in the store.

"I can usually tell who's gonna buy and who ain't. If four guys come in together, for instance, they'll go in the back and browse. And you'll hear them laughing and joking with each other.

"No sale. They're all afraid to buy and let the other guys know. But chances are they'll all come back – alone. That's the way it is in this business."

Like most porn dealers, Curly feels he is being harassed by the police.

"As soon as one thing gets cleared up," he says, "they hit me with another.

"But you learn one thing. You never plead guilty. Pornography is what people think it is."

Apparently, the law thinks dealing in porn is worse than, say, being a burglar.

Several months ago, a shipment of porn films consigned to Curly's store was broken into. When the police investigation was finished, they had caught and released the thief – but charged Curly with illegal transportation of dirty films.

In a store full of hard-core smut, what's the best-seller?

"For a long time it was this one," Curly explained, lifting a copy of "The Sensuous Woman" from a book rack. "But lately it's tailed off.

"The big one now is this one – 'The Happy Hooker.' Every time that Xaviera Hollander goes on a TV show someplace, they come in here in droves and empty the racks."

Even a little humor in a 17-story fall

August 18, 1972

There is little that is funny about falling 17 stories from a scaffolding to an asphalt parking lot, but artist Tony Rich can see a bit of humor in some of his misery.

Like the stumble-bum, covered with paint, who was taken to the hospital in the same ambulance after Tony fell some 200 feet from the side of the First National Building in downtown Detroit last September.

"I never met the guy," Tony explained, "but they tell me he was some kind of sight.

"Apparently this is what happened.

"I was up on the scaffold with my partner, Dave Newsome, working on that giant mural and when the cable broke, I grabbed the lifeline and slid part way down it. Meanwhile, the paint cans tipped over and started to pour through the air.

"While I was hanging on the rope for a couple of minutes, a crowd gathered below me in the parking lot. And this bum came staggering out of a bar and stood there watching.

"Well, the falling paint must have hit him and knocked him to the ground. And after I fell the 17 stories, the ambulance attendants picked him up, too, assuming he was the other man on the scaffold.

"Newsome had crawled to safety through a window, however.

"They tell me that the guy created some furor in the emergency room at Detroit General. They couldn't figure out why he smelled of booze and how he managed to survive the fall without any broken bones.

"Finally, he told them his story and they cleaned him up and let him go."

That is one incident which is certain to find its way into Tony Rich's book – the one he plans to write as soon as he gets his head together and figures out what he's going to do next.

"I've got two volumes of notes right now," explained the 27-year-old artist from Portland, Me.

"And a lot of them have to do with people from this town – Detroit. You know, I think, the people here are about the kindest and most considerate

I've ever met anywhere in the country.

"After I fell last September I spent several weeks in the intensive care unit at Detroit General and then several more months in the Detroit Rehabilitation Institute. It probably sounds corny, but I think one of the reasons I was able to fight this thing was the hundreds of cards and letters I received from people.

"Listen, I'm no kid. I'm 27 and I've been a pretty hip guy all my life and, well, at first I didn't pay much attention to all that stuff people wrote about how they were praying for me.

"But after awhile it started, to sink in. Man, somebody must have been praying . . . or hoping, or wishing or whatever.

"Looking back on it now, I'm sure I couldn't have made it as far as I have without knowing that those people all were pulling for me so hard."

Tony's in a wheelchair now. There are periods when he can walk, with leg braces and crutches, but he'll be in and out of that chair for the rest of his life. He's searching now . . searching for the right way to go.

One thing he's certain of, however, is that he's going to stay in Detroit.

"I wasn't even here long enough to know the names of the streets in this town before my accident," he explained. "I had been in Montreal, where we'd done four of those wall murals.

"At first I wasn't even going to work on this one. The first day I looked at the size of the job – a 25-story building? – I told the guy I worked for there was no way I was going up on that scaffolding.

"Then I got to thinking about it. This is the largest mural ever painted in the whole world. And I was going to work on it. That convinced me. But oddly enough, once I started I felt that it would be my last wall painting.

"I mean, what do you do after that?"

What's next? Tony's an outpatient at Rehab and he spends two hours each morning working on his legs, trying to make them strong enough to handle the crutches instead of the chair.

He receives $79 a week from Workers' Compensation ("Thank God I fell in Michigan," he says. "In a lot of other states, I'd be on my own.") and he's bought a 1964 Olds with hand controls and has rented a roomy apartment.

Tony stiffened his arms and raised his body several inches off the seat of the wheelchair.

"You know, I was a pretty fair athlete, too," he said. "I used to ski and play tennis pretty well. That's what I'd like to do – figure out a way to play tennis.

"If I could hold myself up with my left hand on a rail or something and hold the racquet in my right hand . . ."

Don't bet against it.

But who'd believe it?

February 23, 1973

OK, let's see – we've got to have our first $1 million Michigan Lottery winner. What should he look like?

We'll make him middle-aged, say 53. He ought to come from somewhere around Detroit, because we sell most of the tickets down here. An auto worker? That's stretching it a bit, but we ought to be able to get away with it.

He'll have a wife . . . we'll call her Ann. She'll be short, about his height, and she'll wear a cloth coat and clutch a brown shopping bag.

They have three . . . no, make it five . . . kids.

How about a nice name, something with a twang to it. Like it belongs to a transplanted Southerner, perhaps from Tennessee, maybe a guy who came to Detroit during World War II to work in the auto plants and just stayed on.

Herman? No, Hermus. That's better. Got a better ring. Miller? Mulligan? I've got it. Millsaps.

Hermus Millsaps Jr. That's our guy.

Now for a town. Warren? Too middle class. Hamtramck? A guy like Hermus Millsaps wouldn't live in Hamtramck. It's got to be lower-middle, a worker's town. River Rouge?

Trenton? Taylor? That's it. Taylor.

He'll work at Chrysler. That's a Detroit, sort of hometown factory. Not on the assembly line, though. That's stretching credibility too far. How about a millwright? No, they earn too much.

A sawhand would be better. A sawhand who also can double as a "specifier." After all, our man Hermus Millsaps Jr. has been with Chrysler for 23 years!

He'll have to need the money. Not like we all need a million bucks. He'll have to be down on his luck, owe lots of bills, have an ex-wife, a rundown car and a new house to pay for.

We'll have him live in a matchbox, five-room place in Taylor that's got only one bedroom. He'll have just made the down payment and he'll need more . . . man, always more . . . to pay for it.

What's a sawhand make? Would they believe it, do you think, if we had him hourly rated so he grosses $176.80 a week and takes home $90 or $100 at tops after taxes, Social Security, union dues and the rest of the checkoffs?

We could get away with that, I guess.

Now for the car. It ain't much. The way I see it, it's a 1961 sort of wreck that's patched together with lots of wire and plastic putty and stuff. Tires are bad. Just about bald.

So bad (heh . . . heh) that he can't drive to Lansing for the superdrawing.

So how will we have our Hermus Millsaps and his wife Ann get to the Civic Center? Why, they'll take a Greyhound bus.

Don't tell me that's more than the people will believe. It could happen. It's possible.

Now, how does he get to the superdrawing and have the shot at the semifinal round of 120 and the final round of 10 contestants?

We want to promote the lottery, so we'll have him say later that he bought three or four tickets every week . . . "Mostly wherever I happened to be shopping." "The winning ticket will be from a gas station. No, wait a minute.

Too many people read about that guy who ran a gas station and had all the daily winners. They'll think it's fixed. How about a saloon?

That's plausible. Later on in the script we could explain how Hermus, divorced, and Ann, a widow, had met in a bar in Dearborn where she liked to polka and, as she says, "he's a hillbilly and he'll do anything."

On second thought, a bar's out. Gov. Milliken doesn't much care for gambling, let alone drinking. Our first model millionaire winner can't be a barfly.

A drugstore's more his speed. Preferably one in his hometown.

I've got an idea, but I really don't think you'll go for it. How about if, after Hermus and Ann Millsaps arrive in Lansing Thursday morning, they kill time by shopping in the dime store for a rabbit's foot?

After all, Hermus doesn't own anything that's lucky. He won $70 in the check pool once at the plant. And Ann won a quart of motor oil a long time ago when she didn't have a car.

Do you think they'd swallow the story if it was a chartreuse-colored rabbit's foot? No way, eh. Well, just a plain rabbit's foot sounds so blah.

We'll have him up on stage with the other 10 finalists and when it gets down to just him and, say, a red-haired woman, he'll just stand there smiling like he doesn't believe it when they give the woman the $100,000 and assure him of the million bucks.

When we ask him to say something to the crowd, he'll take the microphone in a wavering voice and say something like, "I appreciate what the lottery did. I'm still going to buy tickets. God bless the ladies and gentlemen here and God bless you . . ."

Won't sell, you say? Well, give me some time to think about it and I'll see if I can't come up with a more believable story.

God Bless America

March 1, 1973

DAYTON, Ohio – There were chuckles all around when Navy Capt. Jeremiah A. Denton Jr. called the good-to-excellent physical and mental condition of himself and most of this country's other returning POWs held in Hanoi a "tribute to American vigor and self-esteem."

Had to he preprogrammed, right?

What else would you expect from a Navy type hard hat? Red, white and blue underwear?

So a guy is locked up in a prison camp for five, six, seven years and you expect us . . . the suave, sophisticated American public . . . to believe that he comes out patriotic, eager to thank rather than condemn his country and his president?

Sure thing, pal. And would you by any chance have a nice used bridge for sale?

I guess what I'm trying to say is that I'm a little bit ashamed of myself. See, that's what I thought, too.

I figured that these guys had to he kidding when they scampered down from those hospital planes in the Philippines and started all that "God Bless America" stuff.

What kind of a man would spend 7 1/2 years penned up in a North Vietnamese prison compound eating rice and all that crud and feeling his teeth rot out of his mouth and then, when asked to make his first public utterance to the free world, would THANK the people who helped put him there?

I'll tell you what kind of man.

My liberal friends are going to gag on this one, but it takes a brave man to say the kind of things that were said, for instance, by Air Force Lt. Col. Robert B. Purcell at Wright-Patterson Air Force Base near Dayton this week.

When Purcell's F105 Thunderchief jet fighter was struck by a SAM missile on a bombing run over Vietnam on July 27, 1965, the girls back home in Louisville were wearing beehive hairdos.

Dr. Spock was writing baby books and Jane Fonda was the reigning Miss Air Force Recruiting. Dr. Christian Barnard was still setting fractured limbs, only musicians were smoking grass and Mary Jo Kopechne couldn't even spell Chappaquiddick let alone consider going to a party there.

While Lt. Col. Purcell languished in his cell in the "Hanoi Hilton," doing push-ups and staring into his tin cup for entertainment, an entire new order was being drawn and redrawn in this country.

Picture, if you will, missing the last seven years of the 6 o'clock news and then trying to hold a conversation in which your companions mention Kent State, Charles Manson, the "Chicago 7," Tom Eagleton – or Joe Namath " taking it all off."

Or The Pill, or Hot Pants, or Biafra, or Bangladesh.

A "bummer" was a kid with his thumb out on the street corner, a "pig" was where you got your bacon and "gay" was the way you felt when you had four drinks and forgot to have dinner.

"I think what has changed most for me," said Purcell, measuring his words like they were ounces of gold, "is the exterior color and decor of America.

"I had been briefed about things changing on the outside. And frankly, I had been mentally prepared for much bigger changes than I have found."

But it is what he withstood in captivity rather than what he missed at home that lends credibility to Purcell's words.

Pressed to describe his overall reaction to 90 months in the Hanoi pokey, Purcell said that the final two years were "the most wonderful experience" of his life.

He said he was extremely fortunate to be leading a group of 49 or 50 Americans for a couple of years and that the rewarding experience came in "watching those wonderful men react to various stimuli."

I think that where you and I get lost in all this is somewhere under the mountains of rhetoric to which we have been subjected in the last 10 years. First the hawks unload, then the doves countercharge. We've been getting it from all sides – each side overreacting in direct proportion to how vehemently the other overreacts.

Unfairly, we assign to men like Lt. Col. Purcell motives that they are incapable of holding. They don't know what we know. They are unencumbered by the tons of verbal baloney that has been dished out by all sides in the Vietnam War debate.

Sure, most POWs are hard-hat types to begin with. If they weren't, they wouldn't have been bomber and fighter pilots. But they have had time in captivity to do little else save sit and think – about the war, about themselves, their families, their country.

When it came to expressing themselves, nobody had to put words in their mouths. And we judge them poorly if we accuse them of being puppets.

A gentle harlot

April 25, 1973

Bad news from the north country today. The only dog I ever cared about has died.

My pal Jets was a tough old girl and she lived a long and enjoyable life, by her standards at least. If there's a dog purgatory, she's probably in it.

But she's high on the waiting list to move up.

Jets was a pure bred English setter, normal size for a female, which isn't too large. Bob Stahl brought her home to the house next door in the spring, 11 years ago, the year his youngest daughter, Tammy, was born.

Naturally, I was afraid of Jets from the very beginning. She was lively and developed a healthy bark and my bravery vanished quickly as she began to grow.

But there was something about Jets that set her a cut above other dogs. She was possessed of a certain gentleness.

It might have been because she was blind in one eye, the victim of a stoning by one of the neighborhood brats when she was a pup. Bob had wanted to train her to hunt until then, but when she lost part of her sight he abandoned those plans.

Instead, she became the neighborhood harlot.

Now that is a tough thing to say about a girl with such a soft heart, but unfortunately it was the truth. Jets, it seemed, just never learned to say no.

As soon as she reached puberty, or whatever it is that English setters reach, she began to have puppies. Dozens of them.

She became a walking advertisement for unplanned parenthood. The ZPG people would have drummed her out of the ranks years ago.

I don't know for certain how many times a year English setters are capable of reproducing, but if it's three, then Jets had 33 litters. The fathers Jets wasn't particular about. She had more casual affairs than Xaviera Hollender. And it is to her credit that she'd never kiss and tell.

Jets not only had a way with the guys, she developed some strong relationships with people, too.

Bob never kept her tied up, so she roamed the neighborhood freely. She would come to the patio behind my house and crawl under my chair in the shade and lay quietly by the hour if I would touch her ears or rub her back.

She would lay on her side under the picnic table feigning sleep. But an unheard sound could set her off and, without so much as a growl, she would be on her feet and dashing wildly toward the woods across the street.

It might have been her walk that turned on the guys. She was very slim and erect and she padded softly on large, graceful feet, with her tail protruding proudly erect. I often wondered, watching Jets, at the symmetry with which God creates His animals.

She was a terrible mooch. Bob owned a butcher shop then, but I swear that Jets did not take two meals a week at home. She was dogdom's version of America's guest.

If she wasn't begging at the patio door during dinner at my house, she was up the street hanging around one garage or another waiting for a handout.

The only thing she enjoyed more than making love, it seems, was digging into a pile of T-bone steak scraps.

One afternoon I was barbecuing in the backyard and caught her up on the picnic table trying to snatch a hunk of meat off the hot grill.

She had some spunk, that one.

Just about a year ago Bob decided to pack it in here, sell his house and his business and move his wife and five kids up north. The Stahls had summered for several years at a cottage on Lake Leelanau at Cedar and Bob added a couple of rooms and away they went, Jets included.

You know those stories about dogs finding their way home from far away places? Well, I sort of expected Jets to come prancing down the street a couple of months after the Stahls had moved.

My vanity. I figured she'd miss me.

But she loved the woods and water and the fresh, clean air and she never looked back.

A couple of weeks ago she delivered (what else?) another litter. This one was small, only two puppies. And then she developed heart worm and began to mope around.

Bob took her for treatment, but it was too late and she died. One of his daughters called me and I talked to Bob.

"I guess she found a boy friend up there all right," I said. Bob laughed.

"Let me tell you about it," he answered. "There was this time last winter in the middle of a snowstorm . . ."

A marked man

July 26, 1973

It was 1 o'clock in the afternoon and I was working the day shift out of The News' mezzanine. The phone rang.

"Waldmeir?" asked a man's voice. I thought a minute.

"Yep," I answered.

"Listen," the voice continued, "I'm a white cop in a ghetto precinct and anybody will tell you that I'm one of the best cops in the city.

"But I'm too honest and somebody's threatened to kill me. I want to talk to you."

I thought for another minute. I'm not a mortician, I reasoned, so it is doubtful that he wants to talk to me about funeral arrangements.

I was in the middle of a tough game of solo tick-tack-toe when he called, and I was in a hurry to get back to it. I named a time and place: 4 p.m. at a downtown bar. I figured that if he had lived this long he'd probably keep another three hours.

"I'm on my way to the bank to take out my money and give it to my mother," he said, sotto voce. "I'll be there at 4."

At 3:45 I sauntered into the appointed saloon and, I thought quite cleverly, chose a corner booth where one with his back to the wall might watch both doors for potential assassins. I ordered a Smirnoff screwdriver and nervously checked my Pulsar computerized wrist watch.

Promptly at 4 the door swung open and he walked straight to my booth. Correct that. He waddled to the booth.

"Bulletproof vest," he said, unbuttoning his suitcoat and tapping his chest. "Normally I only wear it on the job, but I've got it on all the time now."

He slumped back in the chair and as he did his suitcoat fell open even more. I spotted two familiar woodgrain handles protruding from his waistband.

"I have a magnum here," he said, patting the right side of his belly, "and a .38 over here. Carry them all the time. Got a whip in the car, too," he said, and a smile crossed his face.

Doesn't everybody, I thought.

The waiter noticed the addition to my table and strolled over to ask the mobile arsenal what he'd like to drink.

"Bring me a daiquiri on the rocks," he said. "And a Blatz beer, too."

"You expecting company?" I asked.

"Nope," he answered. "I drink the Blatz for a chaser."

I glanced at my watch again. It had taken exactly three minutes to figure out that my mystery guest was wacky. How long, I wondered, would it take to get out of there.

I cleared my throat. "Ah, how long have you felt that somebody was trying to kill you and who is it?" I asked, attempting to make conversation.

"Lemme tell you the whole story," he answered.

Peachy, I thought. Just peachy. Exactly what I need on a hot afternoon is this guy's whole story. There was, however, very little I could do about it.

You tell me how you go about dumping a cocktail partner who wears a bulletproof vest, carries two pistols tucked in his belt AND has a whip in his car.

The story was not only long and involved. It kept changing.

He was a ghetto copper, all right. One night a few months back he was paired with a black partner who, he explained, went into a dope house to "get his income tax done" and didn't come out for 90 minutes.

"I turned him in for leaving me alone in the car that long," said Pancho Villa, "and when I did that he threatened to 'get' me."

Now "get" and "kill" don't necessarily mean the same thing, I reasoned. If he wanted to kill you, wouldn't he have had ample opportunity to make his move by now?

The arsenal smiled, drained the daiquiri glass and ordered another with a beer chaser. "Bring him one, too," he told the waiter.

"None for me," I said, screwing up my courage. "It's after 4 and I haven't written my column yet. Some guys have to drink to be able to write," I said, attempting a joke. "I have to drink AFTER so I can bear to read it."

When the check came, he grabbed it and paid it. I insisted that we split it and he agreed. Then he put two bucks on the table. "If you can name four major league baseball players who played in each of the last four decades," he said, "I'll pay the tip. If not, you pay."

I mumbled something about not being able to remember what I had for breakfast, tossed down the $2 and bailed out. The arsenal was still naming old baseball players as I left.

Joe Don Looney

July 27, 1973

It was the summer prior to the 1965 pro football season and the Detroit Lions were rushing headlong toward disaster while still in training camp at Cranbrook in verdant Bloomfield Hills.

Their rising young star was a 23-year-old half-back named Joe Don Looney, who had come to the Lions from the Baltimore Colts after a checkered football career that had covered four colleges and three professional teams in less than six years.

The Lions' coach was Harry Gilmer and he was having his share of problems. It was to be Joe Schmidt's final year as the team's premier middle linebacker and everyone who was anyone knew that Schmidt was marked for bigger things, perhaps even head coach someday. Much of the Lions' hope for success, however, rested on the strong legs and broad back of Looney. But on this particular afternoon, young Mr. Looney had barricaded himself in his room in one of Cranbrook's residence halls and had refused all pleas to come out.

Looney, it seems, was in a snit over the fact that the Lions had "cut" from the roster a rookie named John Flynn, who just happened to be Looney's best friend in all the world.

Now Joe Don was no dummy. He knew that the Lions were banking heavily on him to rescue their sagging football fortunes. He knew also that they were not likely to punish him too severely for pouting.

He was, of course, correct on both counts. Gilmer was in trouble. Looney wouldn't come to meals or to practice and the rest of the natives were getting restless. So the head coach asked the grizzled old veteran Joe Schmidt to have a talk with the young man.

"I could hear his record player going full blast in the room," Schmidt recounted later, "and I had to bang on the door to get him to open it.

"Finally Joe Don let me in and we sat down and I talked to him like a Dutch uncle.

"Listen, Joe Don, I said, you just can't he missing meals and practice like this. I know Flynn is your buddy, but there are only so many places on the roster and the coaches have to cut some guys off.

"This is a team game, you know. We rely on each other. Why I've been with this team for 13 years and . . ."

Looney held up a hand. "You been here that long, Joe?" Looney interrupted. Schmidt nodded.

"You know, Joe," Looney said, "you really ought to take a day off once in a while."

Ah, those were the good old days . . . back when Schmidt was having fun in his work. The game sort of went downhill for him after 1965.

It takes a temporary upturn tomorrow when Schmidt, recently retired after six years as Lions' head coach, is inducted along with Ray Berry and Jim Parker into pro football's Hall of Fame in ceremonies at Canton, Ohio.

Schmidt was the perfect guy to send to see Joe Don that evening in 1965. He was tough and smart and seasoned and loose, the best damned defensive football player in the game and that covered an awful lot of territory.

And he could laugh, at himself as well as at others.

Joe Don's rejoinder, in fact, cracked up Schmidt so bad that he had to leave the room. "What the hell do you say to a kid who lays one on you like that?" Schmidt asked later.

Joe served as an assistant to Gilmer for two years then took over as head coach for another six. He wasn't good and he wasn't bad. Worse, he was mediocre.

It all might have been rather enjoyable regardless, if he'd been able to maintain that sense of humor. But somewhere along the line, Joe's ability to touch life's funnybone got sidetracked.

When he was a player, Herr Schmidt thought a coach ought to run a team like Sgt. Schultz. After he took over as head man, he decided he would run it like Martin Bormann.

It is a curious commentary that while searching a memory that spans nearly 20 years in sports hereabouts for humorous anecdotes about Joe Schmidt which might suit this auspicious occasion, the guy who comes to mind instead is Joe Don Looney.

It would have been interesting to see what Schmidt might have done to Looney. I shall never forget the infamous afternoon in September 1966, when Looney, having been pulled out of a game in disgrace by Gilmer refused later to carry a play into quarterback Milt Plum.

"If you want a messenger," Looney told Gilmer flippantly, "call Western Union."

If he'd said that to Schmidt, chances are they'd still be finding pieces of Joe Don in the upper deck at Tiger Stadium.

As the years dragged by, the Lions amassed a considerable roster of players who had fallen into disfavor with the head coach. They called it the "Schmidt List."

Joe Don could have been No. 1 on that hit parade. Easy.

Assembly-line blues

August 1, 1973

The current round of contract talks between the UAW and the auto companies stirs considerable nostalgia in these old bones. Assembly-line boredom, the blahs, blue-collar blues – I had them all before they became stylish.

Back in those days "job enrichment" meant working the day shift on the final assembly line at the Chrysler Jefferson plant and afternoons in the trim shop at Briggs on Mack Avenue.

"Job humanization" occurred on those nights when you didn't sleep in your car in the parking lot. And "30 and Out" meant how many ice cold beers you could drink following a steamy afternoon shift before you keeled over.

Now before you get all uptight, I'm not laying the "work ethic" on you. It was a simple matter of economics.

World War II had been over for only a year or so when I first was blackjacked into the UAW. Then, like now, things were pretty tight financially for a kid with bad grades who was working his way through high school.

You had to be 18 to get a job on the assembly line, but they needed workers and the personnel people did a lot of looking the other way.

I was only 16, but my buddy's dad got me a forged birth certificate. I rationalized the lie rather easily. After all, his pop was a policeman, wasn't he?

The summer of '47 brought my first experience on the line. I worked afternoons at Briggs in the trim shop, installing right-front windows in right-front doors.

The money was good although the working conditions left something to be desired. Years later I complained about them to the late Walter 0. "Spike" Briggs Jr., but I don't think he ever really listened.

Anyway, it was hot in June, July and August and the line moved at about 35 cars an hour. After the first 500 or 600 right-front windows in right-front doors, I was tempted to put them in upside down or backward just to see what the foreman would say.

Lunch break became a very big deal.

I packed my own and, I must admit, I got into something of a rut. Each day I would take four slices of bread, butter them and cut enough fat slices of Velveeta cheese to make two sandwiches.

Each sandwich then was liberally spread with grape jelly, wrapped in wax paper and placed in a bag.

By the time lunch break arrived the grape jelly had soaked through the bread, turning the entire sandwich a beautiful shade of purple. The *piece de resistance*, of course, was a carton of chocolate milk to wash it all down.

I was always partial to stuffing my leftovers into exotic places like inside the doors of the cars so that they would be tougher to locate once they started to smell.

Briggs was full in the summer of '48 and since my work record was not what you might call exemplary I applied at the Chrysler Jefferson plant, where I was put to work installing batteries on the final assembly line.

Now there was a man's job. They presented me with a rubber apron and a mallet and led me to a spot on the line where a man was working feverishly grabbing batteries off a greased steel-topped table and sliding them under the hoods of cars that appeared to be moving at least 20 miles an hour down the line.

"We'll do every other car today, kid," the man explained "But you better learn fast, because tomorrow you do 35 and I do 35."

It sounded great. Work an hour, take an hour off. Like most get-rich-quick schemes, however, it had some holes in it.

For one thing I found that I had difficulty doing 35 cars an hour and I was constantly behind in my work. The next man down the line was installing horns and he soon grew weary of leaning over me as I rode fender after fender into his station.

In a week I had the routine down pat, however, and I caught up on my reading the rest of the summer.

Toward the end, however, boredom led to experimenting and then to adventure. Tired of playing the numbers, tired of reading, tired of the long philosophical conversation with my inner-city buddies, I began to fool around.

What would happen. I wondered one day, if I put the negative cable on the positive battery pole and vice-versa? From my greased table vantage point I could see the end of the line. That is where they turn the key for the first time, fire up the engine and turn on all the electrical switches to check them out.

So I put one in backward. Then another. And another. And I sat back to watch what happened.

Smoke happened. Lots of smoke. Sparks, too.

At least I didn't have to eat those damned purple sandwiches anymore.

Happy Times

November 2, 1973

There is no evidence that the late Damon Runyon ever worked for the old Detroit Times but if he had he surely would have collected enough characters to author six more novels.

Runyon had Nathan Detroit down pat all right. But he missed Jack Manning and Jim Trainor, Butch Batchelor and Bud Goodman, Frank Morris and Jerry Petit and at least a dozen others who could spot that fictitious character from "Guys and Dolls" two days, a fifth of Scotch and six points and beat him at any game he cared to name. Nov. 7 will mark the 13th anniversary of the demise of The Times. The News bought the paper in 1960 and folded it.

The first few years afterward the old Times' staffers got together each November for a party. But it always was more like a wake than a reunion – a bunch of guys weeping over a paper that, while staffed by colorful people, never was the great journalistic effort they all thought it was.

A week from tonight they'll huddle at the Detroit Press Club to swap stories. A lot of them are gone now and a lot of them are doing better than they ever did.

But all of them remember . . .

Manning, the managing editor, who had a compassionate streak a half-mile wide because, well, because he was a reporter once himself.

Guys who missed work, particularly if they had been stuck in a gin bottle for a couple of days, were supposed to be "docked" pay. But Manning had another system. He kept a mental record of the time his men owed him for their indiscretions and allowed it to be made up on weekends and holidays.

"I got lost in Cleveland on one assignment," recalls Batchelor, "and I guess I fell asleep in the lobby of a hotel. The cop who awakened me didn't do it very gently and I got unruly and the next thing I know I'm in the can and my eyes are black and my clothes are torn.

"When I finally got back to Detroit three days later I dreaded having to face Manning because I knew he was really going to read me out.

"But he took one look at my black eyes and my cut lip and he says, 'You've been punished enough, Butch. This one's on the house.'

"The day The Times folded, Bud Goodman owed Manning two days, work. Bud called him the next morning and offered to come out and shovel Manning's walk."

Tony Weiss recalls that the Times' chief copy reader was named Monroe and he always wore a straw hat. One night he came in stiff and sent his hat to the composing room. Pinned to it was a note which read, "Head to come."

Petit was assistant city editor under Trainor and he always was impeccably dressed. One day he arrived with a hangover and was considerably bent out of shape. Trainor was furious.

"Get out of here and don't come back until you've had a shave and a haircut," Trainor ordered. Petit obeyed.

Three days later Petit called long distance.

"What the hell are you doing in Chicago?" Trainor demanded.

"This is where my barber lives," Petit answered calmly.

Petit was working The Times' city desk one night when Hank Shurmur and Doc Greene brought a white stallion downtown for a tour of the local saloons. In time they decided to load the horse into The Times' freight elevator and take it upstairs.

When they arrived, Petit was on the telephone attempting to quiet an irate reader. "I'm sorry, madam," he said at length, "but I'll have to hang up now. A horse is nibbling at my ear."

That was one of the few nights when Petit was around. Most of the time he passed his hours in Slim McClellan's old Ringside Bar on Times Square or in the Chandelier Room of the luxurious Lindell Hotel. Don Morris, the night copy boy, frequently was left to guard the fort.

When the time came for young Mr. Morris to take his test as a reporter, Petit balked. "What the hell do you need to test him for?" He asked angrily. "He's been city editor for three years."

Frank Morris was The Times' revered political writer and when he became particularly unruly or obnoxious Trainor simply refused to speak to him. One day Morris arrived in the city room with a pawnshop trombone, which he had purchased on a tour of Third Street bistros.

Morris perched at the telephone switchboard and honked on the battered instrument until Trainor's ire was sufficiently aroused. Trainor called the operator.

"Tell Mr. Morris I'd like to see him, please," Trainor said to the operator. She delivered the message.

"Tell Mr. Trainor," Morris answered, "that this is my day off."

There are, of course, a million stories, some true, some fiction.

In the early days of TV, for instance, Trainor is said to have been sitting in his office watching his tube when he spotted Batchelor scoot out of the Federal Building, cross Lafayette and duck into the Tuebor Bar. Trainor had him paged before Butch hit the stool.

It was Manning, however, who delivered my all-time favorite one-liner. He had disappeared in Chicago while covering a political convention and his bosses called, had him paged, left messages at his hotel and the press room.

Finally, after three days of fruitless searching, a telegram arrived in Detroit from Reporter Manning.

"It always has been my contention," it read, "that the office should seek the man."

The Gypper

December 17, 1973

The prospect of a new professional football franchise for Detroit stirs fond memories of the somewhat haphazard foundation of the old American Football League (AFL).

Harry Wismer, Bulldog Turner, Gene Mingo, Wahoo McDaniel – how are those for names from the past?

Wismer was the operator who put together the old AFL with string and glue and baling wire and borrowed money. Mostly lots of borrowed money. He founded the New York Titans in 1959 and dug up a Texas multimillionaire named Lamar Hunt and talked Hunt into helping to form a pro football league in opposition to the established National Football League (NFL).

Ah, the Titans. What a mob they were when they opened their first season in New York in 1960 before a rousing crowd of 9,000. Sammy Baugh was the head coach and Bulldog Turner was one of his assistants.

"Our crowds were so small," recalled Claude "Buddy" Young, the tiny former Illinois All-American who was one of the original Titans' players, "that we didn't need a public address announcer.

"I told Wismer what we should do is have the players run up into the stands five minutes before the game and shake hands with everybody."

At the conclusion of his first season of operation, Wismer announced the Titans had played before 114,628 customers at home, which prompted one New York sports writer to remark that "half of them came cleverly disguised as empty seats."

Wismer, a former Michigan State student who once worked as a part-time announcer at WJR in Detroit, lived in a Manhattan apartment on Park Avenue, which doubled as the Titans' headquarters and offices. The football team's ticket office was located in a closet, through which one had to pass to get to the bathroom.

"We had all sorts of trouble with the paychecks those first couple of years," Buddy Young recalled. "Wismer would write them all right. But they'd bounce when we tried to cash them.

"There was one string when we hadn't been paid for several weeks and a team meeting was called before an important game. One of the guys got up on a bench in the middle of the locker room and made an impassioned speech about how we'd all let Mr. Wismer down by losing so much and how we ought to dedicate this game to him.

"'Let's go out there today,' he said very emotionally, 'and win this one for the Gypper.'"

By 1962, Wismer had not only worn out his welcome with New York football fans, he'd also worn out his credit. Baugh had been fired and Bulldog Turner, the old-time NFL center, had taken over as coach.

"Bulldog didn't know much about football," Young said, "but he knew a lot about money. One day when the checks arrived before practice, Bulldog called us all together to hand them out, then told us to take one fast lap around the field and head for the bank."

When the Titans went bankrupt in 1962, Wismer reported they had attracted 36,161 fans for their season at home. That wasn't their average – it was their total for the year.

The Miami Dolphins suffered similar growing pains when they came into the AFL in 1966. Comedian Danny Thomas was one of the original owners and I thought for a long while that founding the Dolphins was one of the funniest jokes Thomas ever pulled.

The Dolphins' training camp that first year was located at St. Petersburg, Fla., but they moved after a few days because the players were being constantly distracted by girls in bikinis. Besides, the practice field had been laid over a bed of crushed seashells.

The camp was moved to Boca Raton, where the Dolphins' management promptly made a deal with an oriental restauranteur to cater the training table. Wahoo McDaniel, one of the team's early stars, had enough after the first week.

"If they serve chicken chow mein one more night," Wahoo wailed, "they'll have to wheel me to practice in a rickshaw!"

The Dolphins, of course, were awful their first year and finished with a 3-11 won-lost record. You can't say they weren't thrillers, however.

One game, for instance, ended in a 19-18 loss to the powerful Kansas City Chiefs when the Dolphins' place-kicker Gene Mingo missed three field goals from inside the Chiefs' 17-yard line. Anxious to prove that performance was no fluke, Mingo tried one in a subsequent game from the half-yard line and hit the cross bar on the goal posts.

Both the Dolphins and the Titans ran up huge financial deficits in their first years of operation.

In New York, a drug store chain refused to bring aspirin, tape or other medical supplies to the Titans' training room unless the delivery man was paid in cash. In their first year, the Dolphins were threatened with a cancellation one week when the dry cleaner refused to deliver their game uniforms unless his back debts were paid.

The Dolphins' iceman, likewise, refused to come in unless he got the money in front. And Head Coach George Wilson even delayed cutting players from the roster because the front office didn't have the money to buy plane tickets so they could be shipped home.

The recollections are humorous now. But there is one thing that isn't funny. Both the Titans (sold in 1963 to Sonny Werblin who renamed them the Jets) and the Dolphins have made it big in pro football despite their modest beginnings. Both have been to the Super Bowl and won – which is more than the Detroit Lions can boast.

There is a temptation among Detroiters to scoff at the franchise recently awarded here by the new World Football League. I would caution the doubters, however, not to laugh too hard just yet. The Dolphins and the Titans proved that stranger things have happened.

Hatful of rabbits

January 3, 1974

Clyde Cleveland wore his old tuxedo with the narrow lapels. Erma Henderson's fluffy chiffon dress made her look a little like an overweight Loretta Young.

At 5:45 p.m. Council President Carl Levin, who seems addicted to baggy pants, announced with a wry smile that the "Council is organized" and sent Erma and doddering old Tigers' shortstop Billy Rogell into the wings to fetch Coleman A. Young, the city's first black mayor, to his swearing-in ceremony.

"It may be the only time all year that I can say we are organized," said Levin. But the quip was lost on the serious crowd, which had fought icy temperatures and snowy streets to get to Young's official Inauguration in Ford Auditorium yesterday afternoon.

And so was ushered in a new era in Detroit politics.

Coleman Young . . . we shall wait to pass judgment on him. I give him six months to get organized, a year to find all the holes and fall into them.

It is not how gracefully he falls, however, but how deftly he manages to climb out.

Circumstances could not be worse than they are right now for any political animal. Why do you suppose Ray Gribbs got out?

The energy crisis and the general run of events in Washington have the economy in a nose dive. Last week GM announced 68,000 layoffs. You can bet that Chrysler, Ford and a hundred suppliers in and around Detroit are planning some similar moves.

With the economy skidding, crime is certain to rise. And as crime goes up, people move out and tax collections dip.

Detroit doesn't need a mayor. It needs a magician. And as hip as Coleman Young may be, he didn't pull many rabbits out of the hat in a long career in Lansing.

"He'll buy some time," said former Detroit Mayor Jerry Cavanagh, who is running hard for the Democratic nomination for governor and who came to the inaugural to make certain that he was seen by the downtrodden city folk.

"That's about all a big city mayor can do these days – buy time until things get better," Cavanagh added somewhat gratuitously.

Coleman Young, however, doesn't look like a man who is shopping for anything. And he certainly doesn't talk like one.

Young talks of attacking inflation on the one hand and joblessness on the other. He says he's fed up with crime in the streets, with dope pushers and ripoff artists and muggers.

"It's time to leave Detroit" is his stern warning to them. "Hit Eight Mile Road.

"I don't care if they're black or white," the mayor told the inaugural crowd, "if they're wearing Superfly outfits or blue uniforms with silver badges . . . Get goin'!"

If the same words had been shouted by his mayoral opponent, John Nichols, the crowd would have been on its feet hollering to toss the honky out on his ear. But when the message comes from Coleman Young, some people listen.

Not all the people, however. And therein may lie a stumbling block.

Take the City Council for instance.

The present makeup has four blacks – Cleveland, Nick Hood, Erma Henderson and Ernie Brown – and five whites – Jack Kelley, Dave Eberhard, Rogell, Maryann Mahaffey and President Levin.

There is no absolute guarantee, but Mayor Young likely will be able to count on the black bloc to back his programs foursquare. Mahaffey and Levin are liberals and ought to vote with the blacks.

Kelley, Eberhard and Rogell are the potential obstructionists.

The Young people perhaps count too heavily on support from the man in the street. They point to Coleman's 14,000-vote victory over Nichols as if it were a mandate to go forth and do what he damned well pleases.

It is not, of course. The victory was narrow and the only mandate anyone has is to do his best to save a city that is color-blind in its poverty, crime and a multitude of urban problems.

One thing, unfortunately, haunts Young. In recent months "politician" has become a suspect word in the English language – a word synonymous with graft and cheating and corruption. But Coleman Young is a politician in the true sense of the word.

He knows the mechanizations of making politics work. It is, after all, a profession and not a game. It is give and take.

Political people have a major stake in their own actions. They have precious little protection except their record. They give favors, certainly. But they also collect debts.

I do not decry the fact that Coleman Young is a seasoned politician. On the contrary, I'm glad of it. Ray Gribbs never understood the profession of politics. And Jerry Cavanagh, perhaps, understood it too well and let it get away from him.

Yesterday was a long day for Coleman Young. It began with a 7:30 a.m. prayer breakfast in Cobo Hall and ended last night with a concert by the Detroit Symphony Orchestra and Diana Ross. The first two numbers played by the symphony were titled "Fanfare of the Common Man" and "A Lincoln Portrait," and I could understand the symbolism.

I wonder, however, if the next work – "Dance of Vengeance" – held a message for anybody in particular.

A little old lady's plea

January 28, 1974

They come to the supermarket in pairs, shuffling through the automatic doors and over to the long row of steel carts that are jammed together telescope-fashion in front of the windows.

The men wear baggy pants, felt hats and mackinaw jackets, faded gray wool sweaters that button down the front. The women come in dark cloth coats that are too long, and they wear rubber overshoes with narrow heels.

They struggle with the carts, arthritic fingers often so crippled that it takes the two of them to pull one free. And then they set off down the long, lonely aisles that each week bear fresh disappointments for people who live on what the statisticians choose to call "fixed incomes."

Each section of the store is carefully perused. Labels are studied, sometimes for weight, sometimes for content, always for minutes at a time. Which is the better buy – 14 ounces for 79 cents or 12 ounces for 63 cents?

A bar of soap lasts maybe three weeks, a box of facial tissues a month if you are careful. And if you can find either one. Beans . . . a bag of white Michigan beans. You can do a lot with them.

But what's this? A month ago the beans were 49 cents a bag. Today they're 79 cents. The bag goes back onto the shelf.

Butter? Forget it. Meat? Well, maybe a small roast this week. They didn't take one two weeks ago. It'll stretch for two meals at least and then there are sandwiches and perhaps a small pot of stew with the bone and the scraps.

You watch them and honest to God you want to cry.

The elderly are prisoners . . . prisoners of a runaway economy. Oh, they are free to roam about . . . if there is somewhere to go that's free. And they are free to buy – if they have money left over from the pension check after rent and heat and light and the necessities are paid.

The other day, one of the little old ladies with the too-long coats looked up from studying a label and told a 40-year-old housewife who had happened down the same supermarket aisle, "You know, someone ought to do something about these prices.

"We're too old and too tired to fight. But young people have done it before. You have the strength and the nerve. You have to help us."

She wasn't demanding assistance. She was not asking for a gift or a loan – or even for more money in the pension check. What she wants is for people to know.

And knowing, for someone to care.

The conversation was related to me by the wife of a friend. "How could I tell her," she said, "that I'm not one of those 'young people' she's talking about? I'm strapped just like she is."

The problem is that we all are strapped by inflation. Like the travail of the elderly, it is too far above us. And let's face it: Neither of them are very romantic causes.

Busing – now there's an issue that can prompt housewives to walk to Washington and grown men to chain themselves to schoolyard fences to dramatize their complaints. Or break windows, or slash tires. Or blow up buses.

The Vietnam War was conducted 10,000 miles from Carmel Hall but Detroiters traveled to Washington by the thousands to demonstrate against it in front of the White House.

The Chicago Seven, the Harrisburg Nine – hell, together they got more publicity than the Indianapolis 500. Priests and ministers railed from their pulpits against the injustices of an "immoral" war and then made their point by breaking into draft board offices and spilling goat's blood over records.

Time was when the roar of the crowd ruled just about everywhere. People who couldn't tell Abbie Hoffman from Abbe Lane fell into chanting conga lines and snake-danced across America, griping about the war, the smog, the POWs, even the genesis of a head of lettuce.

When the ecology was threatened, an army was mounted to battle the demons of pollution. But then rescuing a cuddly bunny or a slender sapling is more fulfilling than squaring off against a bureaucratic windmill that is likely to box your ears.

If I sound a bit bitter, perhaps I am. The old woman talked about "young people" needing to carry the fight against inflation, the high cost of living, the plight of the elderly. I, too, am wondering where they are these days.

Could it be that the cause is not personal enough, that they are guilty of the very crimes for which they indicted others during the struggles for ecological enlightenment and against the war – acquiescence and apathy?

Fighting pollution is a "Robin Hood" cause. It is popular and easy to take from the rich and give to the poor when the air you are taking is free and fresh and the air you are giving is mostly hot.

And struggling against the injustices of an unpopular war, which has gone on far too long and has cost everybody far too much in money and lives, is less difficult, too, when it carries with it the threatening menace of a military draft that is likely to snatch your fanny off to a rice paddy.

Sociologists and armchair psychologists look at college campuses today and explain that they are quiet because we have a new generation of students. But that's only partially correct. No one will be drafted, no harbor mined, no village full of innocent civilians napalmed if that little old lady can't afford a bag of beans or a quarter-pound of butter this week.

The mayor's protectory

February 1, 1974

The noise in the reception room at the mayor's office grew louder and louder. Finally, Hizonner called in an aide to ask what was going on.

"I'm sorry, Mr. Mayor," the harried aide said, "but there's another batch of criminals out there who insist that they will surrender only to you personally. Frankly, we don't know how we're going to deal with them all.

"They've been arriving in a steady stream for the last two days. We just sent a busload over to Recorder's Court, but everytime we manage to get the room emptied they fill it up again."

The mayor walked to the door and opened it a crack. There were perhaps 50 of them waiting, lounging on the sofas, sitting on the floor, studying the French-language magazines in the waiting room. One of them spotted the mayor and the chant started. "We want Coleman, We want Coleman . . ."

The mayor shut the door quickly.

"Wake up my press aide and get him in here right away," the mayor shouted. "This whole business is getting out of hand."

Within minutes the mayor's office was filled with his staff.

"Listen," said press secretary Bob Popa, "just because I'm the biggest guy here doesn't mean that I'm going to throw all those people out of the reception room. I'm no bouncer, you know."

The mayor shot him a withering glance. "Let's get one thing straight," he said. "We are not going to brutalize anybody in that waiting room. I got my head whupped when I was young and I know how it feels.

"What we need are ideas to solve this problem. I mean, it was a great publicity stunt when I let that young man from the Harper-Van Dyke gang surrender to me the other day, but I had no idea that every hoodlum in town would read the story and come traipsing in here to ask me to personally guarantee his safety from the police.

"Now let's get our heads together," the mayor said. "Jerry, what do you think?" His eyes searched the room for Police Commissioner Jerry Tannian, but he was missing.

"Tannian will be back in a few minutes," Popa explained. "He personally drove the last busload of prisoners over to Recorder's Court. The TV guys wanted some pictures."

"I hired him to run the Police Department, not to be a bus driver," the mayor grumped. "We need him here to make decisions. What about Superintendent Bertoni?"

"Angelo's in the Wayne County Jail," another aide answered. "Been there since the day before yesterday."

"And what, may I ask, is the superintendent of police doing in jail?" the mayor said through clenched teeth.

"Frankly, Mr. Mayor," the aide answered, "we just plain ran out of police officials to assign to personally accompany each of the criminals who have surrendered to you in the last two days.

"I don't want to say 'I told you so' but I warned you that there might be trouble when you ordered the 11th Precinct commander, Inspector Frank Blount, to make himself personally responsible for the safety of that kid who gave himself up on Tuesday.

"You set a precedent with that order. There are only 80 inspectors in the entire department and we used them all up on the first day we started accepting surrenders and granting safe passage from police brutality.

"When the 80 inspectors were gone we assigned the 18 division commanders. And when they ran out we used the seven chiefs. The last guy left in the rank of inspector and above was Bertoni and you know him – he wouldn't ask his men to do anything he wouldn't do himself."

"But why is Bertoni in the Wayne County Jail?" the mayor asked. Before anyone could answer the telephone rang.

"Coleman?" the voice asked. "Bill Lucas here. Listen, we've got a problem over here at the jail. We've managed to put all the prisoners who surrendered to you into two-man cells with the 80 inspectors, 18 division commanders, seven chiefs and Superintendent Bertoni. But the rest of the inmates are beginning to demand equal treatment. Do you have any inspectors left?"

The mayor slammed down the receiver, but it rang again immediately. This time it was his liaison man with the City Council.

"Things are getting a little rocky over here, Mr. Mayor," the liaison man reported. "The Council is upset about all that publicity you've been getting with the surrenders. I think they'd like to get into the act.

"Nobody has said anything, but I think you could score some points if you sent a few of those hoods over here. Say you let a few of the Irish crooks surrender to Jack Kelley. And maybe the women could give themselves up to Erma Henderson or Maryann Mahaffey.

"Hold the line a minute, sir . . . my other phone is ringing."

The aide was back on the line in a few seconds. "What did I tell you? That was Billy Rogell. He wants to know if any of those people happen to be ex-baseball players?"

The mayor hung up and another aide entered. "I think we've hit the jackpot this time, your honor," he said. "There's a computer expert outside who says he's on the FBI's 10 Most Wanted list." The mayor smiled and rubbed his hands.

"Step aside, my man," he said, "I'll handle this one personally."

The aide frowned. "I don't think you can deal with him, sir," he said. "The man says he wants to give himself up to George Edwards III, the former city clerk. He says he owes George a favor."

Young Billy Bonds

February 20, 1974

When Billy Bonds broke in as a radio newscaster and disc jockey back in Albion in the late 1950s, he earned $1 an hour plus a $5 bonus for sweeping out the station three times a week.

A few weeks ago, he turned down a $77,000-a-year offer to anchor a two-hour nightly news show for NBC-TV in New York and instead signed a three-year contract that will pay him $80,000 this year and $85,000 the next two years to stick with WXYZ-TV, Channel 7 and the ABC-TV network.

"I remember back when I was working in Albion and still trying to get my degree from the University of Detroit," said Bonds, 41, the co-anchorman with John Kelly on Channel 7's nightly news. "I'd go over to Channel 4 and try to talk to Dick Westerkamp, who was the big man here then, but he wouldn't give me the time of day.

"Sonny Eliot was the only veteran guy who was nice to me and he helped me a lot. For one thing, he told me to get out of town and make a name for myself."

Bill Bonds does, indeed, have a name that is easily recognized in Detroit television. Unfortunately, he also has a face that frequently has been too familiar for his own good, particularly in the local pubs.

"I don't know what people expect," said Bonds. "You work most of the day getting the show together, then you've got to be 'up' for the appearances at 6 and 11 p.m. When it's over you can't go straight home and hit the sack.

"A guy gets all wound up. So I used to go out and have a couple at night. But not anymore. It's too much of a hassle. You put 100 people in a room and they'll have 100 different versions of what I said and what I looked like.

"So week nights I just go home and read. It's easier that way."

Billy comes by his reputation as a good-natured rounder honestly. That, in fact, may be precisely what makes him the best TV newsman in all of Happy Valley.

Like Sonny Eliot, Bonds is a homegrown product. He grew up in the neighborhood around 12th and Burlingame, one of six children of an advertising exec named William Bonds. To say he attended school in Detroit is an understatement.

Bonds went to Visitation, Blessed Sacrament, Catholic Central and Berkley High before he quit school in the 12th grade.

"School bored me," said Bonds. "I thought all that memorizing was a lot of nonsense. I wanted the teachers to give me reasons for theories and they kept telling me to be patient. Finally I said to hell with waiting and joined the Air Force."

Bonds says he entered the service to fight the North Koreans and ended up spending 4 1/2 years battling the system instead. "My brother Dick and I both went into the Air Force as privates. I came out a buck sergeant and he came out a colonel."

Bonds got his high school diploma on tests and enrolled in political science at U of D in 1955. Before he graduated in 1959, he says, he had been engaged several times but never made it to the altar.

"I think I spent the first 24 years of my life trying to figure out what I didn't want," Bonds recalled smiling. "I kept getting engaged to girls I didn't like. It was sort of a compulsion."

Finally one came along he did like – his wife, Skippy, who also is a U of D graduate. And the couple were blessed with four children in their first 22 months of marriage. The eldest, Joanie, is now 10. John is 9 and the twins Kris and Mary – are 8.

"We never had to worry about not eating meat on Friday," Bonds said wryly. "Or fish either, for that matter."

Bonds quit the Albion job after his graduation and worked for enough Detroit-area radio stations to fill a case of alphabet soup – WQTE, WPON, WCAR, WKNR – before WXYZ-TV hired him as a "street" reporter in 1965.

From there it was only a short step to co-anchorman on the nightly news with Bonds' old buddy, Barney Morris, and the pair distinguished themselves, particularly during the 1967 riots. Two years later ABC-TV whisked Bonds away to Los Angeles, where he anchored another news show until he got into a beef with the local management and they yanked him off the air one night, never to return.

Meanwhile, things were not going too well for Channel 7 back in the old hometown. So ABC moved Bonds back to Detroit in 1972. Depending on whose figures you choose to believe, the Bonds-Kelly Channel 7 nightly news rates either first or second in this market area.

Several serious questions, of course, have been posed by Channel 7 viewers. Like, is it true that Bonds and Kelly really do not get along off camera?

"I'd have to say that John and I agree 95 percent of the time on news treatment," is the way Billy escapes that one. It is plain, of course, that there is a conflict of egos. And I'd venture a guess that Bonds – with his hefty 80,000-a-year stipend – has the upper hand over Kelly right now.

Frankly, Bonds could care less what Kelly or anybody else thinks. He has his eye upon, and has been tentatively promised, a shot at the host role on a new ABC-TV national morning news show (ala "Today") that is scheduled to begin next January. And if not that, well, Howard K. Smith should be retiring pretty soon.

"And if those things don't happen," said Bonds, "I think I'll go into national politics. Maybe run for senator. I've got a lot of questions I'd like answered and I think there are enough other people who feel as I do. Besides, if Teddy Kennedy is qualified to hold public office, I certainly am."

We had been lunching and Billy dropped me at my car in the early afternoon and said he was headed for his office. "How long," I inquired, "does it take to put together the 6 o'clock news?"

"It takes at least four hours a day," Bonds answered, straightfaced, "to slant all that stuff objectively."

Wearin' the green

March 12, 1974

Councilman Jack Kelley handed Coleman Young a fifth of Bushmill's Irish whisky and placed a bright green cap on the mayor's head. "I hereby declare you an honorary Irishman," Kelley intoned.

Young looked at Kelley and, smiling, rolled his eyes.

A small crowd had gathered in the conference room adjacent to the mayor's office in the City-County Building to witness the official proclamation of "Irish Week," which begins today and endures through next Sunday – St. Patrick's Day.

Kelley, the Council's resident professional Irishman, and Young, the city's first black mayor, hit it off quite well in their first public encounter.

"If you would honor us at our parade next Sunday," said Kelley, "we'll have a green Cadillac for you to ride in, Mr. Mayor." Young grinned. "Just as long as it isn't a green Pinto," he said.

Kelley yielded the floor to the parade's "Maid of Erin," a pretty young lass named Mariann Dooley, whose greeting to Young ended with an excerpt from an ancient Irish prayer. "May the wind always be at your back, Mr. Mayor," she said, "and for you and all the people of Detroit, let the good times roll."

Young glanced at Kelley. "Frankly," he said with a wry smile, "it's not the wind I'm worried about."

The ceremonies finished, Kelley engaged Young in a bit of amicable small talk. Referring to the mayor's much-publicized recent illness, Kelley observed that if Young continued to suffer from the flu "you're gonna turn white."

The mayor smiled. "That's one way of solving the problem," he answered.

He ain't exactly Redd Foxx or Flip Wilson, but Coleman Young has shown in the first 70 days of his administration that he has the ability to laugh at himself as well as with others.

The "honorary Irishman" ceremony could have turned into a skirmish with Kelley, who knows more about using a needle than a lot of acupuncture specialists. But Young successfully parried the gentle thrusts and resisted the temptation to answer them with verbal sword play.

It could be that the mayor was in shape for the joust, having recently scored his first minor triumph as a standup comic before the Detroit Press Club's annual "roast" at the Raleigh House.

It should be pointed out here that normally all remarks made before the Press Club's "Steak out" audience are strictly off-the-wall as well as off-the-record. However, Young's press secretary, Bob Popa, passed along a transcript of the mayor's remarks with permission to publish excerpts from them.

Be advised that they were made entirely in jest. I think.

Following a promise that he might soon sign a "proclamation" declaring the proper pronunciation of p-o-l-i-c-e to be "PO-lice," Young alluded jokingly to the fact that he is having difficulty getting his "100 Day" program off the ground.

"We were delayed," he told the audience, "by a widespread talent search that ranged all the way from 12th Street to Woodward – uncovering few qualified whites. Bob Popa was the only one we could look up to. We gave him a one-question test: Spell 'Renaissance.'

"We had to pass him. We didn't have anyone who could correct his paper."

Young noted some "drastic changes" in city jobs. "Ed Davis," he said, "doesn't know why he was fired as head of the DSR. But The Shadow do. It had nothing to do with philosophy. He simply refused to make Joyce Garrett Miss DSR for January."

Mayoral assistant Malcolm Dade, Young remarked wryly, is an example of the high quality of his present staff. "He found coal in Hazard, Ky.," Young said. "Hell, Jack Kelley could find coal in Hazard, Ky."

Young hailed Detroit as remaining a land of opportunity. "Where else," he asked, "could a boy grow up in the ghetto and by conscientious application of his talent get to surrender to the mayor?"

Hailing "great strides" in his relations with the Police Department, Young quipped that "it won't be long before you'll be able to call any one of 50 police mini-stations and get a busy signal . . . I really don't object to criticism from the DPOA," he added, "but I do resent being referred to as 'The Dark at the Top of the Stairs."

Young jokingly called on the "cop who planted the watermelon" in the backyard at Manoogian Mansion to come dig it up. "And while he's at it," the mayor added, "he can take the pink pelican, that was left by the previous tenant, off the lawn."

Not even the police hierarchy escaped a good-natured poke. "You may have noticed," Young remarked, "that Officer (Frank) Blount entered a plea of guilty to 39 parking tickets, received a suspended sentence on all of them and was promoted to inspector – all in the same week. In this administration, virtue is its own reward."

As for Police Commissioner Jerry Tannian's support of gun control legislation, which Young opposes, the mayor stuck the needle in to its hilt. "Tannian," he said, "is going to find out that his job requires more than his personal charisma.

"Commissioner Tannian and I had a little disagreement over gun control," Young added, "but I'm sticking to Sandy Levin's point of view: Guns don't kill people. Schwartzes kill people!"

And so it went, on and on.

The overflow crowd laughed with Young as well as at him. Gov. Milliken made a few remarks and didn't come off badly himself.

"We Republicans," the governor concluded with mock seriousness, "can see the light at the end of the tunnel. Unfortunately it's a freight train bearing down on us."

Hizonner strikes out

March 19, 1974

I'm disappointed in Coleman Young. I expected him to conduct the business of running Detroit with more class.

I figured Young to be the kind of alert guy who would surround himself with people of knowledge and know-how, black and white. I had him pegged as a man who would move carefully but surely; a guy who would be streetwise but political enough to know that you can't play the Big Con with an entire city and get away with it.

But I'm beginning to wonder.

Young's first 80 days in office have not exactly established his reputation as a statesman. He has been intemperate in his own remarks on the one hand, and has approved of the same sort of conduct by at least one other member of his administration.

Another thing that disturbs me about Hizonner: Apparently he is sicker than the electorate was led to believe, both before and after the November election.

Young, we were informed last week, long has suffered from chronic emphysema, a disease of the lungs that makes him highly susceptible to respiratory problems. Translated, that means be gets a lot of colds, flu and other, more serious, ailments connected with the lungs and chest.

He has missed a lot of work because of illness.

Now, nobody expects the mayor or anyone else to drag himself to the job when he's sick. But when a guy runs for a public office that demands as much personal attention as being mayor of the nation's fifth largest city, it strikes me that the electorate might at least be informed that he's not exactly Vic Tanny when it comes to his health and physical well-being.

Obviously, Young's illness was a well-kept secret. Now that he's in office and can relax for four years, his advisers talk about the emphysema as if the voters knew about it all along but chose to ignore it.

As for Coleman's first 80 days, he's done some good things and he's done some dumb ones. In some cases even the good ones managed to look dumb when he was finished.

Take the fulfillment of his campaign promise to abolish STRESS, the plainclothes police detail that used to troll for criminals in the inner city and too frequently served as judge, jury and executioner rolled into one.

A cornerstone promise of Young's campaign against John Nichols was to broom STRESS just as soon as possible after he set up shop in the City-County Building. That, of course, was the mayor's prerogative.

But Young could not resist the temptation to toss an extra harpoon when he issued the order disbanding STRESS. All policemen, the mayor said, are racist by nature. That was a cheap shot.

Young seems to have a penchant for inflammatory remarks. Perhaps he makes so many offhand statements because during his long career in the State Legislature he could talk to the walls and nobody paid any attention.

Detroit, however, is not Lansing; the city is not his legislative district and the mayor gets listened to a lot more carefully than some senatorial windbag.

A good example of the mayor's conduct rubbing off on his subordinates was the outburst this weekend by James W. Watts, the Young-appointed commissioner of the Department of Public Works. Watts charged that the Civil Service Commission is discriminatory in hiring practices in order to keep blacks in low-paying jobs.

"If the blacks knew what was going on in this town," Watts trumpeted, "they would burn it down."

Gee, that's swell. In his inaugural address, Mayor Young issued a warning to criminals and rip-off artists to "hit Eight Mile Road." A few more loudmouths like James Watts and there'll be a helluva traffic jam at the border.

And they won't all be wearing Superfly outfits.

Maybe it's just poor judgment on the part of the mayor's advisers. It is said that he listens to some bad advice from well-meaning but inexperienced people. But things that would not ordinarily rate remembering, seem to stand out.

Like the surrender of that young east side gang member a few weeks back.

The kid obviously was afraid that the coppers would do him up if he turned himself in at 1300 Beaubien. So he arranged to surrender to Mayor Young.

The cameramen were on hand, naturally, and the young hoodlum and the old gray mayor made a pretty picture. But Young took the opportunity to sock it to the coppers again. "I don't want this young man brutalized," he intoned. "I remember getting my head whupped by the police when I was a kid."

That was cheap shot No. 2. It was as if he was still campaigning for votes in the black community. You're in, Coleman. Give it a rest.

The ultimate in poor judgment, of course, is Young acquiescing in the naming of Joyce Garrett to a $30,000-a-year job as executive director of the Detroit Bicentennial Commission.

Now, Mrs. Garrett doubtless is qualified to handle the job. She speaks at least three languages, one of them being English. However, she's also been linked romantically to Mayor Young by Mayor Young himself.

It has been argued that there is nothing wrong with friends of the mayor being handed fat plums; that if Mrs. Garrett was a male crony of Young's no one ever would notice.

Unfortunately, however, she isn't. And they do.

Nixon speech: A con job

August 9, 1974

All that was missing were the moving strains of the "Battle Hymn of the Republic" playing softly in the background.

Richard M. Nixon couldn't resist giving it to us one more time before he left. The con job, I mean.

There he was on national television, all decked out in the white shirt and the blue suit with the tiny American flag in the lapel. He stared straight into the camera lens and faced this nation's most tragic, shameful moment – a moment he alone created – without batting an eye.

Good Lord, the man even smiled two or three times during his 16-minute speech.

What is it with him? Has he lost complete touch with reality in the last 21 months?

"I've always tried to do what's best for the nation," he began. And then he talked of the erosion of his "political base" and indicated that the disappearance of support in the Congress was the overriding reason that he became the first president in the 198-year history of this glorious republic to be drummed out of office a step ahead of the sheriff.

"I would have preferred to carry through to the finish," he said determinedly. And later he added, hanging tough: "I am not a quitter."

He repeated the familiar litany of much-publicized achievements of his 5 1/2 year administration: Renewed relations with Red China, detente with Russia, the suspension of wars in Vietnam and the Middle East. All the same stuff he's been using for months to smoke-screen his legal troubles.

Along toward the end there was a rambling passage quoting Teddy Roosevelt about the man "in the arena" who toils and spends himself in a worthy cause. If Teddy were alive he likely would have been tempted to wing Mr. Nixon with a corral cookie.

He even had the consummate gall to end his farewell speech with a prayer.

As I watched this incredible tableau unfold before me, I could not believe my eyes and ears. The man looked for all the world like a presi-

51

dent turning over the reins of government to a legally selected successor under normal and usual circumstances.

In case you are confused about what really happened last night, be advised that this wasn't just another State of the Union message.

Your President resigned under intense political and legal pressure because there is grave evidence that he is guilty of having committed high crimes and misdemeanors while in that exalted office.

He quit with more than two years remaining in a four-year term to which he was elected by a landslide vote in November 1972.

He was about to be impeached by the House of Representatives and faced almost certain conviction and ouster from office in a trial by the full Senate of the United States.

He is not some poor slob who has been lynched by the newspapers, radio and TV. He is not the victim of some tangled web of circumstances created by others for their gain and behind his back.

He has admitted not only knowledge of, but also complicity in, the cover-up of a felony.

Under similar circumstances, you or I would long since have been dispatched to languish in the slammer if we had owned up to what he already has publicly disclosed.

More than a dozen men who worked for him, directly for the President of the United States mind you, have either pleaded guilty or have been convicted of crimes punishable by imprisonment. Some of them were thrown to the wolves by the big boss – that patriot who wears the little American flag in his lapel.

If he had bailed out of the presidency months ago, some of them might be walking the streets instead of the exercise yard today.

Of course, he did not admit in his farewell speech that he is guilty of any crime. In fact, he only mentioned twice in passing the Watergate burglary, the mistake which triggered the incredible event that you and more than 200 million other Americans were allowed to witness last night.

Impeachment, the process that has taken up most of Congress' attention for many months, now is a moot point. Said Rep. Peter Rodino, D-N.J., chairman of the House Judiciary Committee: "How many times do you have to kill a guy?"

The remark smacks of cronyism and the public won't buy it.

Ten months ago the Justice Department cut a deal with then Vice-President Spiro T. Agnew that allowed him to escape a felony prosecution by resigning his high political office. Spiro got off far too easy.

Like Agnew, Richard Nixon admitted being party to a felony. Is his penalty simply to be allowed to resign from office, collect up to $78,000 yearly in pensions and retire to write volumes of juicy memoirs?

I don't mean to kick a guy when he's down, but Richard Nixon should not be allowed to escape scot-free simply because he packed it up and left town just as the posse was about to overtake him.

If there was a sliver of doubt left concerning Richard Nixon's innocence, it was erased last night when Channel 7's Bill Bonds interviewed ex-con Jimmy Hoffa, the former Teamsters boss, for his reaction to the speech. As soon as Hoffa gave Richard Nixon a vote of confidence, I knew we had him cold.

So, it's back to the cloth coats for Pat Nixon. But that's not so bad.

Her husband will be lucky if his tailor is not requested to whip up something snazzy in stripes for the ex-prez.

This 'lady' was no lady

August 16, 1974

Jim has lived downtown for years, first in an apartment on Jefferson and later in one of the townhouses in Lafayette Park. This is his town and he loves it.

He's modestly successful in business, wears fairly decent clothes and drives a new car every year. You might call him your garden variety bachelor.

When you sort of grow up downtown you fall into patterns of behavior. You hang out in the same saloons, eat in the same restaurants, stop for breakfast with the rest of the gang after the bars close.

Nobody ever worries about the so-called crime problem. That's something that happens to "other" people, somewhere else.

So when Jim walked out of a downtown joint the other night he smiled to himself when this painted lady of the evening accosted him on the sidewalk. She made her pitch and he bantered with her for a while just to pass the time. And then he said no thanks and proceeded to climb into his car.

Only he made a mistake and hit the button that opens the electric door locks and, as he got into the driver's side, she slipped into the passenger seat.

"Look, honey," Jim said amiably, "I don't want to be rude, but I said I don't care to do any business." His passenger, however, was not to be discouraged.

With a flick of a wrist, "she" produced a seven-inch switchblade knife, pressed it to Jim's throat and commanded him to, "Drive, baby, or I'll slit your throat."

Jim could feel the point of the shiv pricking against his Adam's apple so he followed orders.

They cruised out of the downtown section; out where the apartments are jammed close together and the dim street lights played off the faces of the people sitting on their porches to escape the summer heat inside.

As they drove, Jim discovered that his passenger was not a woman, but rather a man "in drag" – a guy dressed up in women's clothing. Somewhere out in the center of the city the guy with the knife ordered Jim to slow the car, then turn into an alley between apartment houses.

"Stop right here, man," the cat with the knife said coldly. "Now gimme all your bread."

Jim rummaged through his trousers and his suitcoat and produced $27 in cash.

"Don't bull____ me, man," he said. "You got more than that. You cats with the big cars always carry lots of cash. It's in your briefcase, ain't it? You cats always carry the briefcase in your trunk. Open it up."

Jim left the motor running and opened the trunk by pressing a release button in the glove compartment. The two men moved to the rear of the car and looked into the trunk. Jim spotted his golf bag with one of his extra putters laying loose alongside it.

"I keep my briefcase up by the spare tire where it won't slide around," he lied. "I'll have to climb in and get it out but I can't with you holding the knife to my throat."

The robber told him to go ahead, but don't make a false move.

Jim started into the trunk, but reached instead for the putter, grasping it in both hands. He whirled quickly, taking a full baseball swing and caught the holdup man full in the face with the putter's blade.

The man dropped the knife as he reached up with both hands to catch his teeth, which were falling from his bloodied mouth and into the dirt of the alley like so much popcorn. The wounded man screamed in pain and crumpled to the ground.

In an instant Jim was out of the trunk and back into the driver's seat. His instinct was to gun the car straight ahead, but the alley was long and dark and he had no idea where it might lead. Perhaps only to a dead end. So he made a hasty decision.

Jim threw it into reverse and felt the car lurch and give a gentle thump, first with the rear wheels and then thump with the front as he backed it over the fallen robber speedily into the street. His headlights were still out, but he could see the form lying there motionless in the alley.

The screams of the wounded robber had alerted some neighbors and a few of them were crossing the street when Jim pulled out of the alley. He nicked a couple of them on his way up the street in his haste to escape, then turned onto a heavily traveled thoroughfare and drove until he located a cruising scout car. He waved it to a stop.

"I got stuck up by this guy with a knife!" Jim shouted excitedly. "He made me pull into an alley back there and I went in my trunk and I hit him in the face with this putter! Then I ran over him with my car. I think he's dead and you guys really ought to go back there and help him!"

The officer listened impassively, then offered Jim a cigarette to calm his nerves.

"Sir," he said, "let me give you some advice.

"If we go back there and find that man, we're going to have to make out a report and you're going to have to sign a complaint against him. So his friends will know your name and where you live.

"The way things are in the courts these days, chances are he'll never come to trial. In fact, chances are better than even that he'll sign a complaint against you for felonious assault or some other ridiculous charge and you may have to go to court and waste a lot of time.

"In fact, in a few months some smart attorney might even suggest that he sue you for damages and you'll end up selling your business to pay off the claim.

"So I'm going to tell you this for your own good, mister. I'm gonna make believe I never saw you. You get back in your car and go home and wash off that putter and put it back in your golf bag and forget this ever happened.

"And don't worry about him. If he's dead, he'll turn up in the morgue. If he's injured, he'll get to a hospital.

"And if he's smart he won't mess with a guy with golf clubs anymore."

73-24-36

October 2, 1974

It was early morning and Ilana "Za Za" Wajc Stello, also known on the nation's burlesque marquees as Chesty Morgan, had just awakened after a fitful night's sleep.

"Effrywhere I go," she complained in her thick accent, "eet ees zee same. Zee phone eet rings all night long. Men wait at zee motel. Zay call, zay knock at zee door. Watt zay tink I yam? Some kind huff calling girl?

"Een Cliffland some daktor offer me five tousand dollar to go weet heem for zee night. I am married woman. Just because I am stripper zay tink I wanna run aroun.

'Eeets disgosting, I tell you. I move my hotel today."

We were parked in Al Broder's office above the Six Mile theater, deep in the heart of Highland Park's sex Strip on Woodward near the city limits. Za Za, as she prefers to be called, stirred saccharin into her cup of tea and selected a chocolate-covered doughnut from a box on Broder's desk.

"My dy-ett," she said, smiling. "I 'ave to kepp my figure, you know."

I have fought for hours to figure a way to describe Chesty Morgan for you. About the best comparison I can come up with is that she is sort of a top-heavy Zsa Zsa Gabor.

Chesty likes to think of herself as your garden variety housewife – in her mid-30s, weighs 125, stands 5 feet 4, mother of two kids. There the similarity ends, however.

The publicity blurbs present her physical dimensions as 73-24-36, reading from top to bottom. I am here to testify today that the "73" part is no typographical error.

"She's the hottest thing in show biz," said Broder, digging into his breast pocket for a copy of Chesty's contract. "Look at the kind of deal I had to make. And I was lucky to get her."

"Dahling," Chesty said, "don't show heem zee money. Pleeze, dahling."

Broder paid no attention. He produced a document which specified that Chesty is to receive $7,500 for her two-week engagement.

Alas, burlesque, like football, is a game of inches. Give us a competitor who can make the big play and we'll show you a full house every time.

Chesty Morgan has been packing em in all over the East and Midwest for the last two years. She grossed (you'll pardon the pun) $71,000 in a single week in Boston a couple of months ago. Broder, who has run the Six Mile as a burlesque house since early July, expects to break all records with her.

Chesty was born Ilana Wajc (she says it is pronounced Weiss) in Poland. An orphan, she was sent to Israel at the age of 11. "Ilana," she explained, "means tree."

The last time Chesty resembled a tree, however, was at 15. By 16 she was working on the farm on a kibbutz near Haifa and beginning to sprout.

"I was very shy and didn't even want to see zee boys because of my size," she said. "I had to have my clothes special made. It took nearly a month's pay, een fact, to buy wan bra."

It's unclear just when or how, but Chesty says she met an American tourist, married him, moved to the U.S. and bore two daughters. He was killed and she knocked around New York until two years ago when some friends suggested she'd be boffo in show biz.

They were right. Six months ago, Chesty was dancing somewhere in the East, she says, when she met Dick Stello, a National League baseball umpire whom she married. Needless to say, they travel different circuits, but as soon as the baseball season ends they'll rendezvous in Pittsburgh and look for a house.

"People ask me, 'How can you sleep?' or 'How can you work in the garden lak dat?'" Chesty said. "I told dem eet ees easy; I yam normal, joost lak dem."

Chesty's in her mid-30s, but she doesn't look her age. When you're built like she is, you have trouble keeping wrinkles in your brow.

"One ting I tell you," Chesty said emotionally. "I luff America. I tink eet is zee greatest country in zee world."

I suggested that since she bears such an affection for the U.S., perhaps she should have Old Glory tattooed across the most prominent portion of her anatomy and work it into her act. At which point comedienne Liz Lyons, who is working the Six Mile show with Chesty, chimed in.

"Sure," Liz said, "and there'd be room left over for scenes from the Battle of Vicksburg and maybe even the War of 1812."

Jamaica, no problem

January 6, 1975

The wind blows a lot down in Port Antonio, Jamaica. Maybe that's why Jamaica seems to be a favorite vacation spot for politicians and other public figures.

Last week the north coast of the Caribbean island was top-heavy with big shots.

Canadian Prime Minister Pierre Elliott Trudeau and his official party breezed in last Monday and took up residence at a seaside plantation house called Prospect Park.

Sen. George McGovern, D-S.C., was holed up in a holiday residence at Port Maria, near Ocho Rios, seriously insisting to local reporters he does not intend to run for president in 1976.

World heavyweight boxing champion Muhammad Ali spent four days in Kingston and Montego Bay on a goodwill mission for the Black Muslims. Comparing Ali's oratory to an onshore wind leaves a good deal unsaid.

He is more like a hurricane.

And then there was Detroit Mayor Coleman Young, tucked away in a vacation villa some where near Port Antonio, a picturesque seaport on the mountainous eastern end of the island.

It was cloudy and windy and it rained frequently at Port Antonio, out in the boondocks of Jamaica – about 60 miles through the mountains from Kingston and 150 miles down the north coast from Montego Bay.

The roads are narrow and winding and it is safer to fly than drive. I hopped an eight-seat air taxi from Mo Bay, sharing the ride with two other tourists and several boxes of pork loins that were being airfreighted to a plush resort hotel.

They told me before I left Detroit I never would be able to uncover Mayor Young's hideaway, but I wouldn't listen. Remind me to pay attention next time.

Actually, I didn't expect to catch Hizonner doing anything special. It is just that he seems to come and go in the shadows, like the Phantom of the Opera, and the secrecy of his movements arouses curiosity.

Adam Clayton Powell, the late New York congressman, favored the West Indies, too. He owned a home at Bimini in the Bahamas, and he could be found almost any evening at the bar in his favorite hotel on the harbor there.

What I have wondered about Mayor Young is just where he goes in Jamaica and why, how he lives, who pays his bills, etc.

In one year in office, he has managed three lengthy vacations there.

If he pays his own way, which is what most people indicate, the price is not exactly cheap. The villas he has occupied in the past at Montego Bay and Ocho Rios, I discovered, were in the high-rent district – $800 a week and up.

Apparently he doesn't go for the night life or get caught up in the island's social whirl.

The best guess is that he goes to escape the mounting problems of city government and that Jamaica is convenient because of the direct air connection to Detroit.

Also, the island's population is more than 90 percent black and the Socialist government of Jamaican Prime Minister Michael Manley has been warm in its welcome to the black mayor of the fifth largest city in the United States.

It may be said with some certainty that Coleman Young's name is not a household word down there. Neither is that of Joyce Garrett, the director of Detroit's Bicentennial Commission and the mayor's only companion on his latest Jamaican trip. I took with me a couple of recent photographs of the two of them and showed them to cabdrivers, bartenders and innkeepers without reaction.

The mayor's trail led to Port Antonio, a tropical hideaway where the rich and famous hole up in places like Frenchman's Cove, Goblin Hill and the Trident in villas that start at $1,000 a week.

I hit all of the big resorts and most of the little ones in Port Antonio, feeling a bit like a CIA agent on someone's trail. My driver and guide, an elderly gentleman named Jim Brown who pilots a 1957 Chevy, hadn't seen Young around Port Antonio either.

"Whatcha gonna do, mon, when you find him, anyway?" Mr. Brown inquired.

It was a good question but, as it turned out, it was academic. The hills are full of private villas and we couldn't knock on every door.

Last night, as I boarded the flight for the return trip to Detroit, guess who was on the plane? Do you think perhaps he spent the week at the airport?

Who gets GYN?

March 20, 1975

Mayor Coleman Young sat at the head of a large mahogany conference table in the board room at Detroit General Hospital. He was dressed in a long white frock coat. A chrome plated stethoscope hung around his neck.

At his end of the table were gathered most of his top aides – deputy mayor Bill Beckham, political adviser Malcolm Dade, press secretary Bob Pisor, PR director Laura Moseley Jackson and several other heads of city departments. The rest of the seats were taken up by senior members of the hospital's medical staff.

Hizonner rapped his rubber mallet on the table to call the meeting to order.

"I've summoned you here to straighten out the problems of this hospital once and for all," the mayor began. Laura Jackson held up a sign that said "APPLAUSE" but nobody paid any attention.

"The way I see it," Hizonner continued, "Detroit General has been run too much like a hospital for too long. What it needs is leadership and efficiency. That is why I have decided to take personal control and institute some changes."

Laura Jackson clapped her hands and began to whistle the tune to "The foot bone's connected to the ankle bone; the ankle bone's connected to the leg . . . " The mayor rapped his mallet again and she quieted down.

"First," the mayor said, "I want to express my appreciation to my loyal staff members for all of their helpful suggestions. I do agree that several of the hospital's key departments would be managed much more efficiently if directorships were turned over to city hall people.

"This, of course, has created some problems. For instance, we could not possibly choose fairly from among all of the men in my office who have volunteered to take charge of the GYN department. Consequently, if all candidates will stick around when this meeting is over we will draw lots for that job.

"The runner-up gets obstetrics."

The mayor rummaged through his prescription pad for notes.

"There is not time to announce my entire reorganization program here," he said, "so a list will be posted after this meeting. One appointment that I'm sure will be warmly received, however, is that of Mr. Pisor to head the department of proctology.

"I felt that Pisor's long experience in dealing with newspapermen makes him eminently qualified for the job."

This time Laura Jackson held up the "APPLAUSE" sign and there was a polite smattering.

"One problem area has become particularly embarrassing for my administration," Hizonner continued. "In his complaints to the city, the hospital's board chairman, Horace Sheffield, has said that sometimes Detroit General runs out of such items as toilet paper.

"I'm here to tell you that I'm tired of paper-capers and tissue-issues. Ms. Jackson, henceforth you are to be directly responsible for alleviating the toilet paper shortage. I know I can count on you because of the long experience you've had in supplying similar services for Manoogian Mansion.

"As an emergency measure, this afternoon I want you to send Detroit General a case of that French gray tissue you bought me a while back. Frankly, I can't stand the color anyway."

This time Pisor held up the "APPLAUSE" sign and the gathering responded with a standing ovation.

"In the area of public relations," the mayor said, "I've decided on some new programs. One is a series of 'good news' press conferences. We'll hold one every time a patient survives a surgical procedure.

"Staff members who go one full month without being sued for malpractice will have their picture posted on the hospital bulletin board.

"Well, that about covers the announcements," the mayor said, rising. "Now I want to lead you on a familiarization tour of the hospital."

The group filed out of the board room and trooped down to the Emergency Room, where patients were strewn about on stretchers and cots. The mayor approached a police officer who was carrying a middle-aged man over his shoulder.

"And what's this gentleman's problem?" he asked the cop.

"Cardiac arrest," the officer answered, breathing heavily.

"I see," the mayor said, twirling his stethoscope. "I presume you've already informed him of his right to remain silent and to be represented by counsel."

Booster gets the boot

September 15, 1975

The slogan of the "Image Detroit" campaign, which Laura Mosley Jackson dreamed up, carries a simple message: "Get to know me better."

Alas, it appears that Mayor Young finally "got to know" Mrs. Jackson well enough to realize that, for the good of the city's image, he ought to dump her.

Mrs. Jackson, 31, was fired last Friday as director of Detroit's Department of Information. She was paid $28,900 a year as the town's chief publicity agent.

At one time, her department had carried a $1-million annual budget. Recently, she undertook a $30,000 semiprivate campaign, with the city as co-signer, to boost Detroit's "Image" among residents and strangers alike.

Lord knows, Detroit's profile can use all the scrubbing it can get. But Mrs. Jackson was hardly the person to undertake that heavy task.

For openers, Mrs. Jackson is a political hack. That's not too unusual, I suppose, but most of the political hacks at City Hall at least make an attempt to see that their books balance and that their troops are kept sullen but not mutinous.

Mrs. Jackson ran a highly visible department. She should have taken every precaution to keep herself above petty controversy.

It was obvious from the outset, however, that she wasn't smart enough to do that.

Mrs. Jackson has a couple of glaring faults. She can't handle people, and she can't handle money.

Last spring more than a dozen of her highest-ranking employees petitioned Mayor Young to have her removed. They charged her with being incompetent, with conducting witch-hunting staff interrogations and with overstepping her bounds both professionally and fiscally.

Mrs. Jackson complained that the PR office uprising was prompted only because she is black and a woman. To set that straight, however, half of the employees who signed the letter to Mayor Young are black. And half of them are women.

Hizonner, incidentally, never answered their request for an investigation. Later, Mrs. Jackson saw to it that most of the signatories to the removal petition were either transferred or fired.

Mrs. Jackson has plenty of clout in City Hall. She is a close buddy of Joyce Garrett, the mayor's lady friend. Her mother is chairman of the city's Zoning Board of Appeals and her father, a prominent medical man, has been a heavy contributor to Young for years.

Her job was a political plum. With Mrs. Jackson's help, however, it soon went sour.

Months back, Mrs. Jackson was dropped from the rolls of the Public Relations Society of America for nonpayment of dues. She was refused further privileges at the Detroit Press Club for the same reason.

Then she started hanging paper – passing bad checks.

The Press Club had one returned twice for more than $200. Detroit restaurateur Chuck Muer got burned so often with Mrs. Jackson's funny money that he felt moved to circulate an interoffice memo, warning his dining managers to accept neither her charge nor her personal checks.

Ten days ago, while she was out of the city on vacation, it was reported that Mrs. Jackson's office in the City-County Building had been burglarized. A couple of hundred dollars was reported to be missing and records of the "Image Detroit" campaign allegedly had been rifled.

The case was passed from the 1st (Central) Precinct detective bureau to headquarters, Special Investigations, then all the way up to the office of Deputy Police Chief Jerry Hart. Because of Mrs. Jackson's loud outcries, one of the Detroit Police Department's sharpest homicide investigators, Sgt. Lloyd Clemmons, has been assigned to take charge of the investigation.

There is no progress report on what Clemmons has uncovered – if anything.

A week ago, when I wrote a column about Mrs. Jackson passing bum checks, I called her office for comment and was informed that she was out of town. I was put through to her deputy, Tom Killeen, who said he knew nothing about the checks or the break-in and that I would have to consult Mrs. Jackson. End of conversation

Later, I learned that a woman in Mrs. Jackson's office had eavesdropped on our conversation and had called Mayor Young to falsely report that Killeen gave me damaging information about his boss.

Friday, when Mrs. Jackson was fired, it also was announced that Tom Killeen is to be transferred out of the PR department. Apparently, Mrs. Jackson had enough political clout left to take an innocent man down with her.

Something snaps

March 8, 1976

The other day we were discussing the principle of the pressure cooker and how the top locks on real tight and the steam cooks quickly and cleanly.

But you cannot see what's going on inside and are required to watch the burner closely so that the cooker doesn't overheat and explode.

To help avoid accidents, the manufacturer installs a little rubber plug in the lid of most cookers. When the steam rises past a safe level, the plug pops. Instead of a violent explosion, all you get is a wet stove.

People ought to be equipped with safety valves. Then, when the pressure builds up inside, when it gets so intense and unbearable that everything seems like it's going to blow up, the plug could pop before all that inner turmoil causes irreparable damage.

Some of us have improvised our own blowout valves.

When the collar gets really tight, when the world starts to close in, some of us scream.

At our husband, our wife, our kids, our boss. Maybe at customers, fellow employees, the parking attendant, a waiter, a bartender.

But we let it go. We let it out and make asses of ourselves and it's over.

The pressure gauge falls and the crisis passes. And, if we have any sense at all, we look back on how we acted and learn something from it.

After a number of years of watching people who can achieve that kind of instant relief and comparing them with others who seemingly are incapable of allowing the cork to pop, I've come to the conclusion that the hotheads aren't as stupid and crude as they may appear.

They've got the secret that most of us couldn't find if we searched a thousand years.

I know of a dozen people who'd be around today if they could have let it out; if they could have let the safety valve break loose instead of waiting for the inevitable explosion and losing everything.

The problem is that, unlike a boiler or a pressure cooker, there's no accurate method by which to test just how high human steam is rising until it's too late.

A girl who worked downtown a few years back was in love with a guy who kept promising he was going to marry her, but never did. He bought her a nice place and took her out and all that, but he just didn't want to get tied down.

After a couple of years, the out-of-town trips, the furniture for the apartment, the dinner and theater dates just weren't enough. Twice, she threatened to kill herself if he didn't straighten up. She tried twice, too, but only halfheartedly.

He figured she was just being overly dramatic about their love affair.

Then, one evening, she called his apartment and told him again that this was it, she was tired of waiting for him. He told her to take two aspirins and call him in the morning.

Her answer was a single gunshot. When the police got there, she was dead.

On the telephone, yet.

There was a high school kid out in the suburbs. Nice family.

His mother wanted to have a family portrait made to send out to the relatives for Christmas. Everybody was going to be there and, please, wouldn't he get his hair trimmed? Not cut, just trimmed – so that it would look neat for the picture.

The boy objected and the discussion escalated. The kid went to his room and his mother gave him a few minutes to calm down and went up to continue the conversation. She found him hanging in his closet, a belt looped tightly around his neck.

He died a few days later. Go ahead and ask.

For what?

Friend of mine, good guy, an accountant, early 50s. Dedicated to his family and his job.

Never did a thing in his life halfway. The ends were always neatly tied.

But he worried about his work, and his friends and family couldn't assure him enough that things were OK, that life was a roller coaster ride and all of us are on the same shaky train together.

Like that cooker, the steam built inside, undetected. His stomach started to hurt. He couldn't sleep.

Last week, the lid blew.

Some of the men he worked for came to the funeral home. "He was a good man," they said. "We'll miss him."

I've got to hand it to his widow. She looked one guy straight in the eye and asked, "Why didn't you tell him that last week?"

A real shooter

April 8, 1976

The old man died the other night. We buried him yesterday.

He was a shooter. Joe Waldmeir was. The first memory I have of him was wearing a stocking cap on his hair so that the tiny natural waves would stay in place.

Not that I remember an awful lot. It seems that where he's concerned, I recall situations more than personal contacts.

Joe and Helen were separated and divorced when I was a baby, the last of their three kids. We lived in a third-floor walkup apartment on Fourth and Ferry and the old man was tending bar someplace downtown.

He worked a lot of places. I remember the bar at the old Arena Gardens. They had an outdoor boxing ring next to the building and as small as I was - maybe 4 or 5 at the time - I can recall sitting in the grandstand there on a summer evening and watching my first fight.

I remember sitting on the aisle with Joe there, too, for an indoor bout and seeing a young heavyweight named Joe Louis knock a guy out. Years later I took to bragging that it was one of those first-round KO's the Brown Bomber became famous for.

But I really don't know how far you can trust a 5-year-old's memory.

Later Joe worked for a boxing referee and saloon-keeper named Slim McClellan at the old Ringside Bar, which was across the street from the Detroit Times on Times Square. The newspaper guys used to come in there and I'd go every so often - enough so that a lot of them got to know me as Joe's kid.

They had better fights at the Ringside than any the fans ever saw at the Arena Gardens. I guess when I come to think of it, some of the battles in the apartment on Fourth and Ferry weren't bad, either.

Joe wasn't really much for the family life. He seldom paid his alimony or even the child support. My mother raised three kids single-handed, taking in boarders in the apartment on Fourth and working places like Evans-Winter-Hebb.

Joe Jr. - that's my older brother, Joe - helped out, too. He quit school in the 11th grade (maybe he got tossed out, but it doesn't matter much now) to take a job as a clerk with an insurance outfit.

Mom needed the extra money.

Young Joe turned out OK. He managed to finish high school, get his B.A. at Wayne, his M.A. at Michigan and his Ph.D. at Michigan State, and now he's a professor there.

We got out of the apartment and moved around, ending up in a flat on Pennsylvania and Shoemaker. The old man had remarried by then and had two daughters, Mary Ellen and Kathy.

I'd take the Crosstown streetcar, over Harper and down Milwaukee to get to where they lived on East Grand Boulevard and Jos. Campau. Some days the trip would be worth it, some days it would be a disaster.

I guess that when I was a kid I never realized when the old man was in the sauce. Maybe I realized, but didn't want to admit it.

Anyway, it was after a few scenes there in that apartment of his that I just got to the point where I didn't give a damn anymore. I saw the old man less and less in the following years.

I got through grade school, into high school and out, into college, the service, with help from my mother.

All three of us grew up, married, had children. But I hardly ever heard from or of Joe.

Once in awhile I'd run into him downtown. He worked at Mario's on Second Avenue for a long time, then at Vincenzo's up on John R. For a while he tried running his own place, a bar on Mack Avenue just inside the city limits.

But it didn't work. Joe wasn't cut out to be management.

After he retired, he'd drop into Danny's Gin Mill when Danny had the place in the basement back of the Sheraton-Cadillac and I'd run into him occasionally there and have a drink with him. His buddy, Mickey Brown, tended bar at Larco's and he'd see Mickey now and then.

In time a lot of his friends became my friends. They told me what a great guy my old man was and I'd shake my head and agree. But I really didn't know. I didn't even know him.

For a long time I wondered how I'd feel when he died. When he hit 80 I thought about it more and more often.

And then it happened and I felt sorry - sorry that we could not have been closer. But he didn't want it that way and neither did I and that's the way it goes.

I know he had no regrets. And that's a good way to finish, I think.

Welcome to 2000

July 22, 1976

Now that the July 4 Bicentennial is out of the way we can look forward to the nation's next important milestone, Jan. 1, 2000.

I was checking the crystal ball the other day and when the clouds had settled I was looking in on a conference room on the 11th floor of Detroit's City-County Building.

Detroit's Mayor Young, in the middle of his seventh four-year term in office, was seated at the head of a polished mahogany table. He was dressed in faded battle fatigues and his long, white beard flowed into his lap.

At his right hand, Deputy Mayor William Beckham, wearing a gold monocle, thumbed through a stack of papers. On the mayor's left, Press Secretary Robert Pisor sat twirling his thinning moustache.

Occasionally Pisor reached over and gently prodded the 82-year-old mayor to keep him awake.

Beckham rapped the gavel sharply, calling the meeting to order. Startled, the mayor stiffened in his chair.

"Man, can't you use chimes or maybe a little tinker bell?" Hizonner asked. "One of these days somebody's gonna whup your head with that gavel."

Beckham ignored the reproof and dug into the stack of correspondence.

"I think it's appropriate that we begin the 21st century with this message from our governor," he said. Beckham then read a two-page letter that praised the Young administration profusely and congratulated the mayor for more than a quarter century in office.

"And in conclusion," Beckham quoted the governor, "I want to tell you how much I admire and respect the mayor's untiring devotion to public service and I want to reaffirm our strong friendship and close relationship.

"With warmest personal regards etc., etc., signed, Gov. Joyce Garrett."

The mayor's tired eyes brightened.

"I told you people that girl was gonna go far," he said.

Beckham cleared his throat. Pisor smiled.

"Now I've got good news and bad news," Beckham continued. "Which would you like first?"

"We've heard that one before, Bill," Pisor answered, grimacing. "The good news is that the mayor's going to Heaven. The bad news is that he's going tomorrow. Right?"

Beckham looked wounded, then paused to jot another notation beside Pisor's name in his black book.

"For the good news," Beckham began, "Police Chief Cockrell reports that crime was reduced again in 1999. His department reported only eight murders, 11 muggings and 14 rapes.

"Now that may not seem like a significant reduction from 1998, but it averages out to only one murder for every 3,000 people inside the city limits.

"Of course, the statistics have to be tempered by the fact that because of budget cutbacks and layoffs our police force is down to 45 people. Half of them are command officers stationed at headquarters and most of the rest are working on the residency checks or for internal affairs.

"Chief Cockrell also reports significant progress in stamping out street gangs. He says that if we close another 300 streets this year, the gangs will be isolated on Woodward, Gratiot, Grand River and Jefferson."

Beckham passed the report to the mayor, who stamped it with his signature. Next item on the agenda was the budget.

"Why the hell do we need 10,000 gallons of white paint?" the mayor thundered.

"The fences, your honor," Pisor interjected. "The fences we build around vacant city property. We own just about all the land inside Eight Mile Road now and the fences have to be painted at least once every five years or we have to give back the matching federal grant money that helps pay for the paint."

The mayor mumbled something about President Howard Cosell's revenue-sharing policy and moved on.

"This water bill," the mayor inquired. "Isn't it awfully high?"

Beckham answered. "You wanted us to dig that moat around the Boulevard," he said. "And then there was the inner moat around the Renaissance Center.

"You can't fill those things with Cadillac Club, you know. And if you think the water bill is high, wait until you check out the cost of lumber to repair the stockade fences and drawbridges."

Laura Moseley Jackson, the mayor's $65,000-a-year political adviser, took the floor.

"Before we adjourn," she said, "we really ought to give some thought to picking an opponent for the mayor's campaign in 2002.

"We ran Pisor against him in '86 and '94 and Beckham ran in '90 and '98. We should get a new face in there."

"What ever happened to the big Irish councilman who used to climb on the table?" the mayor asked. "Maybe he'd be interested."

"Got out of politics years ago, right after he went on the wagon," Pisor answered. "Said that when he sobered up, the Council wasn't fun anymore. He went to college and now he's a brain surgeon."

I did my time

August 24, 1976

It ticks me off when suburbanites like me are criticized for lamenting the decay of Detroit.

"You don't have roots here any more," we are told. "What gives you the right to talk about Detroit's problems?"

Well, I think that there is something we ought to get straight. Like thousands of others who live in the metropolitan area, I am as much a Detroiter as the stiffs who stand idly by and watch the town slowly disintegrate.

I have lived outside the city for the last 23 years. But I did my time. I paid my dues.

I moved before busing or red-lining or rampaging street gangs forced my flight. When I departed in 1954 I was just looking for space to raise kids.

I fancy myself somewhat of a prophet, in fact. I also quit smoking two years before the cancer scare.

As for roots here, mine are deep and binding. I wonder, in fact, if some of the political high rollers and bellyaching officials presently on the city payroll can match my ancestral ties to this hallowed turf.

For instance, my maternal great-grandparents, the Knudt Nielsens, were married in St. Paul's Lutheran Church in 1880. My mother's father, Pete Nielsen, was a Detroit cop for 30 years; several as a detective lieutenant at the old 8th Precinct at Grand River and 12th Street.

My father, Joe Waldmeir Sr., came to Detroit after World War I. He tried being a cop, too, but he didn't have the patience. He ran a blind pig for a while on Second Avenue across from Burroughs when they made adding machines.

After repeal, he spent the rest of his life tending bar in a series of Detroit restaurants.

I was born on Mark Twain, which seems fitting for a man in my profession.

I have lived in a house on Promenade; in an apartment at Fourth and Ferry, upstairs over a store at Lillibridge and Warren, in a four-family flat on Pennsylvania and Shoemaker; with my late grandparents for a year at Bryden and Joy Road; and in the first house my mother could afford, on Somerset between Morang and Moross.

Mom took sick and nearly died in the apartment on Fourth, my brother Joe was miraculously saved after a bout with pneumonia there. We even called the priest – candles, last rites, the works – for him, but he pulled through.

My roller skate wheels stuck to the asphalt on Kirby when the surface was too hot. Joe hit me in the face with a broom handle and smashed my nose during an alley game called "tippy." We used to chase rats, big rats, in the alley behind Third.

Mom went to old Central High School, which is now Wayne State University. My sister, Pat, graduated from Eastern High. I went to St. Dominic, St. Margaret Mary, Sherrill, Nativity, Denby and Wayne State.

St. Margaret Mary was nice. They had a coal furnace and the place even smelled warm in winter

Brother Joe was a loser. He got kicked out of Holy Rosary and later fired from an insurance company because he was too tight with the union organizers. But after World War II he went back to school, earned degrees from Wayne, Michigan and Michigan State and taught for a while at U of D before settling into the English Department at MSU.

Notwithstanding the old man's penchants for extralegal endeavors, the family always managed to find work in Detroit.

After her divorce. Mom started as a clerk at Evans-Winter-Hebb. Later she was an accountant for a small factory at Clay and St Aubin. Sister Pat worked for Ma Bell until she married.

I sold newspapers, jerked sodas, was a helper on an ice truck, put windows in Plymouths at the old Briggs plant and batteries in Chryslers on the line at the Jefferson plant – all before I left high school.

One summer I unloaded boxcars at the Michigan Central Depot, six nights a week, 3 to 11, Wednesday off. And my girl friend lived in Livonia.

I had my first drink of whisky at the age of 14 at Bill's Marine Bar, where the Roostertail now stands, one summer morning in 1944. The guy who was driving the ice truck bought it for me.

"Go ahead, kid" he said with a wink. "Just take a deep breath and toss it down."

I bought my first drink – a Seven and Seven – at the Blarneystone Bar at Eight Mile and Hayes when Eastwood Park was still across the street. I was 17 then. Suppose the statute of limitations has run out by now?

Oh, yes, I nearly forgot. My other great-grandfather, William Waldmeyer, is buried in Arlington National Cemetery. He was a Union volunteer in the War Between the States.

He died of a fever while encamped in Virginia in 1863, waiting to fight for the freedom of a lot of people he didn't even know. One of them might have been your great-grandfather.

Small world.

So long, Big Louie

May 25, 1977

The night before the Detroit Plaza Hotel opened in the Renaissance Center a bunch of us had wandered over for a cocktail party.

As we prepared to leave, I suggested to Sonny Eliot and Billy Bonds that we stop past the booth where "The King," Lou Gordon, was holding court and pay our respects. After one more drink I talked them into it and we arrayed ourselves single file at his table.

"These guys wanted to leave," I told Lou. "But I said we couldn't go until we kissed your ring."

Gordon glanced up casually from his conversation, then held out both hands so we all could see them.

"That just proves what kind of a reporter YOU are," he snarled. "I don't wear any rings!"

Ah, Big Looie. We'll all miss him.

Say what you will, Lou Gordon – who died yesterday at his home here – was a power in this community and apparently in a lot of others.

I can remember checking into a hotel in Los Angeles, snapping on the light switch and having the TV flash on – with the Lou Gordon show, of course.

At the time I didn't realize that we actually were exporting the Gordon program to other parts of the country. Think of it: the country's first syndicated leer.

Frankly, I repeatedly refused to appear on the Gordon show. In fact, I couldn't understand why anybody did – except that he apparently provided exposure in a lot of market areas for people with a product or an ideology to peddle.

I just didn't like the way Looie edited the tapes. What I mean is, I had visions of him making some lengthy statement about some crime that I allegedly had committed, then breaking for a commercial before I had time to tell him he had the wrong guy.

But I had my fantasies.

In one of them I had resigned from my newspaper job and decided to run for a political office. Somehow I wangled an invitation to appear with Big Looie, but I insisted on the portion of the show that he did live from the Channel 50 studios.

I planned to sit quietly in my chair and fence with him verbally for a few minutes. Then, when he least expected it, I would let out a war whoop, vault over the desk and pounce on him – preferably with Jackie watching – while the TV cameras recorded the entire tableau.

Lou's heart operation a year or so back ruined that plot, however. I couldn't go planning to leap on a guy who wasn't healthy.

Lou always tried to be friendly.

When I first moved from sports to the Back Page of The Detroit News, Lou was writing a column for a batch of suburban dailies and weeklies. Shortly after I switched I received a note from Lou that read, "Welcome to the straight world."

In my answer I allowed as how I must have made a wrong turn if Looie had been in "the straight world" all this time.

Since be had been so kind as to write, however, I deemed it only proper that I dispatch a get-well greeting when he was hospitalized for his heart surgery.

"Your fellow employees wish you a complete and speedy recovery," I wrote. "The vote was 194-183."

Apparently the card was lost in the mail. I never got an answer.

For all of the hassles, Lou Gordon and I never misunderstood each other. In fact, to my constant consternation – and probably to his, as well – readers were forever lumping us into the same ideological category.

I get the mail every week: "You and Lou Gordon," people write, "are the only newspaper columnists who tell it like it is."

As you probably have noticed already, Lou Gordon and I were not the best of friends. But neither were we mortal enemies.

A lot of people in Detroit's mass media field were jealous of Lou's success. I'm not certain that, deep down, I wasn't one of them.

He wrote a column that appeared regularly in these pages. He stepped on a lot of toes and managed to become an adversary in situations where most newsmen would have preferred to remain on the fringes.

Always quick to seize a populist cause, Lou waded into utility rate campaigns with both feet. His TV crew, of course, never was far behind.

It is human nature, I guess, to wonder who will replace him. My guess is, probably nobody.

Looie was one of a kind. And, in the end, that may be a good thing.

A quiet visit to Runnymede

June 22, 1977

WINDSOR, England – Rain had fallen for nearly three days and the wind from the sea was cold and sharp.

The trip out from London followed the motorway for a while and then dipped into a series of small villages and boroughs with strange, hyphenated names.

There is a huge, gray rambling castle here where Queen Elizabeth II and her retinue spend a great deal of time. The horse races at Ascot are nearby, too, and the swells and the punters stream out from London when the meeting is on to take a hunch and bet a bunch.

We were following the Thames River most of the way. Below Windsor it turns into a meandering stream, narrow enough for Evel Knievel to jump on a minibike.

A long, green meadow runs for about a mile alongside the river at one point. I stopped the car about halfway down it, jumped a narrow ditch at the roadside and set off through the high, wet grass for the knoll at the other side.

There is no path, no neon marker, not even a small sign to show the way.

The only sound is an occasional car that passes, or a dog barking somewhere on the other side of the line of trees.

A hundred yards across the meadow I unlatched a gate in the wooden rail fence and found a broad gravel path. It led to a series of wide cobblestone steps – 48 in all – which wound upward through trees, turned bright green from the dampness and lack of sunlight.

At the top, the path spilled out into the light again and at its head rested a large, oblong marble stone gleaming white, even in the overcast and dreary surroundings, and almost completely covered with a chiseled inscription.

Sprigs of pale pink rhododendron, freshly cut from the bushes that flourish all along the pathway up, were laid at the base of the stone.

"This area of Great Britain," the inscription read, "was given to the United States of America by the people of Great Britain in memory of John Fitzgerald Kennedy who was killed by an assassin."

And below those words is inscribed this excerpt from Kennedy's 1961 inaugural address:

"Let every nation know, whether it wishes us well or ill, that we shall pay any price, bear any burden, meet any hardship, support any friend or oppose any foe in order to ensure the survival and success of liberty."

Across a short fence, cows were grazing as animals have here for centuries.

The meadow is Runnymede and it is here – or at least nearby, the historians say – that King John affixed his mark and seal to a document called the Magna Carta in the 13th century, guaranteeing freedom of expression for all men and establishing the basis for the world's common law.

I had been here before – 10 years ago, almost to the day. It was not a pleasant trip then.

The United States was waist deep in the Vietnam War and British antiwar activists were constantly clamoring for its cessation along with their brethren across the Atlantic.

The British pacifists needed a target, someplace to make their mark and get some publicity. So they came out to Runnymede.

Only they came at night, armed with paint brushes and spray cans. And they wrote all sorts of foul things on the peaceful Kennedy monument, then disappeared.

Next morning the vandalism was discovered. The newspapers were called. The TV stations sent camera crews.

And the backfire was heard all over England.

Groups of people, mostly teenagers, volunteered to clean up the mess. Thousands jammed the road along the Thames and beat their way across the meadow and up the path.

They came and stood in silence. Some brought flowers – carnations and daisies and roses – and laid them at the base of the stone. Others wrote messages and pinned them in the bouquets.

"We're sorry," I recall one message reading. "Please forgive us." The monument since has been cleaned and refurbished. There are no initials carved in its smooth backside, no chips from its trim edges.

They tell me that while journalists and TV crews come to London from the United States all the time, but no one ever goes to Runnymede anymore.

The cows graze, the Thames moves inexorably past. And now and then a dog barks.

I cut a branch from a rhododendron and laid it on the pile. It seemed the right thing to do.

Oh, those nuns

August 31, 1977

A group of people who would protect our morals from yet another assault by television has asked Channel 7 to preview a new fall prime time TV series called "Soap."

The request is based on a suspicion that the show contains some irreverent religious scenes. The station's management, understandably, declined.

You will notice that I call it a "suspicion." The group, the Interfaith Broadcasting Commission of Greater Detroit, says it only knows what it reads in the papers.

It based its request on the fact that the series has received some controversial press in advance of its showing.

One objection, it seems, stems from reports that there is a scene in "Soap" which depicts a young lady going into a Roman Catholic confessional and telling the priest, who happens to be a former boy friend, that she's still in love with him and wants him to leave the priesthood and marry her.

That the padre declines the offer apparently makes no never mind.

The commission suggests, without even seeing the rushes, that the series ought to be moved from 9:30 p.m. to 11:30 p.m. "so that it will be beyond children's bedtime."

I read all this with great interest. I have, for years, toyed with the idea of writing a TV series dealing with my early experience with the church.

The first person who objected to the way I depicted my version of my pristine Catholic upbringing would be sentenced, as I was, to 25 years of eating fish on Friday only to be told after all that time that it didn't make any difference, anyway.

Funny they should worry about how the series would affect children. Kids have been handling the Catholic Church just fine for centuries.

It's the adults who have the hang-ups.

I have not lived for centuries, of course. It only seems that long. But I spent eight of my first nine years in school being taught by nuns and disciplined by priests. And, booby, I could tell you some stories that would curl Norman Lear's hair.

Unfortunately, it's too late to do much with mine.

Not that it was an entirely regrettable experience. There were some bright spots.

Attending grade school at Nativity of Our Lord was like playing on a losing football team: They didn't care if you learned much, as long as they could build "character."

I'm afraid that I disappointed them on both counts.

Mass was every morning at 8. Each class would file into the pews in the huge, ornate church and the nun would sit in the last row on the aisle so she could observe who came late.

The boys sat in one row, girls in another. The contest was to see which boy could make the loudest noise, closest resembling a muffled blast on an airhorn, to make the girls giggle – without getting caught by the nuns, of course.

Communion was an event, not because it brought me any closer to immortality, but because I got to bring my breakfast to school. That usually was two pieces of cold buttered toast, wrapped in a napkin.

While the noncommunicants in the class did their work, I was allowed to eat my toast and wash it down with warm orange soda pop.

Actually, discipline wasn't always meted out by the priests. The pastor, Fr. Bernard Geller, only came around to hand out report cards.

His visits, however brief, were memorable. I can recall one session where, following a stern lecture, he belted one kid and knocked him through a door and halfway down the stairs.

The name of the nun who taught the eighth grade escapes me (it's probably something Freudian), but the memory of her is vivid. She carried a slat from a desk, which she used to enforce her version of law and order.

A failure to do homework was punished by 20 whacks with the wooden slat; five on each side of both hands.

We had one big redheaded kid who broke the wrist that served his writing hand. He came to school in a cast. When he failed to turn in his first day's homework, the compassionate sister gave him 10 whacks on each side of his good hand.

By the time I was ready to leave Nativity, my family had moved into the Denby district. The nuns thought that public high school was scandalous and insisted that I would not graduate from the eighth grade unless a solemn promise was made that I would go on to a Catholic high school.

My solemn promise lasted until I was graduated. That'll teach them to trust a 13-year-old.

On second thought, this stuff's too good to waste here. Operator, get me Norman Lear . . .

Hizonner gets a bellyful

September 19, 1977

Smoke rose lazily from the divided oil drum which serves as a barbecue pit on the lawn behind the riverfront Manoogian Mansion. Disguised as a rather plump Kirtland warbler, I was perched in a nearby tree and observed this scene:

Detroit Mayor Coleman A. Young, dressed in a tall, white chef's hat and wearing an apron with "Hizonner" in large letters and "$!#& Housework" written across the front, was tenderly basting the rows of ribs and chicken.

"Not too much sauce on mine, Mr. Mayor," Press Secretary Bob Pisor said, waving the smoke from his eyes. "Gets all sticky in my mustache."

"Man, you gotta have lotsa sauce on ribs," the mayor replied. "Don't they teach you dudes nothin' in those fancy schools?"

A long table had been set up for dinner and most of the mayor's department heads were already warming up with cocktails. The Boss, who once owned his own barbecue, was cookin' up a mess.

"We really ought to go over a few things before we get into this dinner meeting, Mr. Mayor," Pisor said. "Like the debates with Ernie Browne."

The mayor looked at Pisor coldly through the wisps of smoke.

"I said it before and I'll say it one more time," the mayor answered, obviously provoked. "I ain't gonna be provoked by that lying bastard."

"You see, Mr. Mayor," Pisor started slowly, "that's one of the troubles.

"You keep saying that you want to debate on the issues. You insist that no matter how the black-white vote breaks down, you intend to be the mayor of all the people.

"You say that Councilman Browne is a nice man and that there's nothing wrong with being a church-goer and a Boy Scout leader. Or having white folks for friends. Maybe it's not for you, but it's OK for him.

"So you slipped once. So you called him the 'first black white hope.' But you apologized for it later.

"So far, so good. But then you finish off the press conference after the primary election by saying you 'aren't going to be provoked by that lying bastard.'

"I fear, Mr. Mayor, that your credibility has suffered a bit. And I think you're going to get some questions on that during the debates and we'd better have some answers ready."

The mayor scowled and ordered Pisor to hand him a potholder. He glanced at the table and Police Chief William Hart waved.

"We have to get our act together on the Police Department, too," Pisor continued. The mayor furrowed his brow.

"I mean, after The News broke that story a few weeks back about how so many rookie cops couldn't read or pass the state qualification test, we didn't exactly wow the public with our rebuttal.

"Hart goes and tells the media that it's OK because cops don't have to be able to read to do a good job.

"And then," Pisor paused and took a deep breath, "you make a statement that it's all 'lies and sinful slander' and that The News is 'racist' and the writer is full of 'sour grapes.'"

The mayor mumbled and slopped on more barbecue sauce. "So it wasn't lies and slander?" Hizonner asked.

"Not exactly, sir," Pisor responded. "We've had to back down on a lot of the charges because they were true. We ought to be better prepared when the questions arise this time."

"What else . . . what else?" the mayor barked impatiently.

"Well, you ought to get together with Jimmy Watts sometime tonight and find out what's been going on with his department's contract with City Disposal Systems, Inc.," Pisor said, checking his list.

"One of Watts' own men took several garbage trucks to two different places to have them weighed and it looks like somebody's been adding tonnage right in front of our inspectors and charging the city for it."

"Garbage?" the mayor asked. "Who cares about a few pounds of garbage?"

"It's one ton a truck, Mr. Mayor," Pisor answered. "And $7 a ton. The whole thing amounts to about $400,000 a year in overcharges and nobody from our office has said a word about looking into it."

The waiters had begun to serve the guests. Pisor wished he did not have to raise the final item.

"Ah, Mr. Mayor," he began. "There's just one more thing."

"The people who are running the debates say they were reading the paper the other day and got an idea from a story about Jack Anderson starting a new TV interview show.

"Anderson says he's going to have every guest who appears with him take a lie detector test before they . . . "

The mayor frowned and interrupted. "On second thought," he said, "why should we give Ernie Browne the benefit of all that exposure . . . ?"

Wine and talk at Manoogian

October 20, 1977

Coleman Young was late, but that's nothing unusual for a politician on the hustings.

I had parked in front of the Manoogian Mansion promptly at 9 p.m. and rang the doorbell. A tall white man – a police officer from the mayor's guard detail – ushered me into the drawing room.

The housekeeper was there promptly to explain that the mayor was on his way, that he'd be a few minutes late and would I like a beer or a cup of coffee?

I opted for the coffee and wandered into the sitting room, where the World Series was playing on a black-and-white TV set in the corner.

On the way to the meeting I'd been wondering what sort of shape the mayor's mansion was in. People who are supposed to know had said that it was rundown and dirty; that Young's people had not exactly taken pains to look after its maintenance.

Needless to say, I don't usually get invited to the mansion for state dinners, so I had no idea what the place was going to look like.

In fact, I had only been there once before – for a brief visit, when Jerry Cavanagh was mayor.

As usual, the people who know are dead wrong. The riverfront home that millionaire industrialist Alex Manoogian donated to the city of Detroit as an official mansion a decade ago is in fine shape.

The landscaping is neatly manicured, the furniture is scrubbed and polished, the carpets and floors spotless. The place looks like it's been decorated recently, too.

At 9:15, the mayor's car pulled into the long drive and he entered through a side door with his assistant, Malcolm Dade. We shook hands, but there were few formalities other than an apology for being late. Coleman Young is not given to posing.

"C'mon upstairs," Young said, beckoning me to the carpeted spiral staircase that leads to the mayor's private quarters on the mansion's second floor.

We walked down a narrow hallway and he unlocked the door to his private office. It was decorated with a large desk, two chairs, a sofa and doz-

81

ens of plaques and pictures – the collected memories of 30 years in public life.

The housekeeper brought a bottle of rosé wine and three glasses on a small tray. She left, closing the door quietly behind her. Hizonner poured, then chose a chair next to me rather than barricade himself behind the desk.

Dade lounged, crosslegged, on the sofa.

The purpose of my visit was to pass along some information I had gathered about how the FBI had paid a family friend, Willie Volsan, to keep an eye on the mayor. Young listened patiently, then shrugged.

"I don't know what they'd be looking for from Willie," he said. "I don't see him that often and I doubt that he'd be able to say much anyway."

Somehow the reaction seemed to me to be predictable. Coleman Young is not given to fluster, either.

He may drop a four-letter word now and then. And his remarks in the heat of political debate occasionally may he considered intemperate. But he's an old hand at dealing with the government.

No one had told me precisely why Volsan had been hired to snitch for the FBI. Nor, for that matter, what he had been paid. But enough sources had confirmed his association to make it interesting.

Originally, the scenario goes, the bureau thought it could learn something about Detroit's dope traffic from Volsan. He'd been mentioned in Detroit police and federal Drug Enforcement Administration (DEA) narcotics surveillance reports.

Volsan had been living with Coleman Young's sister, Juanita, for several years. Shortly before he ran for mayor of Detroit in 1972, Young had bought into a lounge and restaurant on Livernois Avenue in Detroit.

When he was elected, however, he had to give up the business. So he turned it over to his two sisters, Juanita and Bernice. Volsan came in the deal with Juanita.

"We always were a close family," Young explained, sipping the wine and relaxing. "But we haven't been as close as I'd like in the last few years.

"Since I don't have any kids, I try to see my nieces and nephews around the Christmas holidays. In fact, I've planned to have them all here for the last few years, but it never worked out."

Why would the feds want to have someone watching him that close? Young smiled.

"Years ago they used to tap my phone and open my mail," he said. "I didn't know what they were looking for then, either."

We talked of Volsan and other things. The evening wore on and Young mellowed and told stories of the old days and what it was like to be a black union organizer in a white-dominated society.

There was some cussin' and some laughin'. And we both learned some things of value.

Mom's stuck

November 11, 1977

My right ear was red and puffy. People pointed and giggled as Mom lugged me across the hospital lobby and up to the information counter.

"You stand right here," Mom ordered. "We'll get to the bottom of this once and for all."

A lady with carefully teased hair and wearing a too-tight, white polyester pantsuit looked up from her filing as Mom cleared her throat.

"May I help you, madam?" she asked coldly.

"I would like to see the hospital administrator," Mom answered, her brow knitted in a scowl.

Miss Pantsuit smiled thinly. "I'm afraid that's impossible," she answered. "He's a very busy man."

"Then please get me the chief of obstetrics . . . Dr., ah, Dr. what's his name," Mom said. She finally remembered the name and Miss Pantsuit looked puzzled.

"Dead," she said. "He's been dead for 20 years. Say lady, what's this all about?"

"I'd prefer to discuss it with the proper authorities," Mom answered. "In private."

I had wandered down the counter and was thumbing through a Blue Cross leaflet. "Put that down and get back here," Mom said. I dropped the leaflet and shuffled back.

"Geez, Mom, this is embarrassing," I said in a hoarse whisper. "After all, I'm 47 years old. I mean, this is a bit much, bringing me here like this."

"Never mind," Mom said. "For the last 40 years, I've thought you acted strange. You've never been like the rest of the kids. I want to find out whose child you really are.

"It could be the $1-million question." Now you have to understand that my mother loves me, well, like a son.

She put up with me when I smoked Wings cigarettes at 11; when I skipped nearly half of the eighth grade to ride my bike to Belle Isle; when my high school counselor advised me to drop out and get a job on the assembly line at Dodge Main.

But, when that lady sued Crittenton Hospital for $1 million because she said they gave her the wrong baby seven years ago, Mom's wheels started to turn.

"I used to wonder whether you really were one of mine," she said after reading the story.

"I mean your brother, Joe, and sister, Pat, were always such nice, bright kids. No trouble at all from them. But you . . . skipping school, hanging around the Anchor Bar with those bums from The News. Look at you.

"Your brother's a college professor, reads books, gets his name in the big literary magazines. Your sister works for the church and raises kids."

Mom stared at me and shook her head.

"You don't even look like them," she sighed. "They're both tall, with brown hair and dark eyes. When you had hair, it was blond. And your eyes are blue."

There could have been a mistake, you know. Your father always said . . ."

"Mom!" I interrupted, "I look like you! You have blond hair and blue eyes. I'm yours, I tell you!"

"We'll see," she said. And off we went to the hospital where my birth was registered.

Miss Pantsuit pressed a button under the counter and a man in a long, white coat appeared. He invited us into his office and closed the door.

Mom sat bolt upright on a chair. I slouched on the leather couch.

"Now, madam," the man said. "What can I do for you?"

Mom outlined her theory. The man tilted back in his swivel chair and made a bridge with his fingers while he stared at the ceiling and listened.

"Hmmmmm," he said every so often. "Uh huh. Uh huh."

When Mom had finished, he spoke. "Of course you understand that was a long time ago," he said. "Our records only go back . . ."

Mom interrupted. "You have a footprint!" she said. "I saw the doctor take my baby's footprint right after he was born. Can't you dig it out?"

"Look at the size of him, madam," the man said. I instinctively sucked in my belly. "After 47 years . . ."

Mom pursed her lips. "Well," she said, "thank you for your time and trouble, sir. I guess there's not much more that can be accomplished here."

The man shook my hand limply and I followed Mom back across the hospital lobby. Outside on the driveway, she paused and caught me by the shoulders, turning my face to the sunlight.

She studied my nose and my eyes, then turned me sideways to check my ears and the large red and blue birth mark on the left side of my neck.

"Well," she said, "I guess . . . I guess so. So who needs a million bucks anyway?"

The Bay of Pigs

December 15, 1977

BAY OF PIGS, Cuba – Actually, the place isn't much. I mean, for all the hoopla, I expected at least a monument. Or a picture of Fidel Castro some-place.

"This is a national park now," said Raphael Garcia, the 27-year-old Cuban who was navigator on the 65-mile taxi trip from Veradero Beach.

"The revolutionary government wants it to serve as a symbol, a place where the people can come to enjoy themselves and remember the heroes who died here.

"The workers who earn the trip can come here to relax. That is the way we do things now and it is very good."

Apparently, not many of the workers are producing that well. Or maybe they are, and they just don't care for the long ride from Havana.

But the long, gray, sandy beach that now marks the spot where some 1,500 Cuban exiles tried to launch a CIA-inspired counter-revolution in April 1961, and failed miserably is largely deserted except on weekends.

The Bay of Pigs. Bahia de Cochinos. It's an intriguing name in any language.

Let me bring you up to date.

Shortly after Fidel Castro ousted Cuba's former dictator, Fulgencio Batista, in 1959, a whole bunch of Cubans fled the island. Hundreds of them settled in Florida and other parts of the United States.

Many of them vowed to return to their homeland as soon as they could get up the money to launch a counter-revolution. And when Castro started playing footsie with the Soviet Union, the U.S. government got into the act.

The CIA – guys like G. Gordon Liddy of Watergate fame – rounded up a bunch of the expatriates and hauled them off to a training camp in Guatemala, where they put together an invasion force.

Once the zealots were sufficiently trained, the CIA popped them onto a boat and buzzed them over to Cuba.

What the invaders had in mind was anybody's guess. In the first place, the Bay of Pigs, which they chose for their landing beachhead, was nothing but a great big marsh in the middle of nowhere. There wasn't even a road leading down to it.

And, if there had been a road, it couldn't have led anywhere because the Bay of Pigs is 70 miles from nowhere.

Anyway, the invasion was tipped off and Castro rushed in some defenders. He didn't need many because the U.S. didn't supply much help to the invaders anyway. So they were sitting ducks.

The fight lasted 72 hours, most of the invaders surrendered, a few defenders were killed or wounded and Castro had another example of "imperialist oppression" around which to rally the Cuban people to the cause of communism.

I'd been reading about the place for years. And this week, when I joined the first tour group to enter Cuba directly from the United States, I put it at the top of my list of places to see.

It wasn't easy. For one thing, when a U.S. citizen goes into Cuba, things are pretty tightly controlled.

When I arrived Monday, a government-owned outfit called "Cubatur" picked up my passport and said it would be returned the next day. They held onto it, of course.

There apparently are buses that go to the Bay of Pigs, but there are "arrangements" to be made. Since there are no cars for hire, the alternative was a taxi.

Cubatur said "it would be better" if one of its guides went along. It was an offer I couldn't refuse. Garcia, a properly programed propaganda machine, was the man for the job.

The trip to the Bay of Pigs covered flatlands and rolling hills as we crossed the island from Veradero on the northern beach to the south shore.

About 15 miles from the road that leads to the bay there is a sugar mill which, Garcia says, served as headquarters for the "revolutionary defenders" against the "mercenaries" who hit the beach.

At the entrance to the beach is a large plaque bearing the names of the revolutionary casualties and, all along the road leading down to the bay, there are individual markers, like tall tombstones, commemorating the places where defenders died in the swamps.

The beach itself isn't much. There's an anchor that Garcia says came off one of the invasion ships, a one-man pillbox fortification, which must have contained a very small soldier, and a "machine gun nest" on a sprit of land that looks more like ducks had been nesting there.

There's a small restaurant and a little arcade with a souvenir shop that sells nothing at all with "Bay of Pigs" written on it. But then, the Americans are only beginning to come.

They said what?

February 22, 1978

John Hertel says that the first time he attended a Democratic caucus in Lansing, he arrived early in order to get a good seat at the long table.

"We were all sitting there, talking about one thing or another, when Basil Brown entered the room," Hertel said. "He just walked in, stepped up on a chair and walked down the middle of the table to his seat. Then he climbed down and sat down.

"I was dumbfounded. But what really bothered me is that none of the old-timers even looked up. It was as if that was the way things ought to happen in a Democratic caucus and nobody paid any attention."

State Sen. John Hertel, D-Harper Woods, collects rare occasions in the Michigan Legislature. He was a Wayne County commissioner prior to taking a shot at the Senate, and that's as good a training ground for observing screwballs as you are likely to find anywhere.

Hertel's stories came to mind the other day while I was listening to a crime victim being interviewed on a TV news show. The man was lamenting the lack of police protection in his outer-city neighborhood, and when the TV space cadet inquired about what the citizen would recommend as a course of action, he said, confidently, "What we need around here is a little complacency."

As did Hertel, the space cadet just sort of blinked and went on, without bothering to question the choice of words.

"A couple of years ago, Art Cartwright got really upset with Gov. Milliken during one caucus," Hertel offered. "He finally jumped up and slapped his hand on the table and announced that, 'Smilin' Willie has done it this time! He's created an Einstein!'

"Basil Brown just shook his head and said, 'That's Frankenstein, you asshole,' and Art sat down."

There is indeed much that goes on behind closed doors in the Michigan Legislature which would wither in the bright light of public scrutiny. Some of the legislators' public pronouncements in 1977 were equally absurd.

With apologies to people who have printed them piecemeal before, and to the Lansing press corps, which culled them from a thousand dull and dreary sessions and compiled them, here are a few which I found amusing:

"Let's not rush into a China shop like a bullhorn!" Rep. Mel DeStigter, R-West Olive, advising caution on a bill.

"I'm on both sides of the law-enforcement issue." Sen. John Toepp, R-Cadillac, in one of the more ambivalent stage-setters.

"I appraised an animal once and married her." Rep. Rusty Hellman, D-Dollar Bay. You figure out why he said it.

"It's better to err on the side of being right." Sen. James DeSana, D-Wyandotte, advising caution in voting.

"What we do or say here is not going to have much effect on what two teenagers do in the back seat of a car." Sen. Richard Allen, R-Lansing, during a discussion of birth-control education.

"All we're doing with this bill is more evenly distributing the inequities of our system." Rep. George Montgomery, D-Detroit. No explanation necessary.

"There's no PBB affecting turkeys, but there's plenty of turkeys affecting PBB." Sen. John Hertel, D-Harper Woods, on his colleagues' inaction on PBB legislation.

"I expect that if we had legislation requiring us to be credible, it would die on a voice vote in the Senate." Sen. John Otterbacher, D-Grand Rapids. The cynic.

"This bill goes to the very heart of the moral fiber of the human anatomy." Rep. John Kelsey, D-Warren. And it comes out here. Do da. Do da.

"I approach problems as an idealist and as a pragmatist," Democratic gubernatorial hopeful William Ralls, covering all the bases.

"All we're saying is, 'Let's take a step backwards.'" Sen. Dan Cooper, D-Oak Park. Sideways must have been blocked.

"I've said all I want to say. Now I'm turning on the fog machine." Gov. William Milliken. He forgot to turn it off.

"The House will not allow you to circumvent the rules of this House unless you do it right!" Rep. Gary Owen, D-Ypsilanti, complaining to a colleague while serving as temporary speaker.

"The facts is beginning to submerge." Sen. Art Cartwright, D-Detroit. Do they ever go anywhere else?

There is some support for live telecasts of the proceedings of the Michigan Legislature. It would be a helluva show, as long as they didn't hire any professional actors.

Porn Girl

March 15, 1978

Now that Dallas Alinder has come out of the closet and nobody's hit him over the head, I guess it's safe to tell this story. First, a word about Alinder.

Fearing that he might embarrass his political bosses, Alinder recently quit his job as Philadelphia's cultural director. While temporarily out of work a couple of years ago, it seems, Alinder had taken a bit part in a X-rated movie.

It was a comic role, he says, with precisely 28 words of dialogue capped by Alinder getting smacked in the face with a plate of caviar. Sort of an underground twist to the old Soupy Sales schtick.

At the time Alinder didn't think anyone would recognize him from the film without his white socks and sailor hat. But they did, so he quit his city job.

Later, he said, people told him he had made the wrong move. His landlord offered free rent. A friendly cop shook his hand and told him, "Good luck. You didn't do anything corrupt."

Alinder's revelations this week recalled my first encounter with a bona-fide porno movie star. This was before Linda Lovelace started touring the country to show off her talented tonsils or Marilyn Chambers became the hottest thing on a soapbox.

I was standing around the terrace at the Pontchartrain Hotel one spring evening about four years ago listening to jazz, when magazine distributor Jerry Ludington spotted me. He had this cherubic young brunet in tow and introduced her as a writer who was in town to plug a book she had written.

A 4-H handbook? Perhaps a collection of choir hymns?

She smiled demurely as Ludington reached into his pocket and produced a paperback. "Porn Girl." The title leaped off the cover. "By Tina Russell."

"Tina," said Ludington, "meet Pete."

There was an awkward silence. Tina smiled sweetly and brushed her long brown hair back off her shoulders. The Brookside Jazz Ensemble was drowning out conversation anyway, but I tried, "How do you like Detroit?"

"My first visit," she said. "We've been rather busy lately."

Ludington returned with a bearded young man in tow. The man was carrying a briefcase and looked very businesslike.

"Tina's husband, Jason," Ludington said. "He's her producer and her manager."

Jason shook my hand firmly. "I also appear in some of her films," he offered.

I took a long pull on my vodka and tonic. While she does what, I thought.

Jason flopped his leather briefcase on one of the terrace tables and flipped open the latches. "I've got a press release on the book right here," he said.

"And some pictures of Tina."

He produced a stack of black-and-white photographs of Tina with various friends that would get us all arrested on any street corner in town. Necks craned in the crowd.

"That's nice, Jason, real nice," I said, trying to stay calm. "Put 'em away."

I had come to listen to the music, not talk shop, so to speak. But I couldn't resist the temptation to ask some questions.

"How many uuummm, errr, ahhhh, films have you appeared in?" I inquired of Tina.

"I think we counted 78, didn't we?" she asked Jason. He nodded his head. "Yes, 78."

"But if you're only 23," 1 said, "that's more than three a year since you were born."

Tina smiled sweetly again. "You can shoot the hardcore stuff every week," she answered softly. "You shoot a lot one day with three or four cameras and they just keep splicing in the different angles and stuff."

A star is born. Showbiz.

The interview went on through more vodka and tonic and, ultimately, dinner. Who's the best porn photographer? Tina gave me the name of some guy I'd never heard of, who, she assured me, really knows how to get where the action is.

OK, you can handle a lot of heavy scenes in one day. But how about your leading men?

Is there only one guy? Do they use teams and free substitutions, like pro football?

"The producers used to hire the male leads by the day and they'd have to do at least three scenes," Tina explained. "Then the union organized the guys and now they only have to do two scenes a day."

Thank you, Walter Reuther, wherever you are.

Phone fantasies

March 19, 1978

NUMBER PLEEZE – Florida columnist Ron Wiggins has collected messages that some inventive citizens have taped on their telephone answering machines.

Joy Elliott, a UN correspondent for Reuters news service, uses this pitch: "My dear, in previous incarnations on different continents I was an archivist, high priestess, philosopher-queen. Well, you ask, how come I'm now a mere answering machine?

"I'm being punished for a sin so delicious you'd be sinning just to know about it. To become human again, I must be the best telephone answering machine in the world. So be a dear and leave your name, number and message at the tone."

Not bad. But the late Zero Mostel was more to the point:

"I'm busy translating 'Beowulf' into Yiddish on a grant from the United Arab Republic. Please leave your name and number."

I've got one for a newspaper columnist:

"I am on deadline now and will respond to your call if any of the following do not answer your question: I remember the column, but I can't find it in the files . . . You sure Charley Manos didn't write that? . . . The Rose Bowl was played at Durham, N.C., in 1942...Gale Storm, Ann Sothern and Eve Arden . . . Bill Kennedy had his own hair at the time."

QUID PRO QUOTES – State Sen. John Hertel, D-Harper Woods, recently came up with a collection of his colleagues' more quotable quotes, which I printed.

A few we overlooked:

"That's not only dishonest, it's disfair!" State Sen. Arthur Cartwright, D-Detroit.

"The sun is shining and you're all getting a snow job on this. If you want to vote to increase taxes, go ahead. I'm ready to see this whole ball of wax go down the drain." former State Rep. E.D. O' Brien, D-Detroit.

And, the champion: "If the Indians (of Michigan) don't like it, they can go back where they came from!" State Sen. Tom Gaustello, D-St. Clair Shores.

ELEPHANT IN YOUR TANK – Recent reports that scientists are converting manure into fuel to heat the nation's households reminds me of the first time rotund, loquacious Andy Granatelli showed up at the Indianapolis 500 auto race with a turbine-driven car that he said would run on just about any type of fuel.

"It'll burn gasoline, alcohol, jet fuel, peanut oil, even perfume," Granatelli boasted.

Sports columnist Bob Collins suggested that perhaps they ought to put Granatelli in the car's fuel tank and see if it would run on bullshit.

SEVEN LITTLE WORDS – A while back I wondered in print if any of you knew the seven objectionable words that the Federal Communications Commission has banned from home TV. One guy wrote in to say that he didn't know the FCC's seven, but he suggested that they ban hee, haw, rerun and news four plus four.

THEY'RE OFF! – Debbie Hicks' allegations that there is widespread "fixing" at Detroit area horse race tracks was met with scoffs by some. Obviously, the scoffers never tore up a mutuel ticket that was rendered nonnegotiable when some little weasel pulled his mount up in the stretch.

The late Joe Palmer, who hung around race tracks for a living, told a story about a guy who liked one particular thoroughbred and followed its progress until he was certain it was ready to win.

He bet a bunch on the nose and the noble steed ran well until it got to the home stretch. There, in front of God and everybody, the horse lugged in to the rail, almost threw his jockey and finished fifth.

"A mistake," his trainer assured his backers. "Next time out he'll run straight."

The next time out, of course, the horse did the same thing. In front by five lengths at the head of the stretch, he leaned into the railing, nearly stumbled and finished off the board.

When he did it a third time, the guy who had mortgaged the house, the car and one of his three kids to get up money to get even, accosted the losing trainer in the paddock area after the race.

"I have a solution to that horse's problems," the bettor announced. The trainer listened cautiously. "What's that?" he asked.

"Put three ounces of lead in his right ear," the bettor answered.

The trainer scowled. "How do you propose to do that?" he inquired.

"With a pistol!" the man shouted. "And I'll do it for nuthin!"

Spoiled brats

April 23, 1978

The veterinarian stood in the doorway to the examination room, the bundle of black fur wriggling frantically in her arms. She attempted to mask her disgust, but was not very successful.

"Spoiled," she said, frowning. "Both of these puppies are spoiled. I suggest you try to train them so that they understand that people, not animals, are the boss.

"Perhaps obedience school..."

She could tell that no one was listening and handed over the squirming ball of whining canine to my wife. There followed much cooing and comforting and we beat a hasty retreat to the parking lot.

"Spoiled?" I asked, once we were out of earshot. "What a ridiculous thing to say. Why those puppies are only 6 months old. And there he is with one lady grabbing him and another trying to stick a needle in his little leg.

"Why, if that woman grabbed me like that and tried to stick a needle in my leg, I'd have raised hell, too"

Morgen, the boy puppy, curled up on the car seat, his head resting in its usual place - on the furry collar of my coat. He whimpered softly. I could sense that my wife was on the verge of tears.

"Oh, don't worry about old Morgen," I said reassuringly. "He's a tough cookie. He'll bounce back from this all right."

She dabbed at the corner of her eye with her handkerchief. "I know he's all right now," she said. "But what about his poor little sister? There, all alone in that hospital . . . all night . . . with no one to talk to her?

I choked back my emotions. No time to lose your cool, I thought to myself. I'm the man of the family. At a time like this I've got to be strong.

"Don't worry," I said, confidently, "she's probably got a private room with TV and a telephone. We'll give her a ring after while and see what she had for dinner."

We drove on in silence.

This was the big day. Having reached six months, our female puppy, Carmen, was admitted to the Michigan Humane Society clinic for a doggie hysterectomy. Her brother, Morgen, tagged along for a blood test for heartworm.

The two dogs are inseparable. They came from the same litter and were given to us by a friend, Marge DeBucci, when they were 2 months old. It was one of those things, you understand.

We had wanted a puppy and were going to buy a miniature Schnauzer. I'd even picked out the name - Morgen, which means "morning" in German.

When Marge agreed to give us "a puppy" we couldn't decide on whether to select a male or a female. Marge brought the pair to the house and we compromised - one of each.

Morgen and Carmen have no papers, no pedigree. Marge said she thought they were "sheepdogs," but they look more like cockapoos. I took one look at them when I got home that night and decided they were Polish sheepdogs: mother was a sheep, father was a dog.

Naturally, I commanded that they were to be trained with an iron hand. No table scraps, only Puppy Chow. Go to the john on the paper, or be beaten within an inch of their lives.

No chewing on slippers, begging at meals. No whimpering, whining or climbing on the sofa or the bed.

It's a cruel world. I run a tight ship. Everybody toes the line. Shape up or ship out, dogs.

Where did I go wrong?

As she grew, Carmen's hair became dull and scraggly, a canine Phyllis Diller. Her eyes, however, are ringed with the shiniest silver gray, framing a gaze which begs forgiveness when she cocks her head.

She learned to sit up first. So who cares if she can't always find the newspaper? She tries. She really does.

Tough-cookie Morgen is a pansy. Slap a newspaper against your leg and his sister crouches like a tiger, ready to strike back. Morgen falls down, rolls over, lifts all four legs and closes his eyes, as if to plead, "Oh please, massa, don't beat me no more! I'll do whatever you say, but don't hit me!"

Spoiled? Well, maybe just a little bit.

But if that lady vet thinks that's bad, she should have seen me on the front lawn the other day, leaning against a tree, trying to show Morgen how to lift his leg.

I mean good grief, puppy, you can't go on squatting for the rest of your life. The other boy dogs'll laugh at you.

A neat suicide

June 15, 1978

Detective Dane Richards dug down into the brown paper grocery bag and pulled out two lengths of rope. One was plain hemp, its frayed end tied with garbage bag ties; the other, a piece of dirty white clothesline.

The bag also yielded a pale blue woolen pullover hat and a wool ski face mask, with holes cut for the eyes and mouth, three pieces of lined notebook paper like kids use for penmanship practice in elementary school and a plain white letter-size envelope.

"This is all the evidence that was at the scene," said Richards, a veteran homicide detective with the St. Clair Shores police department. "What with the notes and all, it was a simple case of suicide.

"The medical examiner didn't even do a post on the body. The guy had it all nice and tidy. He must have been planning it for a long time. All we had to do was pick up the pieces."

Richards pushed some papers across his desk for my inspection. I fingered them uneasily and then read the longest note, which was dated May 25.

"I can't go on any longer," it began. "When my wife, Ann, died a lot of my life went with her. Lately I lost my job teaching after 26 years. No one out there seems to want to employ a 52-year-old 'almost' retired teacher.

"With no job or future, the only thing left is to make it possible for my wonderful children to collect my insurance before it lapses and I have nothing left to help them in the time ahead.

"It's very hard," the note concluded, "but it seems the only way left for me to be helpful. With love to my children." The note was signed, "Elmer L. Lepp Jr."

Elmer Louis Lepp Jr., 52, was found hanging by his neck in the basement of his home in St. Clair Shores May 31. He had fashioned a crude noose out of two pieces of rope, one hemp and one clothesline, climbed onto a wooden chair and tied them around his neck.

He tossed the ends of the ropes over the steel drain pipe from the kitchen sink and secured them, pulled the ski mask and the woolen hat down over his face so that the grotesque, distorted death mask, which comes with strangulation, would not shock the people who came to cut down his body. And then he kicked out the chair.

His windpipe pinched, he probably took several minutes to die.

Lepp left two children - a son, Ken, 18, and a daughter, Sherill, 12. He had come to the Detroit area from up north in the early 1960's because Ann suffered from epilepsy and other problems and she could get better treatment here.

For a while, Lepp worked as an elementary teacher in the Grosse Pointe school system but 10 years ago the school system changed his assignment to gym teacher. Lepp was not trained for the new job but he took it.

And there were problems, both at home and in school. But he held onto his job.

Then on Nov. 26, 1971, things started to come unglued. Ann had been acting erratically. She would disappear for hours on end; rise from her bed in the middle of the night and sit silently, staring into space.

That morning Lepp woke up and Ann was not beside him. He searched the house, went to the basement and found her hanging by her neck, dead, her face distorted from strangulation.

Lepp was not strong enough to cut her down alone. He had to call for help from Ken, who was 10 at the time.

Afterward, things got bad at work. Lepp struggled to raise the kids with the help of the grandparents. He was making $23,000 a year on the job and the fringe benefits included $29,000 life insurance, which paid off even for suicide. But there were other debts.

Then last February, began a long series of clashes with the administration at one of the two schools which he served - Poupard Elementary, on the border of Harper Woods, which culminated in his firing May 1.

The Grosse Pointe Education Association, a teacher's union, came to Lepp's defense and appealed the case. The notices went out May 31, the day he hanged himself.

Neat, Richards said. Very neat.

Lepp had tacked a note on his front door, warning his children not to enter the house but to "go to a neighbor" and have them call police.

He left the suicide note, stacked important papers in a briefcase and put his childrens' clothes in two piles, each with a note instructing what was to be done with them.

"It's OK," he wrote on one, "if Ken (my son) drives my blue van. He has a set of keys."

And, to the police who would cut down his lifeless body, he printed, carefully, "God bless you, men."

Expense account fiction

August 28, 1978

Lately it seems everybody's getting in trouble over expense accounts.

In the U.S. Senate, Georgia's Herman Talmadge gets caught writing phony expense sheets and has to pay back $37,000.

State Sen. Art Cartwright gets nailed for kiting expenses and pocketing the overage; U.S. Rep. Diggs does the same and calls the charges "racist." School board lobbyists spend with both hands – frequently, it turns out, on themselves – and keep such sloppy records that nobody ever finds out for certain where all the green all went.

Alas, expense account composition is a lost art whose dedicated practitioners cringe at the heavy-handed methods employed by Talmadge and Diggs, Cartwright and the assorted other amateurs. Truly, people like that give white-collar crime a bad name.

I shall never forget my first encounter with a master of expense-account fiction. It was, indeed, a memorable experience.

At the tender age of 23 (in those days it was tender) I was dispatched by The News' Sports Editor H. G. Salsinger to cover a Saturday afternoon football game involving Notre Dame at South Bend, Ind.

I worked most of the night before covering high school games here, caught a couple of hours sleep on a couch in the employe's lounge, grabbed a cup of coffee at the station and rode the morning train to Nile, where I bummed a ride to South Bend.

I mooched lunch in the Notre Dame press box, hitched another ride back to Niles after the game and caught the train to Detroit, had a sandwich for dinner and arrived about 10 p.m.

On Monday morning I sheepishly presented my expense account to the late Harvey Patton, then The News' managing editor. Patton appraised it grimly - "$8.50 train fare, 15 cents cup coffee, 50 cents sandwich" - looked up from his desk and boomed, "What the hell did you do? Carry your lunch?"

In order that I should not ruin things for everyone else, Patton sent me to the late Sam Greene, a fatherly gentleman who was The News' baseball writer. Sam chewed the stub of his cigar quietly, rolled the pencil in his fingers thoughtfully and corrected my addition.

When Sam was finished I had spent Friday and Saturday nights in South Bend, had dished out $30 for hotels, $10 a day for meals, $17 for taxis and, to my surprise, I even had treated Notre Dame Athletic Director Moose Krause to a $16 dinner!

We all, of course, have our expense-account champions. My personal hero was the late Doc Greene, who may have learned his artistry at the foot of his father, Sam.

As a measure of my esteem for Doc's creative ability, I can only point to the fact that I always maneuvered so that I would follow Doc into the managing editor's office to have my sheet signed, then I'd sprint to the cashier's cage to collect the money before he got there.

The theory being, of course, that by following Doc, whatever I asked for would be considered a paltry sum. Likewise, I knew that if he got to the cashier before I did, there wouldn't be any money left.

Foreign assignments are expense account plums. With great flair, the boss usually gives the reporter a large cash "advance" which he need not account for until he returns.

Several years back when one of the popes fell ill, the managing editor summoned our religion writer and told him catch the next plane to Rome.

With an $800 advance in hand, the writer repaired to the bar across the street to await his plane's midnight departure. Being of a generous nature, he bought several rounds of drinks for his friends and even a few for some strangers.

By early evening, however, the pope's condition improved miraculously and the editor canceled the Rome assignment.

The religion writer was tracked down in the saloon, where he was forced to pass the hat so he could pay back the 800 bucks the next morning.

Taste goes down with ship

November 8, 1978

Everytime you think you've seen the ultimate in bad taste, somebody reaches for a new low.

Friday night at the Roostertail night club on the Detroit River, owner Jerry Schoenith will throw a party commemorating the third anniversary of the sinking of the Edmund Fitzgerald.

The party announcements alone are enough to turn most adult stomachs.

At the top is a sketch of a Great Lakes ore carrier, awash and breaking up in stormy seas. Below the picture, in suitable script, is "Jerry Schoenith Presents...A Reenactment of the Wreck of the Edmund Fitzgerald.

"Wrecking starts at 8 p.m. with: Searchlights, Sound Effects, Costumed Employees."

The admission: $3, with drinks 75 cents from 8 to 10 p.m.

When somebody gave me one of the announcements I thought it was a gag. I mean, who could possible use the occasion of such a tragedy to throw a party?

I called the Roostertail and jokingly asked if I needed a reservation. No, the lady said; the Fitzgerald party will be held in the Palm River Room and no reservations are necessary.

I can't wait to hear the sound effects. Or see the costumes. I wonder if relatives of the victims will be the guest of honor? What will they need? Black armbands?

THE 729-FOOT ore carrier Edmund Fitzgerald broke up in a violent storm on Lake Superior 17 miles off Whitefish Bay on Nov. 10, 1975, with all hands lost. Capt. Ernest McSorley and his 28-man crew went more than 500 feet to the bottom.

No bodies ever were found.

What prompted Jerry Schoenith to seize on such a horrendous event for commercial purposes? I located him in Florida and he defended the party theme, saying he got the idea from the recent baseball World Series.

"The Los Angeles Dodgers dedicated the series to that coach who died (Jim Gilliam)," Schoenith explained. "I figured we'd do something similar with the Edmund Fitzgerald.

"I got interested in the Fitzgerald quite a while ago. We're on the riverfront and I like to do things (put on promotions) which focus attention to things that have happened on the Great Lakes.

"We try to keep things nautical; water-oriented. But I guess there always will be some things that don't come out right."

Schoenith says that the party announcements are not exactly correct. He's not going to record the screams of drowning men for the sound effects or have any bloated bodies floating in the punch bowls.

"Most of that is just hype," he explained. "We're going to have the staff dressed as sailors and have those revolving caution lights going in the big room. I've got a pamphlet about the accident to hand out and we'll play Gordon Lightfoot's "ballad of 'The Wreck of the Edmund Fitzgerald.'"

Schoenith said he's had several complaints about the party theme and that he "can't understand" the fuss. "It must be a dull time in the city," he said.

I suggested that the idea just might be a bit tacky and Schoenith really went on the defensive.

"To stay alive in this business in Detroit maybe you have to be a little tacky at times," he said. "We don't have the Ford Motor Co. behind us, you know.

"I try to come up with different themes. The people who are taking it wrong are those who never have done anything for the city."

Fr. Richard Ingalls, pastor of the Mariner's Church on East Jefferson, described Schoenith's party as "almost grisly."

Fr. Ingalls will toll the Mariner's Church bells 29 times at the noon hour Friday, in memory of the lost souls. If you're in the neighborhood, the admission is free.

Deck the halls with piles of junk

December 24, 1978

My wife rounded the corner into the living room, her arms ladened with Christmas packages, and let out a shriek. I bounded down the stairs from the bedroom and she unburdened herself and grabbed the front of my shirt.

"All right, wise guy," she shouted into my good ear. "What kind of a sick joke are you pulling now? What is that 'thing' standing in front of the picture window?"

I pried her fingers from my throat, one by one, and gave her my best hurt look.

"That, my dear, is not a 'thing.' If you will look closely you will see that it is a Christmas tree. A tannenbaum, if you will."

"I knew it!" she shouted. "They told me if you kept that dopey job one more year you were eligible to go bananas. It's happened, hasn't it? You've gone over the brink!

"That is no Christmas tree, you dummy. That is nothing but a pile of junk with little lights and pieces of tinsel on it!"

I decided that my best defense would be a good offense. But I maneuvered so that the sofa was between us, just in case.

"Caught you again, didn't I?" I chided. "Didn't read Eleanor Breitmeyer's column about how Tom and Diane Schoenith have decorated their house for the holidays, did you?"

She was momentarily stunned. I decided to press the advantage.

"You know that Tommy and Diane always are right up to date with the latest styles. So this year they've put up no less than nine Christmas trees and everyone of them is made by hand and has some significance to their marvelous, close, warm, wonderful, All-American little everyday family."

Marilyn's eyes darkened and her brow furled and she glared at the picture window. "Oh, yeah," she said sarcastically, "I get it. They gathered up all the scraps from the garbage can and hung them around their mansion and so you think we ought to do the same."

"Not garbage," I corrected. "Not junk. Tommy's so terrible creative! One of the nine trees is made up of boxes and bags from stores which he and Diane patronize regularly. Lanvin, Claire Pearone, Bloomingdale's, Courreges, Tiffany, Hattie . . . all terribly expensive, all terribly chic.

"I simply improvised on that idea, and a couple of others."

Marilyn approached the 'tree' cautiously. I had glued and pasted our boxes and bags, I thought, quite artistically for a person with no formal training. She read some of the labels aloud.

"Woolworth, K mart, Sears, Monkey Ward's." She shook her head slowly. "Naum's, Forest City, J.C. Penney . . . Farmer Jack!"

I could hardly contain my pride. "I knew you'd like my selections," I said. "And look . . . there right in the middle. The smokey-colored box with the singed edges."

She strained to read the name, which I intentionally had placed upside down.

"F-e-d-e-r-a-l-s."

Her glance swung to the top of the tree and I blushed as it stopped at the pink bag with the easy-to-enter overlapping hole cut in the side.

"You old fool!" she shouted. "You didn't put that bag from the Tina Marie Shop on our Christmas tree!"

"Wait until you see the way I've decorated the other rooms," I enthused. "I've made a tree for our bedroom out of all the towels and bathmats we've stolen from motels. Days, Red Roof Inn, Dream Acres Motel in Bellaire, the Holiday Inn in Paris, Ky., the Howard Johnson's in Rome, Ga., where they didn't have any cold red wine to serve with my steak.

"And underneath I put the bedspread we heisted from that boarding house in Upper Slaughter when we were in England a year ago!"

"I can't wait so see the kitchen and the other rooms," she said. "Crisco cans, right? Empty Banquet chicken boxes, instant coffer jars, used TV dinner trays?"

I smiled and shook my head approvingly. She was on target with me at last.

"And in the bar," I said proudly, "I've made a tree from our favorite bottles. Kessler's, Four Roses, Seven Crown, Canada House, Boone's Farm, Strawberry Hill . . . along with 200 empty Stroh's cans.

"We'll have the only Christmas tree in the neighborhood that you can turn in for a refund!"

Woody had a lighter side

January 1, 1979

Francis X. Schmidt was on his way to football practice at Ohio State University one autumn afternoon in the mid-1930's when he stopped at a garage to have his car greased and the oil changed.

Schmidt was the Buckeyes' coach at the time and he was famous for inventing new and intricate plays. Anyway, he had been kicking this one football maneuver around in his head all morning and when he pulled into the garage it was just beginning to come together.

The mechanic waved him onto the lube rack but, when he motioned to Schmidt to leave the car, the coach shooed him away angrily. So up he went, still behind the wheel, feverishly drawing his X's and O's and oblivious of the fact that he was seven feet in the air.

Halfway through the lube job, Schmidt solved the football equation. Elated, he stepped out of the auto, fell to the concrete floor and broke his leg.

All of which serves to prove nothing, I suppose, except that Wayne Woodrow Hayes is not the first screwball to coach football at Ohio State and he is not likely to be the last.

Pity poor Woody, out of work for the first time in 28 years after punching a Clemson player in the waning minutes of his Buckeye's loss in the Gator Bowl last Friday night.

It is difficult to be objective when considering the demise of the volatile Hayes, who devoted his life, and made certain everyone who played for him did likewise, to the great gray playground on the banks of Columbus' Olentangy River.

On the one hand, I say good riddance; they should have fired that old bum a long time ago. On the other, however, I grieve at his dismissal because it marks the end of an era.

And I am at the age when era-endings come much too often.

There was a time when I would gladly seize upon this occasion to tap-dance all over The Fat One's behind. But Michigan Coach Bo Schembechler, who seems to have become a shade humbler as the last game of each season approaches, has exhorted us to remember the good about Woody now that he's on the bricks.

I can't remember much "good." But I do recall some humor connected with his long tenure at Columbus.

There was the afternoon on the West Coast, for example, when the Buckeyes were trailing some nondescript team at halftime early in the season. Woody was furious, stormed into the locker room at the intermission and railed at his slovenly forces for 20 minutes.

The room was equipped with a portable blackboard on which Woody had written "WIN" in huge letters. When the signal was flashed for his team to return to the field, Woody shouted, "All right! This is what we are going to do!"

He flung a beefy fist at the blackboard and, to his surprise it smashed clear through to the other side. Unfortunately, Woody was already headed for the door and he was dragging the black-board behind him awkwardly, blocking the team's spirited exit while his assistants pried him loose.

Woody's postgame press conferences frequently could be timed with a stop watch. The record after one loss to Michigan, I believe, still stands at 2.4 seconds.

The Buckeyes just managed to beat Michigan, 7-0, at the end of the 1960 season. When we went looking for Woody he was out behind the stadium in the waning light, scrimmaging the players who would return to the varsity the following year.

Each year writers and broadcasters who cover the Big Ten make a tour of football training camps in the late summer. One September we all showed up at Columbus for a prearranged visit with Woody on his practice field but were barred from entering by guards.

Later, Woody apologized. "I was chewing out some of my players," he said, "and I didn't want to do it in front of a bunch of reporters."

The explanation was published widely. Two days later the tour stopped at Michigan State, where Duffy Daugherty was coaching. When we arrived at the Spartans' practice field, a guard blocked our entrance.

Incensed at the treatment, we demanded to see the coach. Duffy emerged from behind the fence.

"I'm sorry to lock you out," he said, smiling, "but I've been praising some of my players and I didn't want to do it in front of a bunch of reporters."

Come to think of it, now I'll miss them both.

A survivor finds happiness

March 21, 1979

The first morning that Sylvia Gass woke up in Mexico, a man was standing at the foot of her bed, peeling the polish off her toenails.

"I thought, 'Good lord, is that all they can do for me at a time like this?' I asked him what he was doing, but he didn't speak English.

"That was frightening. I knew that something terrible had happened to me, because I could see the X-rays of my legs when the doctor held them up to the light to read them.

"But no one knew how to explain it to me."

Sylvia Gass is a survivor, in more ways than one. She was among 118 passengers and crew aboard a Mexicana Airlines 727 when it sheared off a wing on a railroad trestle moments before touchdown in Mexico City in late September, 1969.

Forty-three people died, including most of the crew. The man in the seat next to Sylvia was killed and her legs were badly crushed.

When she stopped counting, Sylvia Gass had undergone seven major operations and had endured 43 separate casts on her left leg alone.

A piece of her left elbow is missing. She limps. But she can walk.

"I must have been unconscious for only a few minutes," she recalled. "When I came to, I had no feeling in my legs, but I knew what was going on.

"A friend who was traveling with me unhooked my seatbelt and I slid down into muddy water, right up over my mouth. But I managed to prop myself up and keep breathing until some men came and lifted me onto one of the wings.

"They took me to the hospital in the back of a pickup truck. That's where I woke up with the man cleaning my toenails. They told me later it was so they could watch for signs of infection."

It has been a long, difficult haul for Sylvia Gass, before the Mexico swamp and afterward. If you are one to categorize human beings, you probably would class her "spinster."

She came out of St. Thomas High on Detroit's east side in 1945, daughter of a cop named Stanley Gasiorowski. World War II was just over and she and her sister, Mary, went to work for Cunningham's at the 12th Street headquarters. Sylvia was secretary to the manager of the ice cream plant.

Tom Dunn, a New Zealander who had been stationed in Detroit during the war, was the plant supervisor. He knew the sisters and drove them home occasionally.

In time they all parted ways. Dunn moved his family to Miami, then Houston. Sylvia took a job as a secretary with Chrysler Corp. and joined a travel club. Lucky girl.

The trip to Mexico was a bonus. Sylvia really didn't want to go. She did it for a friend.

"I often wondered how people could even consider suicide," Sylvia reflected over lunch earlier this week. "But there were a couple of times when my legs pained so badly . . ."

She caught herself. "No, I don't think I would have done that no matter what. And now look what's happened to me."

Last fall, the phone rang and the voice on the other end had a distinct New Zealand accent. "Is this the same Sylvia Gasiorowski . . . ?" asked Tom Dunn, now 55 and living in Houston.

They talked. Dunn's wife had died of cancer. When the mourning was finished and it was time to pick up the pieces he had remembered Sylvia and searched until he found her.

He flew up for a visit. Sylvia went to Houston. They talk each day on the telephone.

Her legs are no longer pretty and she wears pantsuits a lot. But she will wear a dress on April 20 when she walks down the aisle at St. Thomas Church with Tom Dunn.

A wedding dress.

Jimmy, the provider

September 21, 1979

Jimmy came to this country shortly after World War I, emigrating from a village in southern Italy, on the Adriatic side, near the heel.

He could neither read nor write Italian, let alone English. He was a small man, with thin, bandy legs and strong arms and a chest that would have fit a body half-again his size.

His head was shaped like an inverted triangle and his ears protruded on each side, the tops bent as if they were permanently straining to hear some distant sound. He smiled easily.

I first met him in the early 1950's, after he had been in this country for 35 years or more, and his English vocabulary was limited to a few sentences, quickly spoken and understandable only if you had the patience to have him repeat them slowly.

His given name, incidentally, wasn't Jimmy. It was either Amadeo or something else, no one ever seemed to know for certain. But everyone called him Jimmy – except his five kids, who called him Daddy - and he answered to it and never seemed to mind.

When Jimmy came to this country there were strict immigration quotas and the big trick was to get one member of the family in somehow, have him naturalized as a citizen and then he could sponsor the others. Some men came in the night and married female citizens and then turned themselves in and were deported, returning when their spouses had made the necessary appeals.

It's unclear exactly how Jimmy got here, but a brother made it as far as Canada, where he paid a smuggler and went to South America. His track disappeared forever.

Jimmy ended up in a small town in eastern Pennsylvania, working in a steel mill. In time he was presented to an Italian girl, Lucy, and told they would be married. Lucy told me later she didn't even know Jimmy then, how could she love him?

They bought a small house on the South Side, a short walk from the steel mill, and settled down to raise five kids. And love grew.

Jimmy was a hard worker, a frugal manager, a strict parent and a loving father. Sometimes it was difficult to balance them all equally.

He didn't believe in labor unions and he volunteered to stay locked in the mill and work through strikes. Lucy and the children brought him clothes and food and passed them through the fence and shared the abuse he suffered, not really knowing why.

From the time he left Italy, Jimmy never rode a bus or a train. And he would accept a ride in an automobile only reluctantly, making the sign of the cross whenever he passed a Catholic church. He never took vacations from the mill, preferring to work and earn the extra money instead.

The house was heated with a coal-burning furnace, but Jimmy felt it was a waste to buy fuel. So he carried his lunch to work each day in a brown paper sack, then folded it and put it in his pocket so he would have his hands free to carry scraps of wood, which he scavenged from alongside the railroad tracks he crossed on his shortcut home.

He grew tomatoes and lettuce and other vegetables in a backyard garden and hosed off the porch and the front stoop almost daily during the summer months, when the fly ash from the steel mill coated the South Side and ground into the paint and left a film on the freshly washed clothes that were hung out to dry.

Jimmy ate alone most of the time, either just before or right after the rest of the family. Boiled foods – a potato, some meat, nothing seasoned. Bad stomach, he said. Lucy and the kids endured his idiosyncrasies with patience.

His kids grew up and married and moved away. One boy became a priest. When Jimmy reached 65, the steel mill forced him to retire. He fought it, but it was no use.

After a few months of idleness he suffered a crippling stroke. Weeks later, he died.

Some people just aren't cut out for the easy life.

Eating humble pie

December 9, 1979

When you're a celebrity, everybody's supposed to know who you are. Unless, of course, you are a doctor. Then even your wife – or husband, as the case may be – is duty bound to point it out.

You get to a party and they start the introductions. "This is Sam, Charley, Mary, Bill and Dr. Jones." Doctors don't have first names, even at social gatherings. They even call each other doctor.

That has nothing to do with today's treatise, which is how to keep you humble under difficult circumstances.

Vic Caputo and I were exchanging a couple of humble stories the other night while waiting in the bar for a table at Anton's, the posh new eatery in Grosse Pointe. We were posing near the piano, trying to be tastefully inconspicuous, while Leon Sehoyan, a lesser celebrity and a hairdresser who shows some promise, was entertaining our wives and his own a few feet away.

See, I had just bought a new pair of shoes at Hudson's in Eastland Mall and I was recalling the time a few years back when I arrived just as the store opened one morning to beat the crowd.

I tried on a pair of loafers and gave the salesman my driver's license because I had neglected to bring a charge card. He disappeared behind the curtain to write up the charge slip and wrap the shoes and when he came out I could sense that he had recognized my name and my picture.

Having been in this circumstance before, although not frequently, I must admit, I was prepared to graciously acknowledge that I was, indeed, the star columnist of the universe. No applause, please. Too early in the morning.

"Waldmeir," he said, puzzled, glancing from the picture to my face and back to the picture. "Waldmeir," he repeated.

"You got a brother or a cousin or somebody who sells plumbing at Sears?"

For the record, there is a George Waldenmeyer who works at Sears in the Macomb Mall. I wonder what people ask him?

Caputo, the son of a former Detroit cop who's been a mainstay at Channel 2 almost since television got started in this town, got his comeuppance one day after his home had been burglarized.

The police investigators arrived, surveyed the scene of the crime and made a lengthy list of everything the Caputos had lost to the intruders. At length one officer began to take a personal history.

He noted Vic's name, the address, the phone number and then asked Vic what business he was in. Caputo, of course, was fully prepared to soothe the cop's embarrassment when he answered, "Television."

The cop never looked up. "And the address of your repair shop?" he inquired politely.

Anyway, back at Anton's, Vic and I had become immobilized by the crowd in a small area between the piano player and the end of the bar. There is only one booth in that part of the room and four middle-aged women were ensconced in it, having a toddy before dinner - or, maybe, instead of.

Two of them kept staring in our direction and it passed my mind that they might have recognized either Vic or me. In a few minutes, one of them rose and walked a bit unsteadily over to us.

"We are entertaining a recently widowed lady this evening," she began. I immediately looked for a path through the crowd so we might say hello and, of course, absolutely make the widow's evening by being charming and witty.

". . . And I wonder if you two guys would move out of the way because our lady friend likes the girl who's singing and we can't see the piano."

Kill the messenger

January 9, 1980

My man Marvin stretched and his bones cracked. He had spent all morning cooped up in a Grecian urn in Mayor Young's office, gathering information for this exclusive report:

Jim Graham, the mayor's $50,500-a-year press secretary, stood in front of his boss' $10,000 oak desk, nervously twisting his handkerchief and scuffing the thick pile carpet with the toe of his shoe.

The mayor had his back turned and was gazing out the 11th floor window at the icy Detroit River. Suddenly, he spun his massive chair and fixed Graham with a steely glare.

"You're through!" Young shouted. "Clean out your desk!"

"But Boss," Graham protested, "what have I . . ."

"What have you done?" Young finished the sentence. "You have the nerve to ask that?

"Look at these," Young hollered, shaking a stack of newspaper clippings under his press aide's nose. Young read several headlines aloud.

"'Mayor Vacations at Secret Resort,'" he chanted. "'Young Takes $5,000 Raise Despite Huge Budget Deficit.' 'Federal Judges Run Detroit Sewers and Schools.' 'Mayor's Choice to Run Sewers Under Investigation in Minneapolis.'"

Young's eyes were slits. He was fuming, but he sorted out several more.

"And if you don't like that bunch, how about these?" he asked derisively. "'Arena Bonds Bad Buy, Investors Say.' 'Buses Still Run Late Despite Mayor's Promises.' 'Press Aide Says Mayor Overspoke in $100 million Promise to Help Chrysler.'

"You've done your damage, man. Get out before I have you drawn and quartered!"

Graham picked up the sheaf of newsprint that had been thrown at his feet. He thumbed through the stories numbly.

"But, boss," he protested, "be reasonable. I didn't write those stories. I didn't have anything to do with them. The reporters cover these events and the editors print what they write. Nobody's asked me a question in six months because I never know what to answer anyway."

The mayor wasn't listening to Graham's argument. He ripped out the story on the denial of the $100 million promise to Chrysler and shook it briskly.

"Look at this!" he shouted. "I go and make a big deal out of offering to build a $100 million assembly plant next to the Jefferson plant," Young said, "and that very same day you tell a reporter that 'the mayor didn't speak accurately. He began overspeaking himself.'

"You made me look like a fool!"

Graham straightened. "But Mr. Mayor," he protested, "you aren't building any $100 million assembly plant. You're building a $28 million paint plant! I didn't call you a liar."

"No difference," Young answered, stubbornly. "You should have seen to it that a lot of this junk stayed out of the papers.

"What about all those headlines about me and Mrs. Garrett, about my vacations in Jamaica, my million-dollar office renovation, my pay raises, the mess-ups in sewerage and transportation departments, the sweetheart contract with Olympia Corp. at the Joe Louis Arena? Shall I continue?"

Graham's eyes shifted from side to side. He was searching for a way to explain his position logically.

"Boss," he pleaded, "I swear I never put out a press release on any of those things. I can't help it if things happen and the papers write about them!"

Young pushed a button under his desk and assistant Malcolm Dade entered the office. Both men ignored Graham.

"Get out that list of newspaper people we might hire," Young commanded. "This time get me somebody who's been around, maybe a guy who's politically savvy, who understands how the city works, knows about newspapers and the rest of the media, and knows what it takes to make the mayor's office run efficiently."

Dade thought a moment, then spoke.

"There's only one guy in Detroit who fits that description, boss," Dade said. "And I don't think you two would exactly get along."

Coleman who?

November 16, 1980

Rínggg. Ringg.

"Good morning. The Eastern White House."

"Put me through to the president."

"Who's calling, pleeze?"

"None of your business, lady. Put me on to the man!"

"I'm sorreee, sir. But I cannot do that unless you tell me who's calling, pleeeze?"

"The mayor of Detroit, that's who! Now get movin'!"

"Pleeze, sir. I'm only doing my job." Pause. Silence. Click. Then click again.

"We'll need a little more information, sir. The president wants to know, where is Detroit? And why would its' mayor be calling him?"

Wheeze. Grumble. Cough.

"I'm tired of this messin' around, lady! Tell Old Prune . . . 'er, the president . . . that I'm the guy who Max and Hank the Deuce spoke to him about. Tell him Smiling Billy, the governor, sent me."

"One moment, Pleeeze . . ." Click. Silence. Click again.

"What can I do for you, Mr. Mayor?"

"That you, Mr. Prez?"

"Not exactly. What do you want?"

"Who the hell . . . ???"

"I am the fourth assistant undersecretary for domestic relations, sir. And please lower your voice."

Hiss. Wheeze. Teeth grinding.

"I don't talk to no flunkies, kid. This is serious. When the mailman came today, there wasn't no check for funds to run my city. Now you go find out what happened to my money and be quick about it!"

Pause. Silence. Sound of fingers tapping on desktop.

"It's coming back to me now, sir. You are 'that' mayor of Detroit. Oh, gee. How could I have forgotten? We were briefed on you. Yessiree, Bob."

"The name ain't Bob, sonny! You can start with the $600 million Jimmy promised for my subway . . ."

Papers shuffle. Pages turn.

"Jimmy. Jimmy. Why does that name ring a bell?"

"He was the guy who worked there before your boss, junior."

"How foolish of me. Of course. And here it is. Right here in your file: $600 million for a subway, $48 million for one development, $50 million for another, $38 million from bloc grant funds for an arena, $60 million for a GM plant . . . My, my, Mr. Mayor. You two must have been very good friends."

Sigh. Whimper. Sob.

"Better than you'll ever know, pal. What a loss. What a terrible . . ."

Sound of throat being cleared, loudly.

"Sure. Sure. Too bad. But what do you want from us?"

"My subway, man. My malls, my factory, my high-rise housing, my hotels and office buildings, my . . ."

"Slower, Mr. Mayor. You're going too fast. My boss, the third undersecretary, will want a much more detailed list of your requests and an accounting of where the money has gone so far. And, of course, you understand that the decision is not up to us. It has to go to the second, then the first, then the secretary, then the Cabinet, then through White House channels . . ."

"But I'm broke, man! Busted out! Smilin' Billy and Hank the Deuce said not to worry, that you guys wouldn't carry a grudge!"

Papers shuffle, pages turn again.

"Now run it past me one more time, Mr. Mayor. And let's be serious. Who are 'Smiling Billy' and 'Hank the Deuce' and why on earth would they tell you to call us about money?"

No more honeymoon

January 26, 1981

There is no small irony in Detroit Mayor Coleman Young's lament that continuing efforts to torpedo his plans for a Woodward Avenue subway are motivated solely by "racism and bigotry" and promulgated by suburban politicians who have no higher purpose than "to win votes."

What, pray tell, do you suppose motivates the good mayor in his desire to pour several hundred millions of taxpayers' bucks into a cement-lined tube that will run beneath, above and along Woodward Avenue from the river to 11 Mile Road? A burning love for his fellow man?

C'mon, Yerhonnor. Let's face a few facts.

The honeymoon is over. Your gravy train has jumped the tracks. I remember a few years back when some people were threatening Bill Ford that if he didn't hurry up and climb on the bandwagon to build a football stadium in downtown Detroit, they were going to go ahead without him.

Ford snickered, "They're like the buglers who blow the call to 'Charge!' but when they look around, there's no cavalry to back them up." He wasn't conned. For better or worse, Ford moved his Lions to Pontiac and there's still no new Detroit stadium.

The parallel with Young is unmistakable. A year ago, when Jimmy Carter was still manning the spigot that pumped millions of tax dollars into Detroit to bail out Young's extravagant administration, Hizonner could blow the bugle and back it up with horsepower.

Alas, his horse ran out of racetrack on Nov. 4. Gabriel couldn't toot up enough support for him in Washington these days to get him a taxi in rush hour.

Four years ago Young's re-election campaign contained repeated references to how he had brought "home the bacon" by getting "$600 million from Washington" for public transportation for this entire area. What happened to that boast, Mr. Mayor? Where is all that scratch?

I'll tell you where most of it is. It's still sitting at the Department of Transportation in D.C., that's where. And unless a lot of people who should know what they are talking about are sadly mistaken, the funds for

Young's subway project, at least, are likely to stay right there.

Young's most recent complaint was prompted last week when a review board of the Southeast Michigan Council of Governments (SEMCOG) voted 5-4 to withhold endorsement of a $13.8 million preliminary engineering grant for the subway at the urging of representatives from Farmington, Bloomfield and Plymouth Townships and Monroe and St. Clair counties.

Mayor Young immediately hollered "foul!" and accused the dissenters of pandering to racist and bigoted instincts of their constituents.

Isn't it funny how everyone is expected to consider Mayor Young's eagerness to reflect the desires of his constituents as statesmanlike leadership while those who oppose him always seem to get kissed off as racists and bigots?

On a campaign-style trip around the city last week, Young did very little to dispel the notion that, in this re-election year, he plans to strengthen his power base in the black community by promoting an "us or them" attitude.

Never again, he told a predominantly black audience, will "outsiders" be allowed to "control the political destiny" of Detroit. You don't need a dictionary to figure out what he means by "outsiders."

That kind of rhetoric from the mayor of a city that is 45 percent white is interesting. Young says it's impossible for him to be a racist. I guess if he says so, it's the truth.

The SEMCOG review board's approval is not imperative for the subway funds to be allocated. Young says he's not worried, the money will be there when the time comes. Old Prune . . .'er, President Reagan, won't go back on Mr. Carter's deal.

Like he told the Iranians, Mr. Mayor: The check's in the mail.

A little respect, please!

February 20, 1981

I want to congratulate the president of the Detroit Press Club, for his courageous stand on behalf of decorum and good manners. Frankly, it is long past the time that the hired help in that joint was put in its proper place.

In case you missed it, last week the prez warned the club's bartenders, waitresses and kitchen help to stop calling Press Club members by their first names. The next time somebody slips up they'll have a written warning placed in their file.

Too many warnings for fraternization and they're out the door.

I cannot tell you how long I have waited for a Press Club executive to take that kind of bold, gutsy action. I've never mentioned this before, Mr. prez, but it was precisely because of the ridicule and abuse I suffered at the hands of that scruffy bunch that I resigned my membership in your exclusive club years ago.

Vinny, the bartender. Now there's one who never showed me no respect.

It wasn't so much the impatient way he would insist that I repay the $20 I borrowed from him three months before. What I found completely uncalled for was the disrespectful way he would speak to me as I snoozed, head on my arms, face down on the bar in a puddle of stale Heinekens.

"Petey," he would say, "get up. How many times I told you? Petey, you can't sleep here. Don't you have a home? Gimme your car keys, Petey. I'll call you a cab."

Everyone would be watching him carry me to the curb and he knew it. How cruel and insensitive. Treating a man of my stature like a common drunk.

"Don't call me Petey!" I would command. "It's Mr. Waldmeir to you, pal.

"I am a respected member of the Fourth Estate! I pay dues here, my good man. You work for me! You watch your tongue or I'll see that you're walking a beat in Rouge Park!"

So Vinny's a bartender and not a cop. He understood what happens when you mess with a guy with clout.

And Marty, the waitress. Well, let me tell you; you couldn't put that one in her place fast enough to suit me.

I mean, everybody slips up once in a while, OK? Like, nobody's perfect and I just happen to have bad eyes and a short memory. I told them for years to change the lighting in the dining room so I could see the checks better.

But Marty chasing me around the bar, out the door, into the parking lot and grabbing my keys out of the ignition just because I forgot a little thing like paying my check, well, that's totally uncalled for.

I've never been so humiliated in all my life!

I recall vividly the last time she did it. I was lying there in the parking lot and Marty had one foot on my neck and was going through my pockets looking for money.

"Pete, you lousy creep!" she shouted. "This is the last time you stiff me on a lunch check. You and Jim and George and Charley are all alike. None of you bums knows what it's like to have to work for a living."

"That's it!" I answered ruefully. "You're on report! Leaving your station, assaulting a Press Club member and calling me by my first name! I'll have your order book for this, young lady!"

Alas, in those days the club was run by a bunch of lily-livered newspaper stiffs instead of the PR flacks who are in control now and my complaints fell on deaf ears. One club executive even suggested that I pay up my overdue bills and stop belly-aching.

Naturally, I was affronted and resigned.

Now that law, order, decorum and manners have resurfaced, however, perhaps I'll seek membership again. But first I better check to see if they still post your name in public when you don't pay your bills.

Good riddance

July 20, 1981

Peter Spivak says it is his burning desire to "do something that will help the city and the community."

He's off to a good start. He resigned as a Wayne Circuit judge.

Spivak, the 48-year-old Grosse Pointe socialite, quit the bench to join George Bushnell's law firm and, presumably, make some money. There's nothing wrong with that.

It'll be interesting to see how Spivak operates on the other side of the bench. In fact, there are a couple of dozen sharp attorneys – not to mention some of his former fellow judges – who have been waiting for a shot at him if he ever slipped out of his graduation gown.

I'll say one thing for Spivak: Nobody ever went to sleep in his courtroom.

A lady fainted once. And there have been some interesting lectures to convicted criminals that have caused prosecutors and defense attorneys alike to shrug and roll their eyes.

The lady who fainted was an interesting case in that she was a grandmotherly type who had been brought before the bar of justice for having been apprehended with a pistol in her handbag.

It probably would have been all right, except that she was carrying the handbag to meet a plane at Metropolitan Airport and got caught by the electronic surveillance there.

When the case got to Spivak, he lectured the lady and advised her to plead guilty in exchange for a suspended sentence or some such thing. She refused, saying that she didn't know she had the gun in her purse (she was traveling through the city late at night and insisted that someone else put it there for her protection).

She demanded a jury trial over Spivak's strong objection – and beat the rap. When the foreman announced her innocent, Spivak dismissed the jury panel and called her before the bench to berate her for having wasted the taxpayers' money.

In the course of his lecture, the lady slumped to the floor. When her husband went to her side, Spivak admonished that there was nothing wrong with her. "She's overweight and she smokes too much," he said.

I guess I first started to wonder about Pete Spivak shortly after he was appointed to the Wayne Circuit bench in 1972 by Gov. William G. Milliken. He was re-elected twice since, incidentally, the last time in the fall of 1980.

That doesn't mean much, however. It's been 35 years since an incumbent – either elected or appointed – failed to be re-elected in Wayne Circuit.

A spate of malpractice lawsuits surfaced in the early 1970s' civil actions against doctors and hospitals asking millions in damages for all manner of problems brought on by alleged poor treatment. Wayne County's caseload surged and judges complained privately that attorneys and plaintiffs were trying to hop on the gravy train.

Midst all of this, Judge Spivak filed a $2-million damage suit against Ford Hospital and a dentist who had treated him there, alleging faulty dental work. When I asked the good judge how he arrived at $6,500 a tooth, he said I didn't understand the problem and that he couldn't talk about it.

Some criminals are bound to miss Ol' Pete. If you caught him on the right day, who knows what he'd do?

Back in 1977 a heroin dealer was convicted in Spivak's court, fined 25 grand and sentenced to 10 to 20 years. Having done that, Spivak immediately suspended the sentence, explaining that the probation "is in many ways a more severe sentence than 10 to 20 years in prison. He knows that if he violates probation, he can go to jail for a long, long time."

But my all-time Spivak classic will remain his handling of a guy who stole $36,000 from his boss at an auto dealership and squandered it on fast women and slow horses.

Spivak put him on probation, but didn't order 10 cents in restitution. He made up a long list of restrictions for the embezzler, however, among them being that he "could not commit the crime of fornication" and that he must "buy his present wife the best gift he has ever."

He didn't specify whose money he should use.

Requiem for a Gypsy prince

September 28, 1981

Each night before they retire, Gary Demetro and his wife set a glass of water on a patch of grass in front of their home on Grand River near Cooley. When they rise in the morning, they go out and spill it and watch the liquid seep into the ground.

"It's a Gypsy tradition," Demetro explained. "So our son's spirit will have water."

A few nights each month, the Demetros burn a candle in their bedroom, and they pray by its light that the soul of their deceased son, Michael Anthony Stanley, a "prince" in the Gypsy band once ruled by King Thomas Stanley, will find peace in some mystical afterlife.

In Port Huron and Mt. Clemens, a couple of people who never met Michael Anthony Stanley are following a much less mysterious ritual. They are Detective Charles Neruda of the Port Huron police and Sgt. John Hart of the Macomb County Sheriff's Department and they are not as interested in determining where Michael Anthony Stanley's spirit has gone as they are in finding out who sent it there.

Mike Stanley, 20, a kid without a job who supposedly bought and sold used cars for a living, disappeared May 8 after calling his folks to tell them he was going to stop at Gratiot and E. McNichols for a while before coming to their house.

He never made it. On May 21, a man skindiving in the St. Clair River below the Blue Water Bridge in Port Huron spotted a body snagged on a pile of broken concrete in 22 feet of water.

It was Mike Stanley, dressed in a jogging suit and high-top sneakers, with his hands crossed and tied, a plastic bag over his head and a sturdy sack containing pieces of concrete and galvanized pipe attached to his left thigh with a length of telephone wire. For the weight, dear, as the old song goes.

Strips from a pink blanket and a green sheet were tied around his neck and there was a two-inch hole in his chest where somebody had shot him

121

at close range with a single shotgun blast. The coroner described the small, neat wound as being shaped like it was made with a "cookie cutter."

In tracing Stanley's final hours, Gary Demetro theorized that his son perhaps was the victim of some unfortunate circumstance. A holdup, maybe; a mugging that got out of hand.

But not even Detroit's sophisticated muggers and stickup artists would be likely to take the time – not to mention spend the gas money – to haul a body all the way to Port Huron. They dump their mistakes in alleys, not rivers.

The coppers – that is, Hart and Neruda – have another theory. Actually, two other theories.

They've got a tip that it was a "contract hit," but they can't nail down the assassin or the exact reason. "There are no witnesses, no weapon and no scene," says Neruda. "That doesn't leave much else."

Two of Mike Stanley's pals have come forth with a story that he had been somehow involved in drug traffic. His family told the coppers that they thought he might have been done up by some Gypsies from Toronto because he had been courting the daughter of one of their leaders without the father's consent.

The "Stanley" family – Mike and his mother – both Kept King Thomas' surname – has had its share of trouble. Old Tom Stanley once was kidnapped, stabbed and dumped in a gutter on Michigan Avenue by some folks he described as "a bunch of East Coast Gypsies" who wanted to muscle in on his territory.

A sign in front of the Demetro home advertises "Spiritual Readings by Fatima." In smaller print, it implores prospective customers to "Let me help you solve your problems."

Palm reader Fatima should have checked Mike Stanley's lifeline. She might not be spilling water this morning if she had.

Young love

February 12, 1982

John remembers the first time he saw the only girl he ever really fell in love with.

They both were about 15, freshmen in high school, and he rode the bus home from Nativity to Warren, where his family had moved from the old neighborhood around Gratiot and Harper.

Her hair was dark-chestnut, he thinks now, and it was shoulder length and cut in bangs and sometimes she wore pigtails. She was dressed in one of those plaid uniforms the girls from Catholic school always had to wear and sometimes black and white saddle shoes, two bits of apparel that didn't exactly make her stand out in the crowd of kids.

Except to John, her secret admirer.

She didn't go to Nativity, because she was always waiting in the bus stop when John and his sister got to the transfer point for the Schoenherr bus at Seven Mile and Gratiot. He figured she must have been from St. Anthony's, which was further down the street toward East Grand Boulevard.

Every day, he would look forward to seeing her there, on the corner, greeting him with a shy smile and a friendly hello. But that was it. They were kids and it wasn't cool to get to know too much.

John remembers a lot about the bus. It was the Schoenherr-Redmond or Schoenherr-14 Mile route and usually there were a dozen kids on their way from Detroit high schools to their families' new homes in the eastern suburbs.

He thinks some of the guys' names were Peter and Dan and Curtis and that they were coming from Notre Dame High School, over near Eastland Center. And the driver was a man named Sidney. Good old Sidney. Always joking with the gang in the back of the bus.

His mystery girl's name? She never said and he never had the nerve to ask.

Every afternoon, the bus would go north on Schoenherr from Seven Mile and she would get off at the last stop before East Eight Mile Road and walk down a street that John thinks was either Carlisle or Collingham, where, he assumed, she must have lived.

You'll think I'm strange, he says now, but I loved her. But I could never sit beside her or say more than hello because I was just starting to grow up and I was scared to death of this new feeling I was having.

John dreaded the last bus ride of the last day of school in June 1968. He was transferring to a school in Warren the next year and, when she got off at her stop and disappeared down that tree-lined side street for the last time, a lot of John went with her.

And then it was summer and John and some buddies went out to the Macomb Mall to bum around one day. They were just hanging out, cruising past Sears when, lo and behold, there SHE was – walking toward him in a group of girls.

John knew then that she wanted him to make his move, to talk to her. But he couldn't. He just kept moving, chattering with his buddies. And that was it. The last time he ever saw her.

Idiot! Dummy! Loser! he thought later. Why didn't I at least get her name?

So now it is Valentine's Day 1982. Fourteen years later and John is about to turn 29. He wonders if the girl with the chestnut hair and the plaid uniform and the black and white saddle shoes ever married, had kids, found happiness.

He's got more nerve than I have. I don't think I'd want to know.

Colemanomics reigns

November 4, 1981

Four more years. And four more, and four more, and four more after that.

It's no longer strictly a matter of who can beat Coleman A. Young. It's who wants the job, anyway?

Detroit is a mess, plain and simple. The economy is sour, the auto industry is on its most disastrous losing streak in history, and Reaganomics, right or wrong, has turned off the once free-flowing spigot of funds from Washington.

We are exhorted by well-paid and well-meaning politicians to stop whining and start pulling ourselves up by our own bootstraps. Alas, when we do, they come up to our knees because, while our alligator uppers are so shiny they reflect up, there are no longer any soles in our boots.

On the way into work the other morning, I rescued from a bus stop a member of an endangered species: A native Detroit Irish politician who has managed to keep his job as an elected official, at least until next year, when he has to run again.

He was lamenting the fact that there no longer appears to be any measurable or significant "Irish vote" in the city, or in Wayne County, for that matter. He was right, of course. But he might have added that there also no longer is an "Italian vote" or "Polish vote" or any other ethnic bloc save one.

Coleman Young proved once more yesterday that he has that one locked up for now and ever more, and therein lies a major portion of Detroit's problem.

Young's Detroit is like those alligator boots. It looks great until you turn it over and check the undersides.

Young poured millions in grants and tax writeoffs into the Renaissance Center. It sure looks pretty on a postcard, but it lost $33.5 million last year.

That's OK, Young's people argue, because it created jobs. Sure, that's why shops and office tenants have been quietly packing up and bailing out for months, and the center partnership acknowledges reluctantly that it's looking for a $50-million loan to stay afloat.

Nobody who has studied Colemanomics even batted an eye.

Hizonner has a way of conning his constituents into thinking they are getting something for nothing – and I guess he rates a few votes for that. Take the oft-lamented Washington Boulevard project, for example.

In late September, one Detroit newspaper headlined a story, "Washington Blvd. Gets Plan for Renovation." I thought maybe I'd been in a timewarp. Or perhaps that I had picked up a five-year-old copy from the newsstand.

Washington Boulevard was supposed to have been "renovated" in the mid-1970s, when the city pumped more millions into the five-block mall with the talking fountain, outdoor stage and Gino Rosetti's flame-red lighting system that looks like playground monkey bars.

Construction mismanagement and the attendant delays drove most of the solid old-line Detroit stores and businesses off the boulevard. When they finally finished the "renovation" project, the city had created a boneyard littered with skeletons of once-thriving merchants.

Now they have the gall to proclaim the arrival of "Son of Washington Boulevard." And there will be no shortage of folks to queue up to pump Young's hand and thank him for repairing the mess that his own people made. Slick.

Where does it go from here? Four years of more of the same. Young goes from landslide to landslide, each election adding to his aura of invincibility and each wasted year making the prize less attractive to any right-minded contender for the job.

Walk a mile in his boots? Forget it. You wouldn't get around the block.

So long to 'the Z'

June 23, 1982

"Fred Zollner," Myron Cope once wrote, "is short and stocky, a dapper man sporting peak lapels, a silk shirt, a constant tan and an unruly coiffure that suggests he is about to mount a podium and conduct Beethoven's Ninth.

"He is the sort who would not harm a fly; rather than swat one, he would catch cold holding the door open until the fly got ready to leave."

Fred Zollner died Monday at the age of 81. Although I have not seen him in six years or more, I will miss the old codger.

He taught me a lot as a young reporter.

The Z – that's what everybody called him, behind his back, of course – was a hick with class. I once helped to get him sued for $5 million, a lawsuit that ended up costing him $225,000 to settle.

When I called to apologize for my part in the affair (which was inadvertently allowing some things said off the record to appear in print), The Z accepted my explanation graciously.

"It wasn't much money, really," he said. "I wrote it off."

Fred Zollner helped change the face of professional basketball when he brought the Pistons from Fort Wayne, Ind., to Detroit in 1957. The National Basketball Association was a bush league.

The Z was the league's money man, a wealthy eccentric who was a soft touch for anybody who wanted to borrow a few bucks – or a few hundred thousand – to keep the sheriff out of the locker room.

His fellow owners never failed to take advantage of his good nature and his love of the game.

Zollner owned an executive DC-3 aircraft, appropriately called the Flying Z, which was fitted with such amenities as a bar, reclining easy chairs, a sofa, a "picture window" and booster rockets to help lift it out of dinky airstrips.

Because his team had use of the plane, The Z's team always got the worst schedule in the league. After all, the other owners reasoned, the Pistons didn't have to put up with airline schedules.

I spent many a white-knuckle night on the Flying Z, ducking around thunderstorms, banging out stories on a typewriter set up in the tastefully appointed john in the tail section, listening to Zollner.

One night during a particularly rough and stormy flight, I slumped a bit sickly into the easy chair across from The Z and inquired about our chances to land, as scheduled, at Detroit's City Airport.

"I'll take care of that right now," The Z said, smiling. And he lifted his foot and rapped his shoe in rapid succession several times on the floor of the plane.

"Devil!" he shouted. "Now, you listen to me. We've had enough of this and we want to land. So, open up!"

I looked puzzled, I guess.

"That's that," the Z said. "We'll make it now." And, sure enough, we did.

Zollner loved the identity he got from owning a pro team – even one as insipid as the Pistons. And he delighted in making off-the-wall management decisions.

When the team moved to Detroit, for instance, The Z hired a referee named Charley Eckman as head coach. Eckman admitted he didn't know anything about handling athletes, but The Z figured Eckman would get some publicity.

In the mid-'60s, he appointed Dave Debusschere player-coach. The Buffalo was 22 at the time and was also doubling as a pitcher for baseball's Chicago White Sox.

"To get along in life," The Z said, rationalizing the dual appointment for his wunderkind star, "you have to have a head like a grapefruit . . ."

He meant one that comes in sections, not one that's mushy. I think.

There are so many stories . . . so much to tell. But then, with The Z, there always were.

One of the last interviews I did with him ended the way I might end this.

"That's about all I have to say," The Z concluded pleasantly. "You know me well enough to write it without having to resort to the knife. "I don't need any surgery."

If it's all the same to you, devil, keep the door closed this time.

Praying for Fritz

August 23, 1982

Fritz Crisler was a funny guy. If he liked you, you were home free. The door was always open.

If he didn't, nobody else ever told you first. Fritz gave it to you straight and it would take an earthquake to change his mind.

He was always quiet, steady of voice, direct in his conversation, never wasting a word.

If he said anything before he died Thursday night at 83, it more than likely was "Go, Blue."

There were a few things Fritz despised: Cheating on recruiting or in a game, pro football scouts trailing his players, Michigan State and Notre Dame. They may not have come in that order.

Some things he just didn't care about. Basketball was one of them.

Ozzie Cowles used to tell the story of how he took his Michigan basketball team to the NIT tournament in New York and got blown out in the first round.

"I was prepared to catch hell from Fritz when I got back to Ann Arbor," Cowles said. "But the first time I ran into him, Fritz only asked me where I'd been for the last few days." Cowles quit as Michigan basketball coach.

Fritz was proudest of the men who had played for him at Michigan in a decade in which he raised the Wolverines' football program to the national prominence that it enjoys to this day. His recollections of the 1947 Michigan team would bring tears to the hard-bitten old codger's eyes.

Herbert Orin Crisler was a coaching genius, no less an artist at his craft than Stagg or Heisman, Yost, Rockne, Leahy, Pop Warner, Clark Shaughnessy or Red Blaik. Oh, we've all heard the tale recounted of how he gave the game two-platoon football. But I think he made other contributions of far greater value.

As much as he decried the heavy-handedness of big-time athletics, Fritz was the first college coach to recognize the financial and psychological edge of building a giant stadium and recruiting the best student-athletes to play in it. Michigan has the country's largest college-owned stadium –

101,000 seats – because Fritz wanted it.

When World War II ended, Fritz and a small handful of major college coaches realized there was a vast pool of football talent available among the athletes who had gone away as boys and were coming home as men. He made it his task to take as many of the biggest, fastest and smartest among them and they served as the finest in the country.

Don't get me wrong. Fritz wasn't a sweet guy. He had a mean streak several inches wide and there likely will be a few dry eyes as he goes to his reward.

He drove a hard bargain. Because he had the biggest stadium in the Big Ten, Fritz held a hammer over lesser opponents like Indiana, Northwestern and Michigan State. Indiana would go for years without playing a home game with Michigan. The Hoosiers always had to come to Ann Arbor, or not play Michigan.

When Michigan State first petitioned for Big Ten membership, Fritz tried his best to keep the Spartans out of the conference. He was disappointed when he failed.

A Michigan-Notre Dame football series would have brought millions in gate receipts. Fritz wouldn't play the Irish, however, after he got beat in a game at Ann Arbor in the '40s. "Every priest in Ann Arbor said mass for Notre Dame that morning before the game," Fritz scowled. "I didn't like the odds."

They'll be praying for Fritz Crisler tomorrow morning. I hope it does him as much good as it did Notre Dame.

A bittersweet Christmas

December 24, 1982

I do not know exactly how to face this Christmas Eve. There is so much happiness and so much sadness to be dealt with that my family is emotionally worn to a frazzle.

I will survive. We all will. And with a little luck we will be the stronger for it.

The drumroll of events started in late summer when my pal, Buffy, fell ill again and was hospitalized for what turned out to be his final trip. My mother, Helen, gave us all another lesson in how to be graceful under extreme circumstances and she held my father's hand and comforted him until he went peacefully in his sleep.

A week later we were all back in the same hospital – on the same floor – to greet the family's newest member, my infant son Christopher Norman. Norman was Buffy's square name and if you don't think the combination of visiting that hospital again and hearing that name spoken didn't tear at a lot of heartstrings, well, you probably are as hard-hearted as everybody thinks I am.

We prepared to christen Chris and I got involved in the annual Goodfellow fund-raising drive and paper sale. It's a tough year economically around Detroit and I had read and heard of so many folks who were strapped by hard times that I wondered who was going to accept the burden and come to their rescue.

So I wrote something about this being a year above all years to dig deeper than we ever have. And in a matter of hours the responses – the outpouring of genuine love and caring – started to roll in.

The mail piled up. Friends stopped me in the street or at lunch or came past the office to drop off envelopes.

By midweek I had received nearly 1,100 responses and the total amount donated for the Goodfellows had passed $17,000 and was climbing.

I don't know what dope does for folks to pump up their spirits, but I'll tell you one thing: It can't possibly match the rush you get from seeing one human grab another under the arm and give a boost when it's needed most.

We took a brief time-out in the midst of the Goodfellows campaign to have Christopher Norman baptized. More tugging and pulling.

My eldest son, Peter, and daughter, Patti Ann, had come home to be with my former wife, Dorothy, who was mortally ill and sinking day by day. They missed the christening ceremony, which was conducted by Fr. Vaughn Quinn and Fr. Jim Cokes at the Sacred Heart Rehabilitation Center in Memphis, Mich.

The priests and the "community" at the center, which is a long-term treatment facility for alcoholism, built the entire Sunday service around rebirth and they made a special felt wall-hanging and carved a candle and embroidered a vest for Christopher to wear.

Everybody else among family and friends seemed to handle that one OK. I was the only one who acted like he owned stock in Kleenex.

Like Buffy, Dorothy fought her battle with grace and dignity. Like Buffy, it ended peacefully in her sleep – in the predawn hours Wednesday morning, with Patti and Pete whispering assurances that her journey does not start alone.

She was a good and loving mother, a good friend and a good wife. That we chose separate ways a few years back did nothing to diminish any of those qualities.

A memorial mass will be celebrated by her brother, the Rev. Dan Bastianelli, Tuesday at 10 a.m. at St. Louis Catholic Church on Crocker Boulevard in Mt. Clemens.

I am proud of all my children, as you may have noted on previous occasions, Lindsey and Christopher Norman equally included. But today I am especially proud of the way Peter and Patti dropped everything – careers, friends, personal comforts – for weeks to faithfully stand the vigil at their mother's bedside.

I consider myself blessed because, unlike a lot of parents, I know all four of my kids know how very much I love them.

Merry Christmas.

PART II

Lovable Lynn

May 27, 1983

In all the hassle over putting aging tigers to sleep, altering the monkey community and closing the Great Ape House, one important passing at the Detroit Zoo regrettably has gone unmarked.

Lynn, the 20-year-old Norwegian polar bear who was sort of the Man O'War of his species in a long and distinguished breeding career here, is dead.

It is a mark of the troubles, both financial and public relations-wise, which have beset the city-owned wildlife park lately that Zoo Director Steve Graham chose not to make public Lynn's death from natural causes on May 8.

I discovered his passing yesterday during an early morning tour of the grounds with Graham.

"We just thought we'd let it go," Graham said. "There's so much else that's been going on . . ."

I'm glad Graham's not in charge of The News' obituary page. Here's a male chauvinist polar bear who was the Tommy Manville, the Mickey Rooney of the animal kingdom.

He gave of himself freely and frequently. The record shows he never turned any lady down, no matter how mottled or shaggy she might have appeared.

Knowing Lynn, he probably played over pain, gritting his teeth and performing even when he had a headache.

They called him Lovable Lynn in the good old days, and he was the undisputed star of a polar bear stud stable that became legendary in the 2 1/2 decades from 1950 to 1975.

In that time the Detroit Zoo recorded 40 births of polar bear cubs. Keepers calculated that more than two dozens of them could trace their lineage directly to Lynn, who came to town in 1962 and cut a romantic swath through the female bear population – and back again.

Several times.

Of those 40 cubs, 24 were either sold or traded to other zoos, bringing cash income or other exotic animals in exchange.

This guy was no laggard and he certainly wasn't a slub-a-bed. He earned his horsemeat, or whatever they feed polar bears.

"You'd always know when Lynn was in a romantic mood," Dr. Robert Willson, the former zoo director, recalled. "He'd come out of his den, cuff a couple of females around and then haul one of them back in with him.

"There wasn't much foreplay with old Lynn. He got right to the point."

Three years ago, in the spring of 1980, time began to alter Lynn's disposition. He turned grouchy, then surly. The love-taps that had marked his youthful courting turned vicious and then deadly.

In the span of a few short weeks he wooed three young females and when they spurned his amorous advances, he killed them. The hide of one of Lynn's victims, a 400-pounder named Karen, was to have been tanned, stretched and presented to Detroit Mayor Coleman Young in a bizarre plan hatched by former Zoo Director Gunter Voss.

Voss was fired before it could be pulled off, however, and the hide later was cut into small pieces and now is used in the zoo's education program for the sight-impaired.

Because of his age and sour disposition, Lynn was placed in solitary confinement in a private den behind the polar bear exhibit.

He had been marked by his keepers to be killed, but the flap over Graham's proposal to euthanize four ailing Siberian tigers (three eventually were killed) caused the zoo brass to change their minds about Lynn.

He subsequently was given another chance and had been living peacefully back among his friends and former lovers when he died May 8.

"The keeper found him stretched out on his side that Sunday morning," Graham said, "as if he was asleep." When he checked later he found a small amount of blood coming from Lynn's mouth and nose.

"By the time we got his body to Michigan State it was too late for an autopsy to reveal anything internally. But he wasn't killed by vandals and he didn't choke. It might have been a lung problem or heart failure."

What happened to Lynn's carcass?

"Both MSU and Wayne State have asked for the skull," Graham answered. "But we incinerated the rest. We're not in the trophy business."

Lest we forget: Dauchau

September 22, 1983

DACHAU, West Germany – There is something about this place that freezes the brightest summer day for me.

A few short miles away, in midtown Munich, beefy-armed waitresses in colorful Bavarian dress are dispensing fistfuls of gray-stoned crocks in the frolicking Hofbrau House.

Oktoberfest has begun and men in picture-postcard lederhosen and women in bright dirndls walk the streets arm-in-arm or sit in the sidewalk cafes or thump their thighs in time to a blaring oompha band.

But no matter what they do, no matter how high they turn the music, no matter how much they drink a few miles away, the sun never really shines in Dachau. And the danger is, I find, that somehow that may be forgotten as years go by.

It is a cold, hard reality that at least 31,951 people died in Dachau in the 12 years between 1933 and 1945. I say "at least" that many because those are the only dead whose names are officially recorded in the Dachau files.

Only God and the monsters who conceived and ran this place as a Nazi concentration camp know the proper count.

If there is such a heinous thing, this is the granddaddy of all concentration camps; established March 20, 1933, a mere 11 days after Adolf Hitler made Heinrich Himmler chief of police in Munich.

Located on the site of an abandoned World War I munitions dump, the Dachau camp was built to house 5,000 Communists and Social Democrats, enemies of the Hitler state. Within a month, the German SS had taken command and before the American Army had liberated the inmates in the spring of 1945, more than 200,000 registered prisoners, from at least 30 countries, had passed through its portals. At one time, in 1944, the camp housed 16,000 painfully, cruelly treated human beings, more than three times its capacity.

In the final four months before Germany fell, 13,000 died of illness and starvation. Only 1,600 prisoners were alive when the camp was liberated.

Now, the camp sits on the outskirts of this otherwise pretty Bavarian town, a lasting monument to man's inhumanity to man. And every time I come this way, I stop – I am compelled to stop – to read the names and look again at the long, neat rows of foundation where the prison buildings used to stand. And to remember.

When I passed here eight years ago, things were pretty much the same.

Then, three years ago, I was passing through and noted that suburbia was beginning to creep toward Dachau. Houses, apartments, stores, right across the street.

So, this time, I went back and, sure enough, what I had quietly feared had come to reality.

A couple lounged on the sparse green strip of lawn in front of the concertina barbed wire with a guard's machine gun tower in the background, and had their snapshot taken.

There's no admission, only contributions, and you have to look for the canister. I wondered if the townsfolk bring their schoolchildren here and teach them about what happened. I wondered what it would feel like to be German and live in an apartment across the street from Dachau.

I would venture to say that, nowhere in the world, except perhaps another concentration camp at Bergen-Belsen or Auschwitz or somewhere, not in a cemetery or a morgue or at any monument, would I have the same eerie feeling that the ghosts walked with me.

In the small chapel at the convent that the Carmelite nuns built behind the back wall of Dachau in 1964, there is a place to write messages.

On Sept. 19, 1983, a girl named Michelle Jedder, who left no address, scribbled three words: "It's so sad."

It will be much sadder if the world forgets.

The great jail break-ins

February 10, 1984

Since this is the official date for observing George Washington's birthday, I want to fess up to a couple of tricks that I pulled a few years back.

You doubtless have heard all the fuss and commotion lately about the lady reporter from Jackson who allegedly helped some friends break out of jail. I've twice used ruses to get myself into the lockup. And one of them was the Utah State Prison.

The first incident happened in Detroit several years ago. A friend of mine had been arrested for killing a guy and attempting to dump the body in a river in Macomb County.

He'd been collared by Macomb deputies in the wee hours of the morning, had tried to escape and had been shot and seriously wounded.

Well, nobody wanted the press near him, but another reporter named Bill Matney and I both knew the guy and we figured that if we could at least catch him as they wheeled him into the Receiving Hospital emergency room when he was transferred to the prisoner ward there, we might be able to ask a couple of quick questions.

So Matney and I trotted over to Receiving's admitting room and there was the usual mass confusion. When the ambulance arrived, we managed to work our way right to the truck's back doors.

As the attendants pushed the stretcher out, one handed me the IV bottle. Matney fell right in behind and away we went – straight to the hospital's prison ward.

In the confusion on the dock, the Detroit cops thought we were from Macomb County and the Macomb deputy thought we were from the Detroit police.

The patient was so heavily sedated that we had to prod him to wake him up to ask questions, but he recognized us and spilled his story. When we were finished, we just had the guard open the gate and walked away.

I have to admit my "break-in" at the Point of the Mountain Prison in Utah was a bit more inventive.

I was one of the mob of reporters covering the firing-squad execution of convicted murderer Gary Gilmore. In order to keep the press at bay, the warden had placed everything but the outside fence off limits to the media.

I knew I couldn't see Gilmore, except when they brought him to Salt Lake City for court appearances, but I wanted an idea of what the prison looked like from the inside. So I took a shot and called to see if they gave public tours.

Incredibly, the lady who answered said no, all public tours had been canceled, but added that a group of criminology students from Weber State University was scheduled to be taken through at 9 a.m. the next day.

Well, early next morning I dressed in my Levi's and denim shirt, drove to the prison and waited for the Weber State bus to arrive. When the group piled out, I fell in with them and walked to the gate.

Again, in the confusion, no one noticed me. There are three separate rooms where doors are locked at both ends and a count is taken.

Twice the guard who was counting and the Weber State faculty member in charge got different totals, but nobody challenged me. Each time we progressed.

At the third room, the voice on the loudspeaker barked to the guard who was accompanying the visitors' party. "Charley!" he said, "see that guy in the denim shirt in the corner?"

I froze. All eyes turned my way. I'd been caught.

"Tell him to get over to the prison laundry and get a number stenciled on that shirt. He looks like he belongs here!"

The group laughed; the guards still thought I was with the kids (probably a special ed case) and I'll never know who the students thought I was, but I got in and spent four hours wandering the halls and even talking to prisoners about what they thought about Gary Gilmore, the upcoming execution and the prison system in general.

And when I was finished, I walked back out through the same three rooms with the group – and the count was wrong each time again, but nobody bothered to check.

There are those, I know, who would be happier today if I'd stayed. And a couple who wish there'd been room on Gilmore's lap.

A 'man of letters'

March 4, 1984

Detroit Recorder's Judge Sam Olsen says, "I have found him to possess many fine qualities and productive skills. The past political climate in which he was involved stemmed from over-production in public service, not under-production."

Judge George Crockett III of the same bench, says, "It is my opinion that (he) was unfairly treated . . . for speaking the truth."

Judge Craig Strong calls him "inspirational" and "a community leader," also "a champion of civil rights."

So much for the judges. Now for the politicians.

Detroit City Council President Erma Henderson stops just short of nominating him for the Supreme Court.

"I welcome the opportunity to endorse his efforts," Mrs. Henderson writes. "This right to choose . . . this right to start, stop and start again is so inherent in our basic philosophies . . ."

Councilman Clyde Cleveland joins in: ". . . (he) has consistently demonstrated maximizing the use of available resources. I strongly urge his reinstatement to the State Bar of Michigan."

State Sen. Dave Holmes, D-Detroit, picks up the cudgel:

"Many of his colleagues have stated that his record was and is one of the best in the 100-year history of the courts," Holmes writes. Further, the senator alleges that the hearing "was stacked against him."

Attorney Myzell Sowell opines that he should be reinstated to the practice of law because "he has been punished enough." Sowell describes him as "an energetic, industrious, decent man possessing a genuine commitment to public service."

Republican attorney Dick Durant calls him "Jimmie" in his letter and says he is "glad to act as a reference."

Attorney Ralph Richardson writes that the allegations against him were "frivolous" and that "his conduct was not as reprehensible as depicted in our local papers.

"He should not continue to be punished for acts alleged to have been performed by him which resulted in his disbarment . . ."

These are excerpts of letters that have been received by the Michigan State Bar Grievance Commission and Disciplinary Board in support of the request by James Diego Cohen Del Rio, a.k.a. Jimmy Del Rio, to have his license to practice law returned.

Del Rio, now 59, had his ticket lifted after he was removed from the Detroit Recorder's Court bench after the Judicial Tenure Commission found him guilty of a laundry list of illegal acts and/or judicial abuse.

As I have mentioned before, you name it, Jimmy did it.

His low-water marks, if you can call them that, were illegally returning several thousand dollars worth of forfeited bail bond money to bondsman Charles "Chuckie" Goldfarb, pulling a gun on an attorney in his court and bragging from the bench about his sexual prowess.

If you find it difficult to believe all the nice things that Sam and George III, Erma and Clyde have to say about him, you're in good company.

Jimmy once silenced the litigants in a trial by telling the defense that he wasn't going to have "some smart-assed Jew attorney" come into his court and push him around."

Some might label that an ethnic slur. Judge Strong calls him "inspirational."

The right to "start, stop and start again" that Mrs. Henderson mentions sounds like Del Rio gave up his ticket voluntarily, so he ought to get it back the same way.

The only reason Del Rio even is being reconsidered is that, because of time and pressure five years ago, he was merely suspended and not disbarred. Nothing that went before can be considered in evidence against him.

Only his actions since he was set down can be weighed in the reinstatement proceedings.

The letters? Well, they tell more about the people who wrote them than they reveal about Jimmy Del Rio.

Memories of Jimmy Watts

March 12, 1984

Jimmy Watts wanted to be the head of the Detroit NAACP.

In the last election, he was running against a lady who didn't have his political clout and organization, and he figured that if he played it low-key he was a cinch to beat her.

A couple of days before the balloting, however, I found out Jimmy was on the ticket and I wrote a column about what his election might mean in terms of Coleman Young controlling that old-line civil rights organization. And he got beat.

"Jimmy blamed you for that," AFL-CIO President Tom Turner, a long-time friend of Watts, told me later. "He wanted that job badly . . ."

I never felt bad about Jimmy Watts blowing that post. In a lengthy career as a UAW official, Coleman Young crony and city big shot, Watts missed few tricks.

James Watts died last Friday night after a long bout with a liver ailment. He was only 62, but he was an elder in politics beyond his years.

Some people are larger in death than they were in life. No one will ever say that about Jimmy Watts.

One of the first appointees to come aboard when Coleman Young was elected in the early 1970s, Watts was handed the overstaffed and disorganized Department of Public Works and immediately set some fires with his mouth.

In one of his first appearances at a public hearing, Watts accused the civil service hierarchy of being "racist SOBs" when it came to implementing affirmative action. And he added that if the people of Detroit "knew what was going on, they'd burn the town down!"

Well, Mayor Young didn't mind Jimmy registering his complaints, but he didn't care for the inflammatory rhetoric. He told Watts to cool it and Jimmy never used that kind of talk in public again.

Watts is acclaimed by some as the man who handled the city's toughest jobs: garbage collection and snow removal. Some even insist that his implementation of one-man garbarge trucks saved the city millions.

I'd have to reserve judgment on exactly how much Jimmy Watts may have done for the city. I suspect that he did a lot for Jimmy Watts, Coleman Young and some of their mutual friends, however.

With the help of some of Watts' workers, I once caught a private rubbish hauler adding hundreds of tons to his city bill under the watchful scrutiny of one of Jimmy's inspectors.

The scam went on for months, even after Watts was told about it. And Jimmy signed all the checks.

Jimmy personally supervised the bid specifications and handled the sweetheart contracts for the one-man side-loading trucks.

While he was weighing which trucks to buy, Watts accepted a trip to Denver from a sales rep who flew him out first class, put him up in a luxury hotel and even got him permission to play the posh Cherry Hills golf course.

When I asked Mayor Young's people if they had a code of ethics that covered taking gifts from bidders, they assured me they did. Unfortunately, they said, it wasn't in force when Watts took his junket.

I might add that the Denver supplier didn't get the contract and later blew the whistle on Watts.

The litany goes on. The one incident I think most adequately illustrates Watts' disdain for the public trust was the time he painted a city pickup truck black, removed all of its municipal identification and acquired a "suppressed" license tag for it from the Michigan State Police.

All that so city workers could deliver free firewood to Watts and his friends without neighbors blowing the whistle.

Few people outside his close circle of friends had contact with Watts in the last half-dozen years. He had long since stopped answering reporters' calls.

But sooner or later we all find somebody we can't hang up on.

Gun control . . . fancy that

October 7, 1984

Coleman Young says he's shocked by the widespread use of handguns in Detroit and that he might consider a stern crackdown, perhaps even including putting metal detectors at heavily traveled areas like the entrance to the Belle Isle Bridge, in order to confiscate illegal firearms.

I can just picture the scene:

The long, shiny, dark blue limousine is cruising out East Jefferson, heading for the Manoogian Mansion. Traffic's backed up clear to Mt. Elliott, however, and when the limo can't move for several minutes, Hizonner buzzes the chauffeur to see what's wrong.

"There's a lineup at the bridge, sir," the chauffeur answers. "Seems there's an awful big crowd of people gathered there. I checked headquarters on the car phone and they've sent for backup and some dump trucks."

"These guys say they've never seen anything like this. Your idea sure is working."

The mayor grows impatient. "Turn on the lights and siren and let's get up there and take a look," he orders. The chauffeur responds and they snake their way to the bridgehead, where the mayor gets out and joins the mob to see what's happening.

Suddenly a voice calls out: "You. You over there with the freckles and the gray hair. Get moving through that metal detector."

Hizonner stops and glares at the youthful police officer. "Just who do you think you're talking to?" he says. "Give me your name and your badge number right now."

"Don't get smart, pal," the officer says. "That only works for Annivory Calvert. I'll give you anything you want, including my girl friend's telephone number, just as soon as you do what you're told. Now get a move on."

The officer takes his arm and guides him to the detector. Bells and buzzers start to ring. In seconds, two other cops have the mayor spread-eagled against a wall and are shaking him down.

"You can't do this!" he shouts. "I'm the mayor! Besides, this is illegal search and seizure. You're violating my civil rights. I demand an attorney!"

"What kind of attorney you want?" the copper asks. "We've got 16 of them over in the paddy wagon along with two dozen doctors, 10 grocery store operators, 14 accountants, six nurses, about 20 Teamsters, a priest, two nuns and a whole bunch of city employees. Shook 'em all down and found they were carryin'."

They read him his rights and hustle him to a barbed wire enclosure next to the Naval Armory.

Inside the barbed wire, the mayor is immediately recognized by several folks from city hall. "Charley! Jimmy! Sharon! Mary Jane! What are you all doing here?"

"Same as you, boss," one says. "We flunked the test and you know the rules. You wrote 'em."

"You mean," Hizonner says, "that you were all carryin'?"

"Like you said a long time ago, boss . . . way back when Jerry Tannian was police commissioner and wanted to try gun control . . . everybody in Detroit carries a piece. Even you.

"You gotta understand. We're just like everybody else out there. We follow your lead. If you say it's OK to carry a gun, then it's OK to carry a gun."

"But, all these people . . . all these weapons? In the hands of untrained . . ."

"Like you said, boss, we've all got a right to defend ourselves. It's like they say about Medicaid abortions . . . guns shouldn't be just for the rich.

"Don't worry. We be out of here in a couple of hours. And there's plenty more where they came from.

"Wanna buy a bazooka?"

Detroit loses its fizz

January 23, 1985

One by one, they fold up or leave Detroit. Or both.

Federal's, Sears, Hudson's Crowley's, Sanders, Hughes and Hatcher, Himelhoch's. All the old line names we grew up with and a few we didn't, like Saks.

The litany of dead and dying business goes on and on. Add Vernors to the list.

They fold and leave for a number of reasons and all that's really left when they empty the shelves and fire the people and padlock the doors is the lingering question:

Why? Why Detroit? Why do we have to do without so much quality, so much service, so much history? What is it about this town that drives away the names, the traditions we ought to be fighting to cling to?

Vernors Inc. is not the biggest and certainly not the most successful of those that have abandoned the inner city in the last few years.

But for some strange reason it hurts more than the others. Between the bottling plant on Woodward and the warehouse in Taylor, Vernors will cut loose some 300 employees when it's all over.

The franchises, bottling companies and distributors in 22 states will continue with business as usual. But Detroit, again, loses out.

Outside of Hudson's, and maybe the Stroh Brewery, Vernors was "Detroit." The drink was invented here, bottled here, sold here almost exclusively for some 119 years.

It was bottled for years at the foot of Woodward Avenue, and when urban renewal embraced that part of the city in the early days, the plant was moved north a mile or so to the present site just south of Forest.

Vernors spawned the famous ginger ale float called, for some curious reason, a "Boston Cooler." Out-of-town visitors would sample its taste and bootleg cases of it back to other parts of the country where it was never sold.

Nothing else tastes like Vernors ginger ale. Not Coke or Pepsi or Seven Up or Hire's Root Beer. You pour it over ice cubes and it fizzes high in the glass. And if you try to drink it before the fizzing subsides, the tiny bubbles sneak up your nose and make you sneeze.

I was luckier than most Detroiters. When the Vernors bottling plant was still on the riverfront, I was living in an apartment up on Fourth and Ferry and on Saturdays my brother Joe and sister Pat would bundle me up and take me downtown for some ice cream at the old Vernors soda fountain.

We walked from Forest and Woodward to the river and back because we had a choice: Ride the street car or have a Vernors.

I try hard not to live in the past. Lord, how I try. But every time I think the slide has been checked, the skid has come to a screeching halt, the city has finally struck rock bottom with a thud and is about to rebound like an India rubber ball, somebody drives another spike in the casket.

No matter how much romance may be connected with the name, Vernors is a business. Make no mistake about that. Worse yet, it's a business that's run by a giant conglomerate based in New York; an outfit called United Brands Inc., which does nearly $3.5 billion a year in foods and other consumer products.

Facts get cloudy, so I dug through the old, yellowed clippings, in The Detroit News reference department yesterday, refreshing my memory about how the company first came to be. I wish now that I hadn't, because it only makes me feel worse.

There was this fat dossier on James Vernor Sr., who came to Detroit in 1849, was graduated from the old Capitol High School on State and Griswold, enlisted in the Union Army (actually the 4th Michigan Cavalry) as a private in 1862 and was captured by rebs at the Battle of Stone River.

They shipped Vernor to a prison camp in Murfreesboro, Tenn., and he escaped and hid in an attic and later rejoined his unit in time to become a lieutenant and participate in the capture of Jeff Davis, who was the president of the Confederacy.

Vernor came home to Detroit after the war, opened a pharmacy and later went into politics as an alderman and member of Detroit's first common council. He had been fooling with a secret recipe for a special soft drink that used ginger and, in time, he perfected it as ginger ale.

James Vernor was no Henry Ford, no Ray Kroc, no Col. Harlan Sanders. His product was popular and good, but it never was marketed properly.

In 1966, when the company was 100 years old, its gross sales were a mere $2.3 million and the company was still trading over the counter.

Don't ask what's happened since. That's all on the business pages somewhere, I guess.

All that's left now is the rambling 12-mile-long street named after the company's founder. And in time they'll probably change that, too.

Wakefield – a friend-filled life

August 28, 1985

Jim Campbell recalls the time Dick Wakefield dropped into his office, checked the place over to see who might be listening and quietly closed the door.

It was long after Wakefield had left baseball and the old outfielder really did not do much except shoot pool and go to the horse tracks. But he still liked to drop in at Tiger Stadium once in a while to chat with Campbell, the Tigers' vice-president and chief operating officer at the time.

"I've got good news, Jim," Wakefield told his friend, "I'm getting married." Now that was big news, if true, for Wakefield was an aging bachelor who had lived with his mother most of his life.

"I'm happy for you, Dick," Campbell responded. "Who's the lucky lady?" Wakefield glanced swiftly over each shoulder and answered, "Mrs. Dodge. Horace's mother."

"She's a bit old for you, isn't she?" Campbell inquired calmly, like a guy who had been there before.

"Ya, she is," Wakefield said. "But she likes me and she's got a ton of money and she's going to set me up in business."

"Business?" Campbell asked. "What kind of business?"

Wakefield shot looks over his shoulders again. "Baseball," he answered. "I'm going to buy the Tigers." Campbell smiled patiently. His boss at the time was John Fetzer and, to Campbell's knowledge, the club wasn't for sale.

"Well, that'll be real nice, Dick," Campbell said. "I wish you a lot of luck."

Wakefield bent closer. "I'm going to make some changes, Jim," he began. "Probably do a little housecleaning; fire some people, you know. But I want you to know that I like the job you're doing and you're gonna be my No. 1 guy."

Campbell smiled. "I appreciate your confidence in me, Dick" he said. The two sat and stared at each other in silence. Wakefield rose, shook hands and left.

"Dick wasn't out the door 30 seconds," Campbell recalled a few days ago, "when he stuck his head back into my office. 'By the way, Jim,' he said, 'I almost forgot. I'm coming to the game. Leave me four seats at the box office, will ya? And make 'em good ones.'"

Richard Cummings Wakefield was 64 when he died Monday of heart disease. He was one of the nicest, kindest, gentlest men I have met in a lengthy career, and the people who mourn his passing are a testament to those traits. He attended the University of Michigan in pre-Pearl Harbor 1941 and roomed with guys like Potsy Ryan and Leo Calhoun, Phil Pratt and Butch McGuire at the Phi Gamma Delta fraternity house. He was a star althlete, but he was first and foremost a friend.

His friends will gather tonight at the Charles Step Funeral Parlor on Beech Daly in Redford to swap stories and say farewell. It will be the second time in just a few weeks that the group has gathered to honor Wakefield. Six weeks ago, a couple of hundred of us convened at the Furniture Club in Southfield to roast him. He was thin and his voice was gravelly. And he broke into tears at the rostrum and warned us all not to grieve his passing, when it inevitably came.

"Don't cry for me," he said. "I've had a great life. I couldn't have asked for it better."

And his friends told stories.

"The police raided a small-time gambling joint in western Wayne County once," Bill Cahalan, the former prosecutor, recalled with a broad grin, "and Wakefield got picked up. I knew he was harmless and I left him off the list of warrants and a gung-ho young investigator accused me of favoritism. I told him I have a rule in the prosecutor's office: Anybody who goes four-for-four in an All-Star baseball game and hits .350 one year gets one free ride. No exceptions. Bring me any other gambler with those statistics and I'll let him go, too!

"After that, we called it the 'Wakefield Rule.' Nobody else ever qualified for it, but that's not my fault."

Wakefield was broke most of the last years of his life and part of the roast was to raise money for him, and he knew it. It was a sad occasion when he came to the rostrum that night; grown men with wet eyes paying tribute to a friend whose days were numbered.

Wakefield bent into the microphone and began what was to be his farewell speech. "A friend in need," he said, staring solemnly into the assembled faces, "is a pain in the ass." The crowd roared.

They say he lost everything. But not his friends. And never his sense of humor.

Classic 'stings' have pizzazz

November 1, 1985

Back in the summer of 1982, a group of federal agents and Macomb County sheriff's deputies were running a "sting" operation out of the back of a vacant store in downtown Mt. Clemens.

They were buying everything from hot Corvettes to stolen medical equipment and, because they were hanging around all day, they got to know the town's criminal element pretty well.

There's a bus station nor far from where they operated their bogus "business" and the undercover coppers noticed that some men had been stealing unattended suitcases.

These minor heists technically weren't any of their business. And they couldn't put the collar on the thieves for fear of blowing their cover. So they devised another plan.

The building where they were running their phony "fencing" operation had a couple of previous tenants; two fat, juicy rats. The agents set traps, baited them with strong cheese and caught the rodents.

Then they took a suitcase they had bought from a burglar who had stolen a set of luggage from a store and locked the freed rats inside it.

That afternoon a couple of the agents positioned themselves in an unmarked car near the terminal while another agent, posing as a bus patron, set the suitcase down on the curb and went inside to buy a ticket.

Needless to say, the bait worked.

In seconds, a car pulled up, an arm reached out and the suitcase was snatched up. As the car sped out of the lot, the agents pursued them down Gratiot Avenue.

"The car only went about three blocks," one of the feds recalled later, "then it stopped in the middle of the street and all four doors flew open and the guys came running out. One of them had opened the suitcase to see what was inside and the rats jumped out and scared the hell out of them!"

Now, friends, I submit to you that this is the way "sting" operations should be conducted. With a bit of glitz, a touch of pizzazz.

I was reminded of the Mt. Clemens sting this week when Detroit's new FBI chief agent, Ken Walton, announced that a yearlong investigation by the feds and Detroit police had broken seven stolen car rings and that $1.1 million worth of luxury wheels had been recovered.

Sixty-eight folks were arrested and 45 indicted. Not a bad haul. But the way the deal went down – with a minimum of fanfare after a somewhat drab buy-and-sell campaign – seemed hardly appropriate for a promoter like Walton, who, if you believe his reviews, is the Steven Spielberg of special agents.

Maybe we're spoiled here in Michigan.

Take the deal that went down in the fall of 1977, when Detroit cops and FBI agents collared 126 thieves who had brought them more than $2 million in stolen goods during a six-month period.

When the heat got ready to take that operation down, they invited the crooks to a big party in a hangar at Detroit City Airport and even provided limousine service.

As each limo pulled into the hangar, however, the feds read the passengers their rights and busted them.

Perhaps the most elaborate hoax perpetrated in these parts by federal agents occurred the following spring, when a group of undercover gumshoes from the federal Bureau of Alcohol, Tobacco and Firearms (ATF) and some local police posing as fund-raisers for the Irish Republican Army set up and trapped dozens of car thieves and assorted robbers and burglars in a classic sting in Flint.

In a three-month span, this bunch of ATF actors bought 37 brand new Buicks, some of them driven right from the assembly line to their warehouse front. One guy drove in a haulaway truck loaded with seven cars and sold it for $700.

Another came in with a hi-lo loaded with cases of spark plugs and sold them – hi-lo and all – for $200.

When the feds wore out their welcome on the Flint gig, their leader, an ATF agent named Walt Ryerson, hired a hearse and set up a rendezvous in a supermarket parking lot. Any car thief who brought in a hot item would be paid double if he's willing to join a funeral cortege and drive the car to Detroit.

A dozen crooks fell for the deal and were arrested one by one as they arrived in their stolen cars.

Now, that's showbiz.

Conquering Mt. RenCen

December 16, 1985

I want to welcome you all to the Renaissance Center and tell you how much we appreciate your coming to Detroit on short notice to take part in such a difficult mission.

Our particular heartfelt thanks go to the Japanese team that abandoned its attempt to become the first to ascend Mt. Fuji backward in order to lend a hand here.

So that you all know each other – and a bit about the challenge – some introductions are in order.

"To my left is a group of 10 crack Swiss mountaineers whose specialty is rescuing ropes of inebriated Italians, who insist on trying to conquer the north face of the Eiger in the dead of winter, assisted only by a kennel of St. Bernards carrying kegs of Cella Lambrusco and Asti Spumanti.

"Next to them is supposed to be the Italian team. They arrived this morning from Lugano, but they went straight to the Roma Cafe because they heard that Hector was breaking an age-old tradition and was going to buy a drink. They'll be along shortly.

"The British rope flew in from Mt. Everest and I've got to say a heartfelt thank you to them because I know how much it means for the Brits to participate in this operation. We'll find your Sherpas. Not to worry.

"Now, I know you're wondering why your presence is required here. Suffice to say, we have a major problem.

"You see, dozens of people have disappeared in the last five years. They come to stay in the hotel or shop or just to walk around and they can't find their way out.

"They walk in circles. They ride the elevators up and down, up and down, trying to figure out which escalator goes where. Why do you have to take a small elevator to ride an escalator to get a big elevator in order to go from the garage level to an office building?

"I won't kid you. We have found some on our own – and others have stumbled out of the maze strictly by chance. The stories they tell of how they manage to survive! You wouldn't believe half of them.

"One woman and her small son were trapped for a month on the lower level and survived on chocolate chip cookies from one of the shops. A conventioneer from Pittsburgh who had been lost for four days finally wandered into the Greek restaurant so hungry that he OD'd on baklava and feta cheese before they got him to lost and found.

"We know there are more. Every day, they enter and are not heard from again.

"Last weekend, a group of Explorer Scouts from a troop led by Tony Franco and Gerald Greenwald volunteered to join the search. They entered the complex at Tower 400 with a week's supply of food, water and medicine and haven't been heard from since.

"An elevator repairman who answered an emergency call last July 4 was found wandering in the second level of the parking garage on Thanksgiving Day. Two secretaries from an ad agency in the 200 Tower who hadn't reported for work in three days were discovered huddled together in a corner booth at Nemo's saloon.

"In an effort to head off some of these potential tragedies in the future, we like to debrief the survivors to see just why they entered the maze in the first place.

"Their answer will come as no surprise to most of you seasoned explorers. Some of them say they come to visit a certain office or shop, but most of them say they do it 'because it's there!'

"To my mind, they're our kind of folks. Adventuresome. Spunky. But ill-equipped for the challenge.

"Now that we're all here, let's have an equipment check. Radios. Crampons. Pitons. Rope. Swivels. Axes. Hooks. Oxygen. Food. Sterno. Rocket pistols.

"Remember: Obstacles are everywhere. This place is like the Bermuda Triangle. Don't trust your instincts for direction. The Jefferson Avenue side is never where you think it is. And forget trying to find the river entrance.

"One final word of caution: Don't read the signs. They're only there to confuse you.

"I have your letters to your next of kin and your updated wills have been filed. Good luck.

"And if you happen to run into any of the Sherpa guides who went in last spring, tell them the folks back home in Nepal have been asking about them and National Geographic needs their film and their story for a cover as soon as they can ship it!"

Charade won't change image of real city

May 16, 1986

Dawn was breaking over the riverfront mansion. One by one, the line of limousines carrying city department heads rolled up the driveway to the front door.

Inside, the coffee pot was steaming and the officials gathered in small groups in the meeting room, yawning, stretching and grousing about the hour.

"I know we're supposed to be on our best behavior today because the Boss has brought all those newspaper editors and publishers in from out of town so he can show them the real Detroit," one said. "But this is ridiculous! A staff meeting at 7 o'clock in the morning? Get serious.

"They're not stupid. They know that no self-respecting public servant gets up this early. Why, I was pulling out of my driveway as the guy next door was leaving for work and I was humiliated.

"He rolls down his window and hollers, 'Whatcha doin' out so early, Melvin? Just gettin' home?' I'll tell you one thing: That guy's seen his last load of free firewood from the public works department!"

The French doors swung open promptly at 7 and the Boss' media flack strode in. He climbed up on a chair and raised his arms and, on the downbeat, the gathering began to chant: "COLE-man! COLE-man!"

'That's good!" he shouted. "Very good! Now remember . . . when we're touring your departments today, that's how we want the workers to holler. They love this guy, right? He's their bread and butter, right? Remind 'em of that. And remember . . . none of those obscene hand gestures. You tell those union goons the first one who hollers anything about our big salary increases gets suspended on the spot."

He shuffled the papers on his clipboard. "Let's go over the list one more time. Bill, the cops all know about saluting when the motorcade passes. And you might remind them, too, that if I see one thumbed nose, they go straight to the trial board. The bodyguards have already been briefed about the demonstrations of affection.

"We've been in touch with Central Casting and they're sending in some women to throw flowers and one to swoon when the Boss touches her. We've also hired some Canadian seniors to tell everybody how safe the streets are in their neighborhoods.

"We offered to bus some of our old folks downtown and even buy them lunch. But they were afraid to leave their houses that long. It's probably all for the best anyway. They'd just repeat those same old wild stories about being terrorized in broad daylight by burglars and muggers and who wants to hear that stuff?

"Which brings us to the route of the tour. We want these journalists to see the real city, not the one they read about out there in the boon . . . I mean, outstate. Of course, that puts us under rather severe limitations. The Boss wants them to know that our public housing problems aren't as disastrous as the local reporters make them out to be. On the other hand, we can't hardly take them to the Jeffries, Herman Gardens or Parkside projects, now, can we?

"So, we've decided on a compromise. We'll show 'em Lafayette Park! And if anyone asks about the Boss having a condo in there, tell 'em it's only because he wants to be close to the common folks."

A hand shot up at the rear of the room. "I don't mean to be troublesome, Bob," a voice said, "but how are you going to transport these people?"

"It took a mighty effort, but the Department of Transportation just this morning found us two DOT buses that have brakes. And with a little more effort, they also got them to start.

"You guides . . . remember your lines. If they ask about the People Mover, tell 'em we're going to plant flowers on it if we don't get the money to finish it. We'll try to stay out of the neighborhoods with the bars on the windows and doors, but if they see one and ask, tell 'em it belongs to one of the lunatic fringe who don't believe our crime statistics . . ."

Heads snapped as the Boss entered. He was dressed in white on white; suit, shirt, tie, shoes, spats, even a white Homburg. He silenced the applause quickly.

"What about demonstrators, Boss? Like the people who are against the trash incinerator, or the folks who want us to take our investments out of South Africa?"

The Boss' eyes narrowed. "I could care less about the protests against the trash plant or our South African stocks," he said crisply. "But the first person who holds up a sign demanding that we take our money out of Switzerland will find out just how rough I can play!"

Media bashing

June 9, 1986

Political types and bureaucrats like to complain that newspapers are always "taking things out of context" and "blowing things out of proportion." Then, they take things out of context and blow them out of proportion.

Yet another shining example of that grim truism is Detroit Mayor Coleman Young's accusation, repeated every time the spirit moves him, that editors of both Detroit daily papers orchestrate crime coverage for the narrow purpose of creating "interesting conversation for suburban cocktail parties."

Young cites as the authority for his remarks one memo that was written 10 years ago by a subeditor at The News, a memo which referred to the way a story about a freeway mugging had been played on Page One.

This classic – and, I might add, singular – example of questionable judgment, which has been quoted and misquoted ever since for self-deriving reasons by a whole coterie of political hacks and administration flacks, was begun as a well-done for the author of the mugging story, but got out of hand.

I'm familiar with the details surrounding this particular communication because I was the author of the story. You may have forgotten the details. And you certainly wouldn't recognize them from the version resurrected every time the mayor wants to beat up on the media. So, for the record, let's go back to the summer of 1976.

The crime scene's never too pretty when the weather gets nice enough to make it an outdoor sport, but it was particularly bad that July. The Young administration had reorganized and cut back the police. Young had let it be known that cops, for the most part, were (1) white and (2) racist. He had publicly coddled one young mugger who surrendered to him on TV in the mayor's office after whacking out some old lady, professing fear for his life if he turned himself in to police.

The message was unintentional, but pretty straight: The mayor was a pushover for a sad story. The situation on the Detroit freeway system that summer was, at best, abominable. And God help you if your car broke down.

The 62 miles of city freeways were a no-man's-land because the Young administration had abandoned them in a political tussle with Wayne County and the state over who was going to pay for the police to patrol them. Young wanted the state to give him the money to hire more cops, so he pulled his off in a dramatic and tragic petulant gesture. Bill Lucas, then the Wayne County sheriff, was angling for state funds to take them over. Bill Milliken, the Republican governor, wanted state police, which neither Young nor Lucas would agree to.

Then one July night, on the way home from a 21st birthday dinner for my daughter, Patti, in a downtown restaurant, my wife and Patti and I were caught in a sudden downpour that flooded the I-94 freeway near the Chene overpass. We had two cars. I managed to usher the women up a down ramp in one and told them to wait for me at the top until I could get my car off. Once they were out of sight and I was alone, I was rousted by a car full of guys who demanded money.

I told them to bag it, but I was blocked from going up the ramp. When one called for his gun, I hustled my buns out of there fast. When I returned with a cop an hour or more later, my windows had been smashed and the car looted.

A couple of days later I wrote a column about the incident. Because of everything else that had gone on on the freeway system that summer – and because of the stubborn political stalemate that was endangering taxpayers' lives and the city's economic future – the column was moved out to Page One.

Within days the freeway patrol situation was resolved, Young and Lucas backed off and Gov. Milliken ordered the Michigan State Police to take over. My near-miss and the story about it, I was told later, helped put the final squeeze on the politicians to settle their differences.

I've never heard Hizonner or his apologists ever mention how the freeway crime wave was resolved. But then, as we like to say in the city room, there's no sense letting a few facts screw up a good story.

A man from Co. B

July 4, 1986

Wilhelm Waldmeyer never saw the Statue of Liberty. He never heard the call to "give me your tired, your poor, your huddled masses yearning to breathe free."

The U.S. Immigration people who greeted him when he arrived on these shores in the 1940s didn't even mess with the spelling of his surname. It was, after all, 50 years before Ellis Island was dedicated and the flood gates from Europe were officially opened.

Some of the family changed it after he was gone. Someone couldn't resist anglicizing Wilhelm and making it William, however, and I guess he figured, what the hell, they could have turned him away. Let them have their fun.

Wilhelm Waldmeir sleeps a deep and easy sleep this Independence Day. He rests high on a hill near the westernmost boundary of Arlington National Cemetery across from Washington, with the graves of the Kennedys and Unknown Soldier and beyond them all of the nation's capital spreading out below.

My great-grandfather never saw the lady of the harbor, whose 100th birthday we are celebrating this holiday weekend. But he knew about freedom and he knew about liberty. He was an immigrant who came to America from Switzerland because there was opportunity here and some basic moral principles that he decided were worth fighting for.

He died for them as well, in October 1864, a private in the Union Army, Co. B, 61st Regiment, Pennsylvania Infantry – the Pennsylvania Volunteers.

The old dude was born in 1827 in a village called Hellikon, in the canton Aargau in northern Switzerland near Zurich. He came to Allegheny City, Pa., as a young man, the only one of nine children who left Europe. In 1851 he married Agatha Kans, who had emigrated from the neighboring village of Weggenstetten.

He was a cooper; a barrel maker. They had two boys, William and John and, when the eldest was only 5 their father enlisted in Mr. Lincoln's

157

army as a foot soldier. It was the fall of 1861 and the War Between the States had been going on for about five months.

I have uncovered no precise record of where Co. B engaged the enemy, but the 61st's battle list reads like a Civil War road map: Turkey Bend, Cross Roads, Antietam, Fredericksburg, Wilderness, Salem Church, Rappahannock Station, Gettysburg, Fort Stevens at Washington itself. Its feats were bloody and impressive. The regiment lost more officers in battle than any other in the Union Army: 19. Enlisted battle dead totaled 235.

Another 627 were wounded, and more than 100 died of disease, including Wilhelm Waldmeyer, who died of what the medics listed as "intermittent fever" in a Washington hospital nine months before the war ended.

He had recently re-enlisted, apparently because he thought it was the thing to do. He was only 34, he'd been in this country some 15 years and had left his family for three of them to fight for a cause he thought was just. And he left Agatha and the two boys to survive on a slim widow's pension.

No giant marker commemorates his sacrifice, only a small, white, weathered stone among the thousands in the lush green hills of Arlington. At Gettysburg, however, there is a monument to the 61st Pennsylvania Volunteers that was dedicated in 1888, two years after the Statue of Liberty rose in New York Harbor.

In his closing remarks at the Gettysburg battlefield on that warm July afternoon in 1888, Army Col. Robert L. Orr said: "When the living shall have joined their comrades in the deathless world, this memorial will proclaim to descendants of those who formed the 61st the imperishable honor here and elsewhere achieved by that regiment. And when its monument here and other memorials on this most renowned battlefield of the ages shall have crumbled to atoms, every lover of liberty will yet crown with unfading laurels and burnish with immortal luster the memory of the gallant and dauntless men who won freedom's battle at Gettysburg."

I'll take the kids to the Statue of Liberty one day. But not before I take them to Arlington and Gettysburg to pay homage to the people who made it possible.

Karate Kid, Jr.

Karate Kid, Jr.

October 3, 1986

My son, Christopher Norman, is 4 years old today.

To celebrate this happy occasion, he very likely will hop up on the dining room table, leap from there to the chandelier, swinging back and forth a few times to gain height and speed. He then will dive headlong through the bay window and onto the front lawn to the rousing cheers of his sister, Lindsey, 7, and four of the little girls who live across the street.

He'll be naked as a jaybird, of course. Actually, he may have just a bit of a problem getting his Great Ape act off the ground, even fully clothed. His left arm has been in a cast from the wrist to the upper arm for the better part of two weeks.

On a 4-year-old, however, I have learned, that is neither a very great distance nor a very great handicap.

Oh, how I remember – and will long regret – the night his terrible injury occurred. My wife and family will never let me forget it, I'm sure. At the very moment when Chris was doing his finest impersonation of Evel Knievel diving off the top of the RenCen into a soggy sponge, I was saddled with a terrible decision.

The waiter at the London Chop House was hovering impatiently while I wrestled with whether to order the filet of Dover sole meuniere or the rack of lamb for my entree. An unavoidable business engagement had kept me away from home for the evening – and away from the St. John Hospital emergency room, as well.

By the time I arrived home, Christopher was huddled in his bed for the night, alternately whimpering and groaning while his mother cooed and fidgeted over his tiny body. It was a great act and I thought, wow, that heavy plaster cast on his arm will keep him off my back awhile.

Wrong, of course. Within hours he discovered that it was merely an arm that had been broken, not his legs. And the cast? Well, nature could not have provided a 4-year-old lad with any more effective weapon in the constant struggle against sisterhood, among other scourges.

In two days, the bulky sling, which Blue Cross had provided for a hundred bucks or so, was discarded. A silk-scarf substitute lasted a couple more days, and then there he was, ready to do battle – a miniature NFL tackle, properly prepared to hand The Refrigerator his retirement papers.

Fathers seem to have an uncanny sense of timing when it comes to avoiding home-grown crises. I can say with all honesty that I've managed to miss just about every major catastrophe that has occurred at my house, save a flooded basement or two.

I don't plan it that way, mind you. It just seems to happen.

I've only missed the birth of one child: my eldest son, Pete. In my defense, he arrived several weeks ahead of schedule, and I happened to be 500 miles away at a remote base in the Marine Corps when he decided to drop in unannounced.

He never would have known I wasn't there if somebody hadn't told him, so I never felt too guilty about it.

My second child, Patti Ann, was thrown from a horse and broke an arm before she was 10. Her mother hustled her off for surgery and casting while I was on the road covering the Tigers or performing some other such intellectually strenuous task.

Later, Pete was hauled to hospitals twice with high school sports injuries – one a severe shoulder separation, which also required surgery – and for some strange reason I was away on business both times and missed the action.

Come to think of it, Lindsey's first and only major crisis came and went while I was playing tennis one steamy morning in Florida. By the time I got home I found my frail 1-year-old daughter recuperating from a battered lip and mouth, suffered when she took a dive out the trailer door onto the concrete pad below.

I'd like to reminisce some more, but I just heard a crash and a scream in the kitchen that sounded like Chris laid a karate chop on the dishwasher.

He'll survive. At this stage I'm worried about the dishwasher.

Oliver North's world

July 13, 1987

Guys like Oliver North scare me. Always have, always will.

Superpatriots. People who listen to a higher message, who profess to be tuned in to life's complex symphony but who, when decision time comes, hear loudest the beat of some mysterious drummer.

Folks who have my "best interests at heart," whether or not I have asked for or even appreciate their help. Those who would save me and my family and everything that's good for America – by their standards, at least – even if it means skirting or subverting the rules and, on the bottom line, mocking the very freedoms they insist they have accepted a mandate from destiny to protect.

Listen, they tell you with glistening eyes and quivering chins, the Constitution of the United States is a marvelous document. Men and women have fought and died to protect and uphold it. Look there, at the rows of bright ribbons on the broad chest – irrefutable proof that this Marine lieutenant colonel has done his part.

So, all you grunts, get off his case. The problem is that you do not understand that what this steely eyed military man has done may not have been exactly kosher, but sometimes you have to bend the rules to get the job done.

It's not right, for instance, to mug an elderly lady. But if she's drowning and you're the lifeguard trying to save her, it's perfectly proper to coldcock her to facilitate the rescue. In the military, you must understand, there is a concept of "acceptable losses."

As North might say, cutely, while he characterizes an illegal arms deal as a "neat idea," everybody wants to go to heaven but nobody wants to die. What was it Barry Goldwater said about extremism in defense of liberty being no vice? Well, it was something like that. Ollie's likely got the quote tattooed on his biceps.

Today was to have been the final day of Oliver North's testimony before the congressional committee investigating the Iran-contra arms sales. The hearings frequently have been tedious theater, but I am glad they have gone on this long. I'm glad North has been pressed so hard to explain his motivation and reasoning. What has emerged is the portrait of a military man who sincerely, and some might say fanatically, believes he knows "what's best" for America.

It is almost Strangelovian to watch his back stiffen when the topic turns to patriotism, to see his jaw set when he talks of "brave Nicaraguan freedom fighters," to see him stare straight into the cameras and say, yes, he lied about what he did; yes, he shredded and shredded and shredded. His eyes narrow as he recounts his version of the "communist takeover of Central America" and uses his paranoia to somehow justify covert, and some may say even illegal, counteractions.

Those are the times when the image becomes frightening, when I am jarred back to the reality of what's going on in all this mess.

The reality is that unknown to you or me or the majority of our elected or even appointed officials, a shadow government has been operating for months, perhaps even years. It has had no mandate save one that has been rationalized (some might say fictionalized) as, save America from itself.

North talks mockingly of the "efforts made to work with the Congress on some programs." He accuses the elected bodies of being "unfair" and laments the fact that they "have been permitted to make the rules . . ."

On the one had, he professes to be merely a tool of his superiors. On the other, he stridently lectures on how much better for all of us the world according to Ollie would be if we just gave him a shot at running it.

When it's all over, TV likely will make a film of North's life and, as the Marines would say, the whole lash-up. Martin Sheen probably will play the lead role, because he has that same piercing look.

It's a shame Peter Sellers isn't around. I can see him now at the witness table, teeth clenched, one hand constantly fighting to keep the other from rising to salute, suggesting who among us should be chosen to propagate the survival generation when it comes time to go into the bunkers.

Old Duff was a winner

September 27, 1987

Duffy Daugherty liked to tell the story of the prostitute's funeral.

There weren't many folks there and at the end the minister asked if anyone wanted to say a few words about the deceased before she was buried.

There was a long silence and finally her ex-boss stood up.

"Margie," the madam said, "was one of the finest little hookers who ever worked for me." As she sat down, another of the ladies in attendance broke into loud sobbing.

"That's the trouble with this business," she wailed. "You have to die before somebody says something nice about you!"

One thing about old Duff: You may not have thought him the greatest football strategist who ever lived, but there's never been a shortage of people saying nice things about him, here or gone.

Hugh "Duffy" Daugherty, son of a Barnesboro, Pa., coal miner who coached football at Michigan State through some of the Spartans' most glorious and also their most disappointing seasons, died Thursday night in California at 72. He'd been retired since the early 1970s.

I was a sportswriter early in Duffy's career and covered most of his historically significant games. I also heard his complete repertoire of stories and anecdotes, most of which I remember with more clarity than his coaching achievements.

The thing about Duff that set him apart from most other big-time college coaches was that he always tried to keep the game in perspective and seldom passed up an opportunity to poke a little fun at himself.

So that I don't get into Joe Biden's bind, allow me to point out here that I refreshed my memory of Duff stories with a quick run through the autobiography that he co-authored several years back with Dave Diles. But the stories have been repeated so many times that they're almost in the public domain.

Duffy was sensitive to criticism but sought to difffuse the bitterness by making his own shortcomings the target.

"We're losing a game and I think we're getting a real jobbing from the officials," Duffy recalled a few years back. "I've got a running battle going with the referee from the sidelines and he warns me twice about illegally signaling plays to the quarterback.

"The third time he blows the whistle and marches off a five-yard penalty against me for coaching from the sidelines. Now, I got him."

"'That shows how dumb you are, Ref!' I holler. 'Sideline coaching is a 15-yard penalty, not five yards!' He calls time and walks over where he's sure I can hear.

"'For the kind of coaching you're doing,' he says, 'it's only five yards.'"

Duffy recruited a whole series of players from Hawaii, among them a barefoot placekicker named Dick Kenney, who won several games with his bruised toes.

"We were coming off a couple of rough years," Duff recalled, "and I decided to spend some practice days really stressing punts, kickoffs and place kicks to show how a poor kicking game can really hurt a team.

"After I go through all this for two days we have a skull session the night before the opener and I point to a sophomore lineman and ask him if he can tell me where most games are lost?

"The kid doesn't bat an eye. 'Right here at Michigan State, coach,' he says."

Duffy's coaching and personal style was in sharp contrast to Ohio State's Woody Hayes. An OSU fan once suggested that Duffy might improve the Spartans' record if he emulated Woody's practice of leading his players in singing the Ohio State fight song before every game.

Duffy squinted impishly but shook his head. "Impossible," he responded. "I don't know the words to the Ohio State fight song."

His dry wit and unpretentiousness may have been Duffy's most important contribution to college coaching. One early fall as football practice was beginning, he was musing about how he had made a significant move to improve his stature with a sullen alumni body.

"You see those two kids over there?" he said, pointing to a pair of huge linemen who were working out. "I've decided to have them carry me off the field after every game this year, no matter what the score is.

"That way the alumni can say, 'Well, he may not be much of a coach, but his players sure love him, don't they?'"

We all did, Duff. Win or tie.

So, shed a tear

October 4, 1987

So Pat Schroeder started to weep the other day when she announced that she would not announce that she was running for president.

Big deal. I cry at least once a month, regular as clockwork. When the Hudson's bill arrives.

Tears have been a big thing in my family for a long time. In fact, I always have felt that there was something wrong with people who can't cry when they are struck with a personal disappointment or tragedy. Or when they just feel moved to do it, for that matter.

I have long wondered, for instance, how Jackie Kennedy could possibly keep her cool so completely throughout the terrible ordeal in Dallas and later during the endless rounds of memorial services for her husband, the father of her kids, after President Jack Kennedy's assassination in the early '60s.

I would have been a basket case if I were in her shoes. So would most of us. But somehow Jackie bit her lip under her heavy veil and never shed a discernable tear in public.

It is not a sign of weakness to cry. Ed Muskie did it in New Hampshire during the 1972 presidential primary. Muskie's were tears of frustration, however. A Democrat, he and his wife had been targeted for political and moral annihilation by the state's largest and most vociferous reactionary Republican newspaper, William Loeb's Manchester Union Leader, and he couldn't do much about it.

Edsel Ford didn't weep, but his voice cracked and he came within a tear drop in an emotional scene before the TV cameras the other morning when he faced the media to announce that his father, Henry Ford II, had died a few hours before.

There should be no embarrassment at a time like that, no reason to hold back. But young Edsel's no dummy. He's seen the TV clips, the Page One pictures, the closeups of people in tears.

Some people cry for no apparent reason at all, at least none that is readily evident to others. My wife, Marilyn, for instance, sometimes cries in church, occasionally during that part of the service where the priest asks the congregation to greet each other with the sign of peace and sometimes during the sermon or some special prayers as well.

She doesn't sob, mind you. She just stands there, erect, thinking about what's being said, and the tears run down under her glasses and she tries to look nonchalant as she dabs at them with her Kleenex.

Inevitably, our 5-year-old, Christopher, waits until the quietest part of the service and then breaks the silence by asking, "Why are you crying, Mommy?" The people in front usually are polite enough not to turn and stare, but I feel the eyes of those behind burning into my neck and transmitting the unspoken question, "What have you done to that nice, young family, you gray-haired old geezer?"

I once attempted to defuse the situation by suggesting that if she attended church more often, perhaps it wouldn't be such an emotional experience for her. She responded by whacking me over the head several times with her Gideon Bible.

Some events, some people I've known bring tears just thinking about them. I was in the hospital room the night five years ago when my stepfather, the old Buffalo, Norm Seurynck, died. My eyes well up just writing his name.

New Year's Day 1972 in the Rose Bowl. The Vietnam War has been grinding on for far too long. The rag-tag irreverant Stanford University marching band shows up dressed in red sports coats and white pork-pie hats. A new breed of college kids who don't give a damn for conformity, for so-called traditional values.

No precision drills. The Stanford drum major blows a whistle and the band scatters wildly, racing to each new formation. Cool. Laid back.

Time comes for the National Anthem and the crowd stands, hushed. One Stanford trumpeter begins, solo, with the first couple of bars. Then another joins in. Then another, and another until the entire brass section is playing.

This tremendous brass crescendo is building and I look to the East and low over the San Gabriel Mountains I see a flight of jet fighters streaking toward the rim of the Bowl. At ". . . the home of the brave" the Navy's Blue Angels, flying the gapped-V "missing man" formation, streak over the field with a deafening roar and burst skyward like a cluster of Roman candles.

Later, I blamed my burning eyes on the smog. And no one bothered to point out that it was a beautiful, clear day.

Members only

November 18, 1988

The long black limousine with the smoked windows pulled up at the front entrance to the Detroit Golf Club. As it glided to a stop, two men in dark glasses emerged and hit the ground at a trot.

One of them grasped the rear door handle as soon as the car halted, then opened it gently and stood at rigid attention. In a moment, a man in a gray pin-striped suit, wing-tipped shoes and a homburg stepped out.

The parking attendant emerged from his hut and studied the visitor.

"Hey, he shouted, you can't leave that car there. Get it over to the employee parking lot. We got a lot of important folks coming today."

The man in the homburg lowered his head and glared disdainfully. "My good man," he said, ignoring the order, "would you be so kind as to direct me to the reception desk? I'm expected."

The attendant tilted his cap back and put his hands on his hips in exasperation.

"You don't want the reception desk," he answered. "They don't fill out job applications there. What you want is the manager's office. But the first thing you got to do is get that car out of here and into the parking lot behind the building.

"Then, you go in through the back entrance and turn left to the second door."

He paused to appraise the visitor more carefully. "You sure are a sharp-looking dude with those pin stripes and the rented limo. What kind of job you looking for? No, don't tell me; lemme guess.

'I know you're not a clubhouse man because you don't have shoe polish under your fingernails. You're too old to be a caddy and your back's too straight for a waiter.

"What's that leave? You dress nice. Maybe a maitre d' ? Say, you ain't a parking attendant, are you? I need this job."

The man in the homburg snapped his fingers and the two men in dark glasses shut the limo's doors and moved toward the club entrance. The chauffeur moved the car slowly over to the side of the drive.

"Hey, listen," the attendant said softly, his eyes shifting suspiciously between the three advancing strangers. "You just cool it now. These folks see the three of you coming in the front door and they'll hit the 911 button so fast you'll think it's a breakout at Jacktown.

"You look like nice guys and I don't want to see you get tossed in the slam for trespassing. So, why don't you just let me . . ."

He held out a hand and made a move toward the man in the homburg. Immediately one of the bodyguards stepped in.

"Cool it!" the bodyguard shouted. "Don't you recognize who you're talking to?"

The man in the homburg removed his dark glasses and the attendant stepped back, stunned.

"Mr. Mayor? Is that really you? What are you doing here? I thought this would be the last place you'd ever want to . . . well, you know.

"I mean, I read that newspaper story about those friends of yours nominating you for membership, but I figured it was a publicity stunt. I never thought you'd be serious enough to really do it."

The advance stopped and the attendant paused, looked around, and then lowered his voice. "Lemme tell you something, just man to man. This ain't your kind of joint. If you play golf, it's OK. But the food's no match for Greektown and the sitting room's so full of stuffy old folks it looks like a wax museum.

"I read where you told your press agent that you never learned to play golf because there weren't many courses in Black Bottom. You're a regular Redd Foxx."

The man in the homburg glanced around and lowered his voice. "Don't worry about me joining," he said. "It's all noise.

"I just want to look the place over in case we ever get the casino gambling bill passed.

"I like some of these folks, all right, but like Groucho Marx once said, I don't think I'd care to belong to a club that would have me for a member."

Bricking up Santa's entry

December 16, 1988

The truck from the brickyard was blocking the drive, and my wife leaped out of her van and told the driver in no uncertain terms that he'd better move it.

"You've got a lot of nerve pulling that truckload of bricks in here," she shouted. "You wait until my husband . . ."

I heard the commotion and rounded the corner. The truck driver was standing with his hands on his hips, glaring at me like he expected me to have an answer.

"Honey," I began calmly, "this gentleman is not turning around in our drive. He's making a delivery."

She circled the truck slowly, appraising the load suspiciously.

"Bricks, eh?" she said. "What happened? Don't tell me. You went to confession and the priest told you to make a novena."

The driver rolled his eyes. I gave him a don't-blame-me shrug.

"You haven't ordered any construction materials in years," she continued, her lip curling. "You won't even fix the toilet when it runs over. Now, 10 days before Christmas, you order a load of bricks? What's up?"

"Fireplaces," I responded. "They're for the fireplaces."

She made a sour face.

"We never have enough wood as it is," she said. "And you want to build more?"

I shook my head somberly.

"No, dear," I answered. "Actually, I'm going to brick them up."

This time she looked at the driver and he shrugged. She decided to humor me.

"I get it," she said. "You're tired of hauling the wood and cleaning out the ashes. I can live with that. But really . . . aren't you overreacting? Why don't we just send this nice man away," she said, signaling the driver to leave with a jerk of her head, "while we talk it over quietly?"

"Stay!" I shouted. "The bricklayers will be here in a half-hour.

"Read this," I said, thrusting a newspaper clipping into her hands, "and you'll understand why there's not a moment to lose!"

Her eyes raced over the text of a Gannett News Service story that reported that government tests have determined that fireplaces and wood stoves pump millions of tons of unhealthy microscopic pollution into the atmosphere every year and that authorities in some states are recommending that homeowners block or remove existing hearths and stoves.

"It's inevitable," I said. "You know the government. They'll make us do it sooner or later. And then we probably won't be able to buy bricks, let alone hire bricklayers because the demand will be so great. So I decided . . ."

". . . To do it the week before Christmas?" she finished the sentence for me. "Listen, buster, this is a very noble idea. But what do you tell the kids?"

I looked puzzled.

"Kids? Why tell 'em anything? This is an executive decision."

Her eyes narrowed.

"Christmas, Mr. Scrooge," she said. "Give it some thought: Who comes down the chimney at Christmas? What does he come down if there's no chimney to come down?"

I bit my lip.

"That," I said somberly, "is an issue that society will have to address once we've done away with the chimney menace. There are certain trade-offs . . . certain acceptable losses in any major decision-making process."

She shook her head disgustedly.

"We're talking kids and Santa Claus, not George Shultz and the PLO," she interjected. "Look, it says here that some substances are safe to burn. Compacted wood pellets, some other things. Maybe we could roll up some of your old col— . . ."

The truck driver shook his head.

"I've read his stuff, lady," he broke in, "and they'd probably arrest you for fouling the neighborhood. I live downwind of here. If that's the only alternative, I'll give you the bricks for nothing."

Near miss haunts holidays

January 4, 1989

On balance, this should have been one of my best holiday seasons ever. Instead, it was the most emotionally draining that I've spent.

Not that I didn't have plenty to be thankful for. The family was all home, healthy and sound. The grandparents, this one included, were all operating on their own steam. Santa was kind to the children and adults alike.

I even managed to hook up the Nintendo game right.

My problem was, I couldn't quit waking up each night in the wee hours, thinking about the terrible tragedy that we missed by a whisker and wondering how all those hundreds of others who were so much less fortunate were coping with their grief.

I've never been through such a helpless, hopeless time in my life as the one I went through on Dec. 21, when Pan Am flight 103 from London to New York and Detroit blew up over southern Scotland, killing everyone aboard and several people on the ground.

For hours my family and I were under the impression that my daughter Patti, 32, a journalist who works for a British newspaper, was on her way home for Christmas on that same 747.

The plane was reported crashed around 2 p.m. and it was at least five hours before we managed to root out the fact that her name was not on the passenger manifest.

But there was no way of confirming she had made the same trip on another plane because it was en route to New York. So we went roughly from 2 p.m. to 10 p.m. before a couple of very considerate and thoughtful people, Linda Jones of The News' staff and Mike Holfeld of WXYZ-TV Channel 7, both physically spotted her on the ground at New York's Kennedy Airport and had the message that she was safe relayed to me at home.

I thought it would end there, that the sheer joy and relief would swiftly overtake the twin demons of grief and remorse and drive them out. But it didn't work that way. They remained imbedded somewhere deep inside, filing the edge off of joy, hollowing laughter.

In this business you talk to a lot of victims of tragic events – and even more surviving relatives and friends. It never is easy, interviewing parents or other close relatives of children who have died of some sudden illness or accident.

I've stood there many times, making notes, gathering all the necessary facts: age, schooling, job, hobbies? And just what kind of kid was your daughter, m'am? A musician? A good student?

You get so that you despise the task of talking to the red-eyed survivors who are so choked with emotion that they have all they can do to whisper their answers. It's almost ghoulish. The editor wonders if we could borrow a picture?

What has always struck me is that the bereaved generally are so understanding, so polite; not exactly eager to cooperate, but perhaps so numbed by the circumstances and the aftermath that they have no stomach for confrontation.

I had a rare insight into that foggy, frustrating world. I spent a half-dozen hours trying to cut my sorrow with faint hope, wondering what to do next.

I didn't want people coming to my house to collect pictures, if that was necessary. I asked a friend to take one from my office and have it copied.

My stomach burns even thinking about it now. God help all those others who didn't get the good news I got.

As fortunate as I am not to share their deepest grief, I know that some of it surely will visit me each year at Christmas for the rest of my life.

Papa Young misses out

May 21, 1989

I was lying in the lower bunk bed in my 6-year-old son's room the other night, thinking of Coleman Alexander Young.

Now, before you get any strange ideas, let me make clear right now that this definitely is not a common occurrence – unless I happen to have consumed a plate of pickled herring and half-liter of chocolate milk before I retire.

It is one of the small pleasures of parenthood that one is asked on occasion to lie in the dark with small children until they fall asleep. Inevitably, the conversation runs to topics one seldom discusses in daylight.

This particular evening, for instance, Chris had a burning question that needed to be addressed.

"Dad," he called in the hoarse stage whisper that we use in the night to keep our conversations from his sister's prying ears down the hall, "did everybody in the world go to the bathroom today?"

I have learned over the years always to weigh each of these gems with a jeweler's precision and, above all, never to respond immediately. It is crucial that a parent at least appear to bestow a full measure of contemplation on such serious matters.

If you snap off an answer or respond negatively, you may flick off the switch and the creative process will slow another tick.

So I paused thoughtfully and then said, "Well, Chris, I have not considered it until now, but I suppose everyone in the world probably did."

"Unh, unh," he said, quickly challenging my answer. "The dead people didn't. And Jesus didn't."

We kicked that one around for several minutes, considering what one Detroit bureaucrat last week coined as "the reasonableness of the reason" behind our two positions.

In time, Chris fell asleep and I fell into thoughts of what Forever Young is missing by not having his son around the Manoogian Mansion – or wherever – so he might learn from his inquisitiveness, benefit from his company and just plain have someone who doesn't risk getting fired if

173

they disagree once in a while.

I know that I've joked a lot about having the 70-year-old mayor for an assistant coach on my kindergarten soccer team. Or getting him into the rotation of parents who are assigned to bring the "treats" for our green-shirt Giants in the T-ball league.

But in truth, I feel sorry for the old guy. And I even felt a twinge of pity when I read the quotes from his Friday statement, acknowledging for the first time that he is the father of the youngster named Joel Loving, who was born to Annivory Calvert in October 1982.

It's a curious coincidence that little Joel and my son Chris were born only a few days apart. In his remarks to the media Friday, Young talked of having to "painfully reappraise" his position regarding fatherhood. And while he quickly moved to correct himself to call it "responsibility," he spoke of his "guilt" having been established by the blood tests.

He'll pay up, he promises, once his lawyers and her lawyers attach a price tag on Joel that he can agree with.

Pain. Guilt. What a great way to look at fatherhood.

Young was in California for several days prior to his return on Friday. If he stayed where he says he stayed, he was only a few miles down the freeway from his son. He says he didn't go to see the boy, however.

Frankly, the boy's probably just as well off. In the long run, he's not the one who's really missing out on their relationship. His father is.

'Rip' played by the numbers

March 18, 1990

It's too bad that Rip Koury couldn't have read the obituary we ran after his death last week. He'd have had a good chuckle at being described as a "retired grocer."

Louis "Rip" Koury, who died Monday at 86, may indeed have spent time in a grocery store in his life. He certainly was familiar with those large, brown grocery bags – just the right size for a day's cash and receipts from a numbers house to a mutuel bank.

Rip Koury was a career gambler. A friendly, likable guy, he was a diminutive Runyonesque character who wore his hair slicked down and always chomped a long, fat cigar.

He also was a trusted member of one of Detroit's most infamous, multimillion-dollar betting rings, and in 1977, at age 74, he went to prison for 18 months after being convicted of conspiracy and violation of gambling laws.

Even the veteran federal prosecutors who pressed the case and got the evidence against Rip were convinced that he took the fall for somebody else; that he figured that, what the hell, at his age they probably wouldn't put him away for long.

For Rip, everything was a crap shoot.

One day during a recess in that same gambling trial in Detroit, he clamped his cigar in his teeth and approached a lawyer he recognized who at one time had ties to the federal Organized Crime Strike Force.

"Listen," Rip said. "I got a bet with a guy that you went into private practice. Right or wrong?" The man said yes. Rip's lawyer stepped in.

"Quit worryin', kid," Rip said. "I didn't say I bet money. Besides, I won."

The man who introduced me to Rip was Jim Ritchie, a U.S. Justice Department prosecutor who once ran the Strike Force locally. We sat at the kitchen table in Rip's Union Lake home one night and talked about the numbers business in Michigan.

For years Rip "made the Detroit number."

You see, the numbers are not like the Michigan lottery.

No random drawing to screw up on TV. Assorted numbers houses that belong to one ring pay a set fee for protection and other services. They also get a uniform winning number.

Time was when the numbers banks paid off each day on the last three digits of the U.S. Treasury balance, which was printed in the newspapers. But the printers who gambled soon fixed that.

Then the numbers guys went to a more elaborate system of adding up the payoffs on certain horse races and paying a specified three-digit combination. But it didn't take long to rig that, too.

So the Detroit outfit decreed that Rip would "make the number" every day. The "bank" operators would call in each evening to report the numbers that were heavily bet and to say how much they stood to lose if those numbers won. Rip would sort out all the information and select the three digits that wouldn't break the banks.

"We gotta have winners," Rip said, "or people don't play. We just don't gotta have big winners."

What's ironic is that in those days before crack cocaine, Young Boys Inc. and Maserati Rick, Rip and his friends were considered "gangsters."

How times change.

Time to retire

November 14, 1990

This is it. I've had enough.

They won't have old Pete to kick out any more. No more abuse, no more name-calling. I'm done. Finished. It's over. My blood pressure needs a rest.

I'm retiring.

Who'll write the column? Wait a minute. Don't get your hopes up that high.

I didn't say anything about quitting work. I'm retiring as coach of my son's soccer team.

Actually, I've been pondering this decision for the last few weeks. I'm not getting any younger you understand. And trying to keep up with a bunch of youthful assistant coaches, not to mention a gang of rambunctious 7- and 8-year-olds is no menial task for a guy who's pushing the big Six-O.

The idea first hit me the Saturday morning that I got kicked out of the game by a kid referee because I tried to get attention in a rather loud manner. Now, before you jump to any conclusions, I did not call him a $#@%&*$@ or a %$*&@!$%$ or even question his ancestry.

Not out loud, anyway.

But he apparently found my demeanor distracting, if not downright obnoxious. So he banished me not only from the playing field sidelines, but later to the parking lot, the latter because he apparently thought I was "sending in plays" or something equally illegal by a series of clandestine hand signals.

If you have ever seen a second-grade soccer team, in this country anyway, you will realize how ridiculous that is. It is a major chore to get this pride of young lions all moving in a formation that resembles anything save a Rugby scrum.

Send in a play? Now that's funny. It would be easier to teach them to translate Shakespeare into Chinese by tapping out the instructions in Morse code.

Lest the impression be left that I am hanging it up on a sour note, let me say at this point that the abuse and the name-calling mentioned above usually were directed by me at someone else. Getting the hook one day was an insignificant glitch in an overall marvelous experience that spanned three years and a bunch of great kids and their families.

When I began this sentimental journey, my son, Christopher, was in kindergarten. I've been permitted to watch him and a lot of his friends grow and, strange as it may sound, mature, over the last 30 months.

There were so many surprises. And I learned so much, not only about human nature but about kids in general.

My first kindergarten team had one boy who was considerably overweight, and I figured he'd be slow and probably quit. Another kid was so small I hesitated to even let him play for fear he'd get hurt. So much for stereotypes.

The chunky kid not only had surprising speed, he had a nose like a rock and he didn't mind sticking it into anybody who came his way with the ball. And the little guy? Well, one day he squared away and kicked the ball so hard that we had to stop the game while a child who tried to block it caught his breath.

The boys learned from each other. They came from varied backgrounds: Irish, Scottish, Polish, African American, Puerto Rican, Chinese, you name it. Nobody cared. In the coaching tradition of the late Vince Lombardi, who built an enviable winning record, I vowed to treat them all alike: Like dogs.

I didn't, of course. I grew to genuinely love and respect each one as I love and respect my own son. But it's time for me – and them – to move on.

We had an undefeated season this fall, and Chris scored the winning goal on the day of his eighth birthday party. It doesn't get much better.

What's this? My pal, Ted Hadgis, wants to know if I'll help him coach basketball? Well, lemme see. It's two points for a field goal and one point for what?

Hey, I'll learn.

Upgrading the trash

November 26, 1990

I was taking my coffee in the kitchen when my wife coaxed the dogs out into the backyard for their morning visit. I heard Marilyn rustling around on the back porch and when she returned she looked puzzled.

"Something strange is going on," she said, wrinkling her brow. "Did you hear any noises on the porch last night?"

I dismissed the question without looking up from my paper. "Nope. Not a thing. Just your imagination."

She brought in the green plastic bin that the city left with instructions about how to clean, sort and bundle our bottles, cans, newspapers and other recyclables for pickup on rubbish day.

"Well, get a load of all this stuff and tell me somebody hasn't been fooling around," she said. She dug into the bin and plopped a stack of newspapers onto the table.

"The New York Times, The Washington Post? And look here . . . LeMonde? It's all in French, for crying out loud. Where'd that come from?"

She didn't see me wince as she dipped deeper.

"Hey, check these out!" she exclaimed, holding up an empty can of truffles in one hand and a flattened tin of Beluga caviar in the other. "Somebody's got awfully good taste, all right. And check the wine bottles.

"Chateau Petrus '82? An empty jeroboam of Dom Perignon '63? We couldn't afford to pay the freight to get them here. How did they wind up in our trash?"

She stirred in the green bin some more and it yielded several issues of New Yorker, the Grosse Pointer and Gentleman's Quarterly. The unusual collection of newspapers continued to pique her curiosity.

Per the recycling instructions, they had been bundled in shopping bags. But these were from Lord & Taylor, Saks, Gucci, and I. Magnin.

"Whoa," she said, rolling her eyes in my direction as she reached bottom. "I think I'm catching on. That 'prowler' not only left us a whole bunch of high-class trash, he took ours!"

She shook the empty bin. "Where are the copies of Playboy and Penthouse I found under the bed?" she demanded. "What happened to all those big green jug wine bottles you drank? The two empty fifths of Seven Crown? The Spaghetti O's and creamed corn cans that I flattened and pitched out?

"And those copies of the National Enquirer that I put into a Farmer Jack bag with your old Detroit Newses? All of a sudden they're gone and we get the New Yorker and Le Monde in a Gucci bag?

"This crime has your fingerprints all over it, buster! You'd better come clean!"

Cornered, I attacked.

"Yes, I did it!" I said proudly. "But I did it for you . . . for us!" Marilyn appraised me suspiciously, but I went on.

"Ever since they made us put these awful open bins at the curb each week, everyone in the neighborhood knows what everyone else reads, what booze they drink . . . and worse yet, how much. What canned goods they use, where they shop. It's an insidious invasion of privacy!

"I see the neighbors cruising the streets checking out the trash. Look at the Waldmeirs, they laugh. They eat Spaghetti O's? They shop at Kohl's and Service Merchandise? If the truth was known we'd be finished socially in Grosse Pointe.

"I couldn't put you and the children through that. So I went out early this morning and picked up all those bottles and papers from other trash bins and replaced them with ours.

"I'm glad I was wearing my dark glasses. A lady in one of those mansions on Lake Shore Drive saw me picking through her stuff, called me a 'poor thing' and made me take one of her husband's old vicuna topcoats!"

Details, details

February 11, 1991

Barbara-Rose Collins once told a newspaper reporter that her IQ was among the top 2 percent in the world and that because of that, she was a member of an elite society called Mensa until "it moved to Milford."

Also, she said, "I am personal friends" with science-fiction author Isaac Asimov. "I can discuss Einstein's theory of relativity with the best of them," Collins added.

The fact that neither Mensa nor Asimov had ever heard of her didn't faze Collins, now the freshman congresswoman from Detroit's 13th District. She brushed off Mensa's denial saying: "I thought I was a member. I was misled."

She hinted Asimov had a bad memory. But she altered the "personal friends" quote to a statement that she had met him once, "maybe in Cleveland."

Or was it Mensa in Cleveland and Asimov in Milford? Details, details. The next thing, investigators will be wanting to know why she asked people representing companies that do millions of dollars of work for the city of Detroit to co-sign $75,000 worth of illegal loans to her political campaign last summer while she was still a member of the council.

Ms. Collins, 51, is either one of the dumbest elected officials in the city's history or one of the sleaziest. Here is a lady who spent 15 years on the Detroit council, a job she won by overseeing election campaigns. She had run for the U.S. Congress once before.

If she didn't know that taking bundles of money as personal bank loans co-signed by city contractors was not only unethical but against campaign finance laws, she had to be stupid.

If she knew it and did it anyway, then she's just plain dishonest. You make the call.

What Collins did is this:

Seven Democratic candidates were in a cavalry charge race last spring for retiring Rep. George Crockett's seat in the 13th district, which encompasses most of Detroit's lower east side and two of the five Grosse Pointes. The Aug. 7 Democratic primary winner would get the job.

In mid-July, Collins took out a pair of "personal" loans totaling 75 grand to finance her run to the wire. The "person" who made them, however, was Detroit's First Independence National Bank.

Within days, the Federal Election Commission (FEC) was on her case, asking tough questions about the loans.

Collins managed to stall the FEC until two weeks after she'd won the election. Then she quietly admitted that the co-signers were Jim Sharp, Don Barden and Cara Woods, each of whom are indebted corporately to Coleman Young and the City Council for multimillion-dollar contracts.

Barden, whose wife, Bella Marshall, is the mayor's finance chief, holds the exclusive contract for cable television in the city. Sharp is the top political operative for City Management Inc.'s millionaire owner, Tony Soave.

Woods runs a lower-profile construction company.

Divisions of City Management each year compact, haul and dump millions of dollars' worth of Detroit's solid waste and incinerator ash under exclusive deals. The company also holds large contracts for the city's sewer construction work.

Collins last week "confessed" that she had "turned herself in" to the FEC and professed ignorance of federal campaign laws. She also admitted she kept $14,000 of the $75,000 for "personal" expenses and that City Management execs later helped pay off the loans with "contributions." Hmmm.

Why cheat? Collins did it because she knew that once she won the election, she could plead stupidity and probably beat the rap because neither Congress nor the FEC is eager to punish a U.S. representative for something like improper campaign finances.

And guess what Collins' first House committee assignment is? She got Public Works, she said, so she could help bring more federal construction contracts to Detroit. Like her buddy Albert Einstein says, everything is relative.

An un-American dream

July 7, 1991

William G. "Bill" Herbert, a convicted embezzler whose computerized parking ticket collection firm holds one fat Detroit city contract and almost got another to go with it, says all he's trying to do is "share in the American dream."

His choice of words is interesting. The last time I heard that phrase used in connection with a Metro entrepreneur-was when Mafia boss Joseph "Joe Z" Zerilli died in the fall of 1977. Family members bought a full-page ad in The News to attack a column I had written about the man whose "family" controlled organized crime in this area for years.

Herbert, a former Detroit water commissioner and Coleman Young appointee, has been on the hot seat since 1988, when he was convicted in a jury trial of stealing $140,000 from a subsidiary of Blue Cross-Blue Shield.

A portion of the money, Herbert said, had been used to establish Tixon Corp., which in 1986 had won a rich city contract to collect overdue parking fines.

Herbert was sentenced to three years' probation and paid a fine of his own – $2,500 – on the embezzling beef.

He also was ordered to repay $131,500 of the missing $140,000.

He subsequently turned over "ownership" of Tixon to his wife, Amanda. Now he's only the general manager.

Responding to continuing criticism of the Young administration cozying up to Herbert despite his criminal record, Herbert wrote to The News: "It is the hopes and dreams of starting a company like Tixon that can provide the incentive for our inner-city youth to . . . work hard so they can share in the American dream."

Swell. The American dream message is steal money, set up a company and everything is cool. Sounds just like Joe Z.

Joe Zerilli was a long-retired Mafia "don" when he died at 79 of natural causes in 1977. His passing coincided with the death of 22-year-old Curtis Randolph, the first black Detroit firefighter killed in the line of duty.

I wrote a column comparing the contributions made by the two men, lamenting the fact that Zerilli had given so little to society while Randolph had given so much.

The Zerilli family wrote letters. They called me and The News' then-editor, Bill Giles, demanding retractions, my firing, whatever.

Finally, after a two-week avalanche of complaints, the frustrated Giles told a family representative to buy an ad if they wanted more "positive" comment about Joe Z.

And that's exactly what they did. They put together a full-page ad, which went for $5,000 to $6,000 in those days, and it ran on Sunday, Dec. 11, 1977. The thrust of the message: Joe Z was "someone who helped make this country great. His extraordinary contribution to mankind belongs to history."

And, of course, the inevitable "he believed in the American dream," which, in Joe Z's case, meant being free to run numbers and other illegal gaming operations, oversee prostitution and drug trade, and control loan sharking in several counties.

To put Bill Herbert in Joe Z's class, however, might provoke the family to buy another ad. Actually, Herbert reminds me more of Jimmy "Occo" Tamer, now an elderly legitimate Mt. Clemens businessman who's been in and out of jail so often he still gets one-day service on his laundry.

As a youth in Flint in the 1930s, Tamer once turned $150 into $5,000 in a few hours.

He bought a machine gun and held up a bank.

Dead meat

July 14, 1991

Coleman Young emerged from hibernation to holler at the media again the other day, accusing them once more of exacerbating Detroit's sorrowful image by telling the truth.

But nobody gives a damn what he says anymore. Not the press, radio, TV. Not the general public or other politicians. Those who do listen no longer believe what he says.

The guy is a tragic-comic figure – an emperor who either cannot or will not accept the fact that his empire no longer exists, that his power is on paper, that the uproar he hears outside the walls is a leering mob and not a cheering crowd.

Personally, I'm tired of writing Young's political obituary, tired of describing him as a wounded, aging lion heroically fighting off the hyenas.

The guy's no heroic lion. He's dead meat. And the only thing that's powerful about dead meat is the aroma.

The media actually should be the least of his worries. But the frustrated Young is cornered, and that's the easiest place to launch a counterattack.

Two of the city's last three big-league sporting shows, the Grand Prix auto race and the Tigers' baseball franchise, are threatening to pull up stakes and blow town unless he meets their demands.

He doesn't want the Grand Prix on Belle Isle, and he doesn't want Wayne County Executive Ed McNamara controlling a new Tiger stadium, which would have to be built with county money because the city's broke. But the powerless Young has no choice and he knows it.

If he gives in on either or both ultimatums, he loses face. If he doesn't, Detroit takes another step down the tubes.

Mainly because of his lack of hands-on control, nepotism and cronyism have riddled the upper echelon of Young's administration. Competent appointees like Zoo Director Steve Graham and Budget Director Walter Stecher grow tired of long hours and impossible tasks and quit.

Stecher goes at a time when the city is coming off a $42-million deficit and heading into a projected $100-million short-fall. You think Coleman's upset now, stick around.

Young's once-mighty political clout likewise has faded. He backed Carolyn Cheeks Kilpatrick with money, people and pressure in the recent Detroit City Council special election. Outsider Kay Everett, an independent, beat Kilpatrick by a mile and Young lost certain control of the nine-member council.

Young wanted Art Carter as Detroit's superintendent of schools. The school board thumbed its collective nose and Carter didn't even make the final-four list.

Then came the infamous fireworks fracas, where two women were severely beaten and their attackers were identified on video tape, and the tape made local and national TV.

Striking out this week, the frustrated Young accused the Detroit media of creating a "burlesque show." For those of you too young to remember, burlesques were theaters where comics told stale jokes while ladies shed their clothes on stage.

In this case, however, it's the comic who's missing his clothes. But the show's so bad, nobody really cares.

Just for laughs

August 12, 1991

People ask if I envy my colleague, George Cantor, who recently switched to writing a sports column. My answer's simple: No.

I spent more than 20 years in sports, and I don't think I've missed a whole helluva lot since I switched. Jocks are still jocks. There are just more of 'em. Making more money.

When I started in sports, there were six teams in the National Hockey League, 16 in major league baseball and nine schools in the Big Ten. You figure that out.

Gordie Howe had all his front teeth, Jack Nicklaus was in grade school and the Pistons were part-time semi-pros in Fort Wayne, Ind.

About all I miss are the characters. Either there aren't a lot of funny people around anymore or the writers have lost their ear for humor.

I recall golfer Lee Trevino, for instance, recounting his tale of poverty in Texas. "My family was so poor," he said, "that we couldn't afford a mother. The lady next door had me."

After the Dallas Cowboys' Danny Villaneuva picked up a kick he had blocked and ran with it during a game one Sunday, I stupidly asked him what "he was" in high school. Villaneuva smiled. "I was a Mexican then, too," he said.

A guy named Bert Sugar once compiled a whole book of crisp sports quotes that I pick up (and borrow from) on occasion, just for a little relief from the woes of the world.

Pitcher Tug McGraw, years back, on signing his first big contract: "Ninety percent I'll spend on good times, women and Irish whisky. The rest I'll probably waste." And on whether he prefers grass vs. artificial turf: "Can't say. I never smoked turf."

Former Lions' great Bobby Layne, inviting me to visit him at his home in Lubbock, Texas: "Bring a clean shirt and a $50 bill, and you won't change either one." SMU All-American Doak Walker on Layne's leadership: "He never lost a game. Once in a while, time ran out on him, that's all."

All-Pro Detroit tackle Alex Karras on his college career: "I only spent two terms in college at Iowa: Truman's and Eisenhower's."

Some of my favorite quotes came from doubletalkers like the Yankees' Yogi Berra. Berra on baseball attendance in New York: "If people don't want to come out to the park, nobody's gonna stop 'em." And on a Manhattan saloon where the sports crowd used to meet: "It's so crowded that nobody goes there any more."

Then, of course, there's always Danny Ozark's classic: "Half this game is 90 percent mental."

The late Branch Rickey, on senility: "First you forget names, then you forget faces. Then you forget to zip your fly. Then you forget to unzip your fly."

Boxing manager Chris Dundee on middle age: "It's when you start for home about the same time you used to start for someplace else."

When Notre Dame's Lou Holtz was coaching football at Arkansas, the fans demonstrated their pleasure at being invited to the Orange bowl by pelting him with oranges. Said Holtz afterward: "I'm sure glad we didn't get invited to the Gator Bowl."

Entertainer Connie Stevens was asked if she would date New York Jets' quarterback Joe Namath. Her response: "Who wants to go with a guy who's got two bad knees and a quick release?"

And then there were some words of wisdom from a pair of departed columning colleague, Edgar C. "Doc" Greene.

Responded Greene one day when I inquired how many columns he had prepared in advance:

"Never write ahead, kid. You might die and get stuck with 'em."

The Shadow knows

September 9, 1991

It was 2 a.m., and when Marilyn got up to let the dogs out, she found me sitting alone in the dark in the family room. "You've got to get some sleep," she said, softly. "Forget about it. It never happened. It's either a cruel hoax or your mind is playing tricks on you again.

"You're overworked, that's all. And when you're tired, your mind does strange things."

My eyes narrowed and my jaw set firm.

"I'm going to tell you one more time woman," I said through tightly clenched teeth, "I SAW him! It WAS him! Don't patronize me! I'm not the doddering old lout you make me out to be.

"Besides, how could I be overworked? I just got off two weeks' vacation. I'm in great shape."

"Pete, Pete," she said, stepping behind my chair and rubbing my shoulders. "We've all noticed it. The kids, the rest of the family, our friends. You're under so much pressure. He's all you think about. He occupies too much of your mind.

"No wonder you think you saw him on the streets of Detroit. He's like Elvis. People who aren't nearly as debonair and intelligent as you report sighting him everywhere.

"Why just the other day, a secretary from Blue Cross who was having lunch in Greektown told Channel 7 she had seen his image in a pita pocket sandwich stuffed with Greek salad! Swore it was him."

My head drooped. Why, oh why, I thought, can't I make them understand.

"I'll say it one more time," I said. "Call me mixed up. Call me overworked. But I SAW Coleman Young. It WAS him. Out in public. Alive!"

Marilyn shook her head slowly.

"I know it's difficult to accept," she said, "but you've go to face it, Pete. The man doesn't go out in public. That couldn't have been him. And on the streets of Detroit? Get serious, will you. He's smarter than that."

My eyes shifted nervously as I frantically tried to recall the details of the sighting.

"He was in a dark suit," I said, squinting hard to lock in the picture, "Gray hair, puffy cheeks, no hat. And there were five . . . no, six, seven, eight people with him. All of them nodding their heads yes whenever he said anything."

Marilyn was listening hard now. It almost made sense.

"The cars," she said. "Tell me about the cars."

"Three," I said, "just like always. The one comes out from Gracelan . . . I mean, the Manoogian . . . first. One cop. A lady. Car's all shined up. She gets to the center lane on East Jefferson and waits and then the limo comes flying out with another scout car behind.

"Heavy duty artillery. Must be a tough neighborhood he lives in."

Marilyn looked puzzled. "But you just saw cars? How do you know it was him inside? Maybe it was a decoy, a stand-in."

"He was at the Millender Center that morning. With some U.S. senator from Iowa who's running for president. Made a speech. Introduced the dude. The crowd cheered at the drop of every four-letter word."

Marilyn shook her head slowly. "Now you see, that's the part that's hard to believe. Not the cheers or the cussing. The fact that the man would take the time to introduce some politician nobody ever heard of, but he doesn't get out on the streets and threaten those punk car-jackers with holy whatsis if they don't quit ruining his city.

"Face it, Pete. Do you honestly believe the real Coleman Young would just sit by and let all this go on without knocking some heads? Naw, that couldn't be Hizonner.

"Get some rest. The next thing you know, you'll be trying to crack the kids' piggy banks because Howard Hughes left a stock tip on your voice mail!"

Magic didn't invent sex

December 4, 1991

Once upon a time there was a young, tall blond lady nicknamed Chicago Shirley who lived in the magic kingdom called Detroit and collected professional athletes. And I'm not talking about their pictures on bubblegum cards.

I never did know what Chicago Shirley did for a living. Or what significance Chicago held, for that matter, except maybe she had lived there once.

She may have been a secretary or a heart surgeon by day. But once evening fell, she customarily sallied forth to a popular local saloon, which shall remain unnamed for the purposes of this discussion, to pursue her avocation, which I'm reasonably convinced had nothing to do with typewriters or scalpels.

She would park her car discreetly in a darkened area of an unattended lot adjacent to the pub, which was a known hangout for visiting-team athletes of all disciplines, races, nationalities and persuasions.

And, as evening turned to morning, she would parade a series of young and not-so-young jocks, managers, coaches, trainers – you name it – back and forth from the bar. The first time I saw her leave and return with a half-dozen or more different guys, one at a time, I thought perhaps she was selling something out of the trunk.

It turned out, however, that she wasn't selling anything. She was giving away smiles, free of charge, and she kept an unlimited supply stored in the back seat.

Chicago Shirley comes to mind today because of the revelations that Los Angeles Lakers basketball star Earvin "Magic" Johnson probably contracted HIV by sleeping around with a series of sex partners that he barely knew at the time and hasn't a prayer of identifying now.

Some people appear shocked at Johnson's frank admission. If you're one of them, I have some alarming news for you: Contrary to what you may have been led to believe, Magic Johnson did not invent sexual escapades on road trips.

I believe, in fact, that the practice predates the original Celts – and I don't mean the team that plays basketball in Boston.

The moral aspects of Johnson's indiscretions aside, he has turned a spotlight on an area where few athletes – or sportswriters, for that matter – previously have dared to venture. I mean, let's face it: Do you think I could get away telling stories about Chicago Shirley in any other context?

This kind of activity has been going on, and discreetly hidden or masked over, for years. But before the AIDS scare surfaced, nobody gave much of a hoot.

Frankly, I'm amazed that many more jocks and many more of their sex partners haven't been infected before. Maybe the numbers are greater and we just haven't been told. Who knows?

Perhaps in Chicago there was (is?) a Detroit Shirley carving notches on her steering wheel and wondering whether that guy with the big smile that she entertained six months ago could have been . . . ?

Chicago Shirley, alas, was relatively democratic in that she displayed few prejudices. All she asked was that her athletes, whatever their sport, came to play. Not so with a contemporary who earned the nickname "The Fiddler" because she carried a violin case for an overnight bag and frequently moved into the local hotel that headquartered visiting hockey teams, preferably from Canada.

One night during the 1968 World Series here, The Fiddler broke ranks, so to speak, and invited an out-of-town sportscaster, who also shall remain nameless, to accompany her to her suburban home, where she lived with her parents and her kid brother.

When he awakened in the morning, the visitor found the brother standing over his bed, holding a pad and pencil. "Hey, mister," the young man asked anxiously, "are you a hockey player?"

Hart's no hero

May 11, 1992

Something vital was missing in the aftermath of the Bill Hart trial, which concluded last week with the former Detroit Police chief's convictions on four of seven felony counts in federal court:

Anger. Outrage. A demand for answers and accountability.

Detroit's so-called civic leaders expressed "sadness" for the man, his family and for the city. Swell. All that was missing was some guy in a toga on a balcony at 1300 Beaubien shouting, "The Crook is dead! Long live the Crook!"

Hart's successor as chief, Stanley Knox, declared that he was "shocked" at the jury verdict, which ruled Hart guilty of stealing $2.6 million in taxpayer funds and failing to pay federal taxes on the money he swung with illegally.

This is the cop who's supposed to be in charge of cleaning things up and he's shocked? Yo! Stanley! Anybody home?

"The results of this case represent a personal tragedy for an individual who served our community with distinction for so many years," said the government's top prosecutor, U.S. Attorney Stephen J. Markman. Well, well. Millions in government money. Fifty-one days of trial and testimony, 51 hours of jury deliberations.

What's the buzz, homey? You nail the wrong dude?

"I regret what has happened," solemnly intoned Mayor-for-life Coleman Young, the official who appointed Hart 16 years ago with a mandate to reform a morally, socially and, some said criminally, corrupt police department. "Bill Hart was a good man and a good cop."

And Hizonner added with the incredible revisionist hindsight that a politician who's trying to justify a horrendous mistake always seems able to muster: "He rendered good and faithful service to Detroit."

Good and faithful service, eh? If that's good and faithful, I'd hate to see what Young's idea of bad and unfaithful service is.

On second thought, no I wouldn't. By these standards, the price would be astronomical.

As for the "personal tragedy" explanation that tempered Markman's victory celebration – publicly, anyway – I have only one question: What does that make Hart's violations of the public trust, not to mention his rape of the public treasury? An impersonal tragedy?

Let us face facts, folks. The jury decision is in. Bill Hart is a common thief. Not only that but he cheats on his old lady – and even on his multiple mistresses – and gambles illegally.

Remember the $20,000 Hart proclaimed "poker stash" that fell out of the kitchen light fixture? You keep 20 grand on hand for friendly bets, don't you?

If he'd been a street cop taking a few bucks a week in protection money from a bookmaker or dope dealer this whole cadre of cluck-cluckers would be reviling his criminal avarice and calling for his head and those of his permissive bosses.

But Bill Hart was no ordinary cop. He was a member of a privileged elite, an affirmative action appointment who got every break in the book and took 'em all.

During his campaign for mayor several months back, candidate John Conyers was asked for his appraisal of the litany of charges against Hart. "He's either the dumbest cop on the force, or the crookedest," Conyers responded.

After 10 weeks of court testimony, the verdict on Conyers' assessment came back as a tie. With $2.6 million in embezzled funds, Hart easily outstripped any other (convicted) crook among Young's phalanx of appointees.

And judging from the picture painted with a modest degree of success by his own defense team, he was a bumbling dolt who couldn't find his own fanny with both hands – but didn't have much trouble finding plenty of others and paying for them all with public money.

Save your sympathy for Bill Hart. If the court is brave enough to send him to the slammer, he'll get what he's got coming.

Trickle down integrity

November 9, 1992

What is ironic in most of the official comment following the death of Malice Green, apparently at the hands of two Detroit police officers last Thursday night, are the repeated references to how "professional" the department has become in Coleman Young's 20 years as mayor.

To hear administration officials and police brass tell it, the alleged beating of the 35-year-old Green by veteran undercover cops Larry Nevers and Walter Budzyn was a total aberration; two bad apples run amok in a huge barrel of occasionally bruised but otherwise unspoiled fruit despite the dedication and diligence of their superiors.

Sure.

After all the work Young's people have done to improve the department's professionalism, after fighting and winning the long struggle on tough issues like affirmative action and residency, the officials express shock and amazement at how something as cruel and brutal as the attack on the unarmed Green could be perpetrated by members of such a highly skilled, highly trained and magnificently led police force.

The sad part, I guess, is that Young and his brass don't just say all these things. They really believe them.

The truth is that there has been a distinct absence of leadership and massive abuses of power in the department's upper echelon for most of the last 10 years.

Talk about trickle down economics. Trickle down integrity is what's been sadly lacking there.

Scandal after scandal has surfaced. None involved such terminal street injustice as that allegedly meted out by Budzyn and Nevers. But other incidents reflect a pattern of abuse, an arrogant disdain for law and order that could encourage and even tacitly condone more outrageous behavior elsewhere.

William Hart, the department's longest serving chief under Young's administration, is serving a 10-year prison term for stealing $2.6 million from a police undercover fund.

Former civilian Deputy Chief Ken "The Professor" Weiner, who once served as a close confidant of Hart and security specialist and financial adviser to the mayor, likewise is doing time for stealing $2.3 million from the city.

Last May, Patrolman Gene "Moon" Mullins, once the undisputed command pilot of the Detroit police "air force," was convicted of six counts of witness tampering and obstructing the investigation of a grand jury looking into allegations against the department's aviation section.

Mullins' boss, retired Cmdr. Alfred J. Dabrowski, also admitted altering flight logs during testimony against Mullins. But when a judge wouldn't go along with a deal cut by federal prosecutors in exchange for Dabrowski's testimony, Dabrowski walked.

Like Weiner and Hart, Mullins was a friend and longtime associate of Mayor Young and was so close to the administration and the watchdog Detroit Police Commission that he was married by Young at the Manoogian Mansion while he was under federal indictment.

And if that weren't bad enough, Odson Tetrault, executive secretary to the Board of Police Commissioners and the man who is supposed to investigate and ferret out wrongdoing in the department, signed the license as a witness.

All that happened after Mullins was indicted by the U.S. Attorney, but before he went to trial.

What kind of vibes do you suppose that sends to street coppers?

Honesty is the best policy?

So what's all this got to do with two white cops allegedly beating a black motorist to death with their club-like flashlights on a street corner in southwest Detroit? Maybe nothing, maybe a lot.

But one thing's certain: Nevers and Budzyn didn't just materialize out of thin air. They are passengers on a sizable iceberg of incompetence, and the more city officials and police brass pat themselves on the back and ignore it, the closer they steer to even more disastrous tragedies.

'Outing' old Charlie

March 1, 1993

Let me set the record straight right off the bat. Charles Beckham owes me and a lot of others who had absolutely no say and no control over the way he took payoffs, illegally steered at least one sweetheart sludge contract and mismanaged the Detroit Department of Water and Sewerage before he finally went to jail in June 1988.

He owes us money that will never be repaid, no matter the size of his fines; money wasted on the increased costs of the services to the city and suburbs that resulted from his misfeasance and malfeasance as the highest-ranking official in a Detroit municipal department that holds a virtual monopoly for the sale of water supply and sewerage disposal over dozens of captive suburban communities.

But above that he owes us an apology for illegally squandering millions of federal taxpayers' dollars and for causing hundreds of federal agents and government attorneys to sort through a maze of lies and distortions to get at the truth, to wit:

Despite all his protestations of innocence, Charles Beckham was a bribe-taking, crooked appointed official who violated the public trust to further his own financial fortunes and those of at least one very close friend of his boss, Detroit Mayor Coleman A. Young.

Jailbird Beckham's got a bug in his baggies because I pointed out his prison record a month ago when he surfaced as executive director of a new self-help group called A3BC, the acronym for African American Association of Businesses and Contractors.

I "outed" good old Charlie for several good reasons. First of all, nobody else brought it up.

Maybe it was because they didn't know. There are folks in the local media these days who can't find Woodward Avenue, let alone remember Darralyn Bowers and the VISTA Disposal scandal from a decade ago.

Maybe the ones who did recognize the name confused Charlie with his brother, William Beckham, who is a respected local businessman.

But maybe . . . just maybe . . . it simply wasn't considered P.C. to bring up Charlie's record, what with his political connections and all. Hey, listen, Mayor Young thinks he's a great guy.

Maybe so. But the A3BC ain't exactly some soup kitchen. Charlie's charging $175 to $2,500 for memberships. People who are asked to come up with that kind of scratch ought to know exactly whom they are dealing with. Warts and all.

In a letter to The News last week, Beckham accused me of having "distorted" his history and attempting to "demean" his "efforts to help minority and urban-based businesses prosper in Detroit."

He also questioned my motives and my "need to regurgitate an issue whose origin is 12 years old!"

In addition, Beckham said it was "ludicrous" for me "to suggest that Charlie Beckham is any different than Ivan Boesky, Michael Milken, Denny McLain, Ollie North, G. Gordon Liddy, John DeLorean, Pete Rose and on and on."

For the record, I never mentioned any of that creepy collection of zealots, swindlers, gamblers, dope peddlers and con men in the Beckham column. But if he chooses to be grouped with them, he can be my guest. And the only time I regurgitate is when I get my water bill.

As for distorting history, there's no need in Charlie's case. It's all on file in the federal courthouse and prison system. A federal jury convicted him of racketeering, fraud and extortion. He did two years of a four-year prison term and got out in June 1991.

The highest-ranking Detroit public official ever sent to prison prior to Police Chief Bill Hart's 10-year term for stealing $2.6 million, Charlie labeled my Feb. 3 column "suspect, offensive and unredeeming." He concluded brusquely: "I am currently discussing it with my attorney."

Make sure your mouthpiece doesn't have the meter running, Charlie, because you'll be wasting the worst kind of money: Your own.

Now for some fresh ideas

June 23, 1993

There is no euphoria, no glee. Only a touch of sadness.

Not sadness that Coleman Alexander Young has decided to hang it up after an unprecedented five terms as mayor of Detroit.

Sadness that he really didn't accomplish all that he might have accomplished in the last 19 1/2 years. And sadness that he stuck around too long and didn't let somebody else give it a try back when there still was a lot more left to work with.

Young, 75, announced late yesterday that he will not seek a sixth term. For some reason, he waited until the final minute of the final day to call together the media, most of whom he disdains but tolerates, so he could play the starring role in yet one more of his absurd political charades.

He has accomplished so much, he bragged at the outset, ticking off a list of things for which he took credit; some correctly, others not. There is so much left to do, he added plaintively, ticking off a list of unfinished projects.

Well, I thought, standing in the room as he droned on, what the hell does all this mean? It was past the 4 p.m. filing deadline. Was he in? Or was he out?

Finally, after milking a live broadcast and eating up several hundred feet of TV and audio tape, he announced anti-climatically, "I've decided that 20 years is enough. I shall not seek another term as mayor of Detroit."

I wondered at that point, just what is going through this man's mind, if anything? Did he think that the comparatively small crowd that had gathered in his media interview room was going to buy all of his claims? And when he bowed out, did he think they'd cheer? Boo? Hiss? Weep?

If there was any reaction apparent, however, it was sort of a collective sigh of relief.

Finally . . . finally. He's done. He's tired. He no longer has the stomach for the hassle. He's through.

The job is open. Let's move on. There are new opportunities. And certainly no shortage of pretenders to this gilded throne.

Not relief for the media. We'll survive, no matter who wins in November.

But the city – our city – needs to escape the political, economic and social paralysis that has immobilized it for nearly a decade.

Now, let it really move forward. Let us give new meaning to all those signs Young's toadies have plastered around the city for so many years.

How does that get accomplished?

First, Detroit elects a mayor who can talk to people. Not yell at people. Talk to them.

Logically. Intelligently. And when they, the citizens, ask legitimate questions, that man or woman responds with something more than a "Trust me, I'll get it done."

"Trust me" doesn't work any more. People are too astute, too involved. And they're too smart of be conned by the blanket excuse that the reason Detroit can't make mutually profitable deals with suburban governments is that all the suburbs want to do is rip off Detroit's "jewels."

Make no mistake. Coleman Young was a politician whose time had come when he was elected back in the early 1970s.

Detroit never really had recovered from the 1967 riot. The black population was playing tag with a 50 percent majority.

A black mayor and the reforms he could bring were ripe for election.

Young was strong, tough, unbending – all the qualities the city's new majority required and appreciated. He had cut a wide swath, made radical changes and, in the process, intentionally scared the bejabbers out of the middle class white taxpayers who didn't vote for him but found him controlling their affairs anyway.

The time now has come for reconciliation. Call it ego, call it stubbornness, call it loyalty . . . the guy hung on too long.

Nobody wants this monarch dead. They merely want a new monarch with some fresh ideas.

A real mayor

November 3, 1993

Let the future begin. Let the word go forth that Detroit, once more, is open for business.

Tell the money changers to clear out of City Hall. Send the message that the municipal management no longer is treading water, marching in place.

Tell the laggards, the gold-bricks, the screw-offs that the caretaker government, run for the last half-dozen years by surrogates who are more interested in protecting their turf than serving their masters, no longer is in control and to pack their bags.

The office of mayor is back, for real.

The "You go, girl!" went and the man who's in charge is Dennis Archer. He has a mandate from the people, and he's kickin' tail and takin' names.

Once the celebrating ends, let the healing begin.

Let the bitterness, the rancor, the name-calling end. Let brother embrace brother. For that matter, let brother embrace sister, sister embrace sister. Hey, whatever's politically correct.

Let the future begin.

Let the ministers come together. Let the Rev. Jim Holley embrace the Rev. Wendell Anthony and the Rev. Charles Adams, and have them all keep their fingers, legs and eyes uncrossed. And the first guy who smiles, scratches or shuffles has to go a month of Sundays without passing a collection plate.

Let these ecclesiastical heavy-hitters direct their tremendous financial, spiritual and political energies to forging a coalition that will truly raise their brethren up and set them free.

Let the union leaders bury their hatchets and not in each others' skulls. Let the UAW's Ernie Lofton, who zealously backed Sharon McPhail, welcome and forgive Detroit Police Officers Association President Tom Schneider, who helped roll out the vote for Archer.

There is so much raw power in offices like theirs and the other labor organizations. Just think what they could do for Detroit if they pulled together with the same force they expended during this campaign to pull apart.

Let the healing begin. And let it spread across all boundaries: Geographic, social, political and financial.

Let Oakland County Executive L. Brooks Patterson and Sharon McPhail seek common ground, let Wayne County Executive Ed McNamara embrace Wayne County Sheriff Bob Ficano, let Pete Waldmeir snuggle up to Coleman Young's soon-to-be-unemployed flack Bob Berg . . .

Wait a minute! Hold It!

I'm all for letting the future begin . . . but let's not get carried away!

This is, indeed, an exciting moment in Detroit's history. It is a time to mend fences, build bridges, join hands and to move forward behind a man who should know how to lead.

Move Detroit forward. How many times have you seen and heard that empty credo during the last 20 years? If this has been forward maybe we ought to try reverse for a while.

How soon can Archer get it moving forward again? That depends. First he has to stop the slide and that'll take not only time and ingenuity, but effort and money.

Detroiters will have to remember – and keep remembering - that they elected Dennis Archer, not Harry Houdini; that it took 20 or more years to get the city into the shape it's in and it'll take at least 10 years and maybe more to check the skid and turn it around.

But it is worth the effort.

Where will I be while all this is going on? Well, I did have my misgivings about keeping this job once Mayor Coleman Young departed the Manoogian.

But despite the fact that Sharon McPhail lost and I'm destined to be stuck with pursuing Archer for at least the next four years I have changed my mind about retiring. Heck, I'd just sit around and throw things at the TV set.

Let the future begin. And deal me in.

McPhail's McFoibles

November 5, 1993

Before we leave the topic, hopefully for good, permit me one final musing on the Detroit mayoral campaign conducted by Sharon McPhail and why she lost to Dennis Archer.

As she stood at the podium in the ballroom of Greektown's International Marketplace on election night blaming media hostility, a lack of money and everybody but L. Brooks Patterson for her defeat, McPhail made a statement that was about as misleading and incorrect as anything she said during her lengthy struggle to become Detroit's first African-American woman mayor.

"This (the campaign) has never been about me as a person," she said, her hoarse voice cracking with emotion. "It's been about us . . . all of us."

After all this time, after all that's been said, written, charged and proven, McPhail still doesn't get it.

The loss was about her and only her. But she continues to deny her role and to shift the blame, trying to turn her defeat into some kind of a conspiracy to discredit women in general.

McPhail brought her personality, programs, promises and policies to the people and asked them to trust her. And they decided not to.

When the final tally was in, Dennis Archer had won a victory of mandate proportions – 57 percent to 43 percent. But, you know what?

Even though he outspent her by a couple of million bucks and campaigned two years longer than she did, Archer could not have done it without a large measure of help from McPhail. She had a legitimate shot at a stunning upset, and she self-destructed.

And unless she stops mouthing and believing those tired alibis and makes a genuine effort to understand what actually went wrong, this lady whose advisers talk brashly of running her for the U.S. Congress against veteran Democrat John Conyers never will get elected to anything, in Detroit or anywhere else.

Not that she doesn't have talent, intelligence, voter appeal, you name it. In fact, if she's really serious about going to Washington, McPhail should forget Conyers and run against her pal, U.S. Rep. Barbara-Rose Collins. McPhail could go in a revolving door behind Collins and come out in front of her.

Assistant Prosecutor McPhail has got to stop thinking and acting like a criminal lawyer. Loop-holes, theatrics, wild charges, conspiratorial enemies – hey, they all can be important tools to hammer away with when you're trying to convince a jury.

But courtroom tactics and courtroom rules don't work when you're running for public office.

There's no judge to order the panel to believe this and ignore that. If you say or do something and it's wrong, no amount of legal or rhetorical maneuvering is going to make it right in the minds of the voters.

Everything is relevant in the political arena.

And that goes for moonlighting on a public job, fudging stories about where your kids go to school, or standing by and refusing to distance yourself from irresponsible charges and insults leveled against your opponent by persons close to your campaign.

No matter how brazenly you attempt to dismiss or minimize your shortcomings, they all count against you in the court of public opinion.

While she's taking her reality check, McPhail also would do well to ponder the fact that while she was being soundly defeated, several black women fared far better.

Wayne County Commissioner Jackie Currie upset five-term Detroit City Clerk James Bradley. Kay Everett was returned to her seat on the Detroit City Council, where she'll be joined by newcomers Alberta Tinsley-Williams and Brenda Scott.

Two other women, Council President Maryann Mahaffey and rookie Sheila Cockrel, make the council's four males a minority.

Her defeat wasn't about blacks, and it wasn't about women. As tough as it may be for her to swallow, it was about Sharon McPhail.

Archer enters with class

January 4, 1994

Dennis Archer said all the right things, pushed all the right buttons, tugged all the heart strings.

He shouted, he whispered, he threatened and he coaxed.

This wasn't the same extremely intelligent, mild-mannered, soft-spoken, dull, mechanical guy in the plain dark suit and winged-tipped shoes who took on Detroit's Mayor-for-life, Coleman Alexander Young, in a do-or-die struggle some three years ago.

Full of the confidence and bearing that only victory can bring, Archer hugged his wife and he rubbed his son's back when young Dennis, a college student, choked back tears during his father's introduction.

He was what any of us – hey, all of us – could ever hope to be on such a historic day.

He wasn't afraid to laugh – or to cry, for that matter – with his family and the hundreds of campaign workers, well-wishers and just plain curious who snuggled into the ornate Fox Theatre on a cold Monday morning to pay homage to the new mayor of Detroit at his swearing-in ceremony.

But while he was shouting and exhorting his followers and others to go forth and change the city's destiny, he maintained his customary measure of class. The only four-letter words that passed his lips were work, love, hope and pray.

Welcome to 1994. Welcome to the Dennis Archer era.

The list of dignitaries in attendance was impressive. And it said something about Archer's pledge to build coalitions and bring people together.

America's guest, Jesse Jackson, arrived with Detroit NAACP President the Rev. Wendell Anthony, an early supporter of Archer's defeated arch-rival, Sharon McPhail. Michigan's two Democratic senators, Carl Levin and Don Riegle, were there, coatless on the sidewalk out front, despite the freezing temperatures.

Washington politicians, it seems, all must have studied meteorology under former Ohio State football coach Woody Hayes.

Speaking of Riegle, one of the reluctant pretenders to his soon-to-be vacated job, former Michigan Gov. Jim Blanchard, who now is U.S. ambassador to Canada, breezed through the crowd pressing flesh. His successor, Republican Gov. John Engler, had spoken at a prayer breakfast earlier.

Another loser, Wayne County Commission Chairman Arthur Blackwell III showed up, too. "We're both Democrats," Blackwell said, "and Dennis now is the leading Democrat in Michigan. I want him to quit being just another nice guy. I want him to take his place now as a leader."

Plainly, this was no day for partisan politics for the Archers, however. It was a day of triumph, a day of thanksgiving.

Actually, for some of us it was a day of atonement as well. I mean, let's face it: I never really thought Dennis Archer would ever be elected mayor of Detroit.

Not that he isn't eminently qualified for the job. Not that I didn't think he was the best of the long list of candidates.

I just never, really, honest-to-God believed that he could pull it off.

As I sat there in the cavernous Fox Theatre on Monday, watching and listening, however, I was reminded of just how wrong I'd been about him and a lot of things; how I had misjudged and underestimated not only Archer, but the people who brought him to this day of triumph: the voters.

I figured that after 20 years of street-smart Coleman Young's bombast and confrontation, Detroit was too calloused to embrace an even-tempered former state Supreme Court justice as a leader of anything more important than a Boy Scout troop.

Archer, I predicted with the confidence that only ignorance can muster, had risen so high that he couldn't possibly get down with the people. Detroit, I said, would never trust a man, or a woman, who didn't whiz around in a big, black limo and talk trash.

Monday was only the beginning. The task will be long and difficult. Detroit may, indeed, be beyond rescue.

But then, I've been wrong before – as Dennis Archer will readily point out, I'm sure.

D.J. makes life miserable

February 20, 1994

Marilyn bunched up the newspaper noisily and threw it on the floor. "That does it!" she said impatiently. "Now I'm really angry!"

I lowered my paper and peered over my glasses, trying to spot which story had set her off this time. I didn't think it was the Kerrigan-Harding tussle. She had been eating that up for days.

Could it be the Sex Lady telling teen-agers, again, how to have the most fun while making out? Or another glowing tribute to Rosanne Arnold's depiction of American family life?

Naw. She stopped reading that trash a long time ago.

I stretched my right leg, fetched the paper casually and uncrumpled it with my toe. There on page 4C was a picture of Grosse Pointe interior decorator D.J. Kennedy along with a story about him being selected to refurbish the Manoogian Mansion for Detroit's first couple, Mayor Dennis Archer and his wife, Trudy.

I glanced up. Marilyn was glaring at me.

"Don't act like you don't know what I'm talking about," she snapped. "This is the last straw. D.J. doing the Manoogian, indeed! He'll probably be doing the Big Boy restaurants before you break down and hire him, you cheapskate!"

Having been through this before, I fell into my customary defense.

"Please," I said, "don't get personal. I just don't happen to think this place really needs D.J.'s touch, that's all. I mean, look what one of his competitors says right here in the story:

"'I guess D.J. will do a good job if you like that Old World look.' Who needs to pay him all that money? We already have the Old World look."

Marilyn's eyes narrowed. "Old World?" She bit off the words. "You betcha. And old carpeting, old drapes, old furniture, old wallpaper . . . Old garage sale, that's what we have!

"From what I've read about what's happened to the Manoogian over the last 20 years, it sounds like you must have decorated it for Coleman Young."

Losing ground, I went to the attack.

"Actually," I sniffed, "it's not the money that's kept me from hiring D.J. It's his whole schtick. I mean, what did they tell us when we moved to Grosse Pointe. Less is more, remember?

"Bare wood floors, one big picture on each wall, all white kitchen appliances . . . pearls with basic black . . . before you leave for the evening always take off one piece of jewelry. That's why I don't wear my earring anymore.

"But with D.J., more is better. Overstuffed sofas, lots of knicknacks. If I didn't know better, I'd swear he made money on every stick of furniture he put in his design."

Marilyn's eyes misted. "But the elegance, the style, the ambience . . . " her voice trailed wistfully. "Remember the Christmas that he decorated the Grosse Pointe Yacht Club . . . ?"

I rolled my eyes. "Sure do," I answered. "Flowers everywhere. On the steps, in the halls, on the tables, on the bars, in the johns. I hear he even had poinsettias in the showers in the locker room. I kept looking for some place to sign the condolences book and make out a mass card.

"I wish Dennis and Trudy a lot of luck. But if that's the look they like, they could save a bundle if they hired O'Neil Swanson or Charley Verheyden to do the Manoog."

Watermelon and hookers

May 11, 1994

Freddie Guinyard's obit was so-o-o-o sterile when he died recently at 79.

He had this collection of Joe Louis memorabilia, it said. And he worked for a travel agency and he went to church.

Not a word, mind you, about hookers and blind pigs, bribing cops or scalping tickets to any event you could name.

Or, for that matter, no mention of numbers guys counting betting slips on one floor while lawyers, judges, doctors and politicians – hey, a couple of mayors, a few sports writers and even the odd police commissioner – were drinking illegal hooch in the kitchen and frolicking in the boudoirs of Freddie's sedate old brownstone on Orchestra Place.

Freddie was a hustler. Nothing wrong with that. He also was one of the kindest, gentlest human beings I ever had the privilege to know.

He grew up in Black Bottom, Detroit's Harlem of the '30s, and he was a teen-ager when another neighborhood kid, a strong young boxer named Joe Louis Barrow, was starting his career in the ring.

Freddie hooked up with Louis and the Brown Bomber's first manager, Detroit numbers impresario John Roxborough, and he traveled for years with the heavyweight champion as Louis' "private secretary."

"Roxborough liked me," Freddie once told me winking, "because I could read and write."

Guinyard had many other talents, among them the gift of discretion. After Louis quit the ring, Freddie opened the blind pig with ladies of the evening on Orchestra Place near John R. It was a classic.

You didn't need to mess with the ladies. In fact, you seldom even saw them. He never sold booze, but he kept a well-stocked cupboard and friends and guests were welcome to go to the kitchen and help themselves.

In the summer Freddie kept watermelon in the fridge because Sam Greene, The News' veteran baseball writer (and father of columnist Edgar "Doc" Greene) would drop in from time to time and Sam liked it, with straight Jack Daniel's for a chaser.

Freddie was open all night after the legal bars closed and he had very few rules, but those he had, he enforced.

No matter how well-known or important you were, you had to call before you came over. His number was in the telephone book, but he also handed out business cards which bore his name, number and self-styled job description: "Freddie Guinyard. Light and Heavy Hauling."

Freddie wasn't worried about the cops raiding. It was guests meeting guests. The precinct cops and vice squad from downtown were leery of dropping in unannounced for fear they might encounter a judge or politician.

I hesitate to drop names here, but I once accompanied the late Detroit Mayor Jerry Cavanagh and his Police Commissioner, Ray Girardin, on a nocturnal soiree which ended with a pit-stop at Freddie's.

Ah, memories. I saw my first baseball game on color TV in Freddie's living room. And my daughter, Patti, then a skinny 8-year-old, fell asleep on Freddie's lap on the plane ride back from Miami the day after Muhammad Ali won the heavyweight title from Sonny Liston in 1964.

"Mr. Guinyard is such a nice man," she said. "What kind of business is he in?"

Freddie was the last of the old guard when he died April 28. Roxborough died in 1975 and Joe Louis in 1981. Ted Talbert is planning a party to mark Louis' birth anniversary, with a cake and all, in the Louis memorial room at Cobo Center Friday from noon to 5 p.m.

If Freddie was alive, he'd be there.

Goodbye to Carmen and Morgen

June 8, 1994

Some time this week I have to go pick up the dogs.

Well, not exactly the dogs. Their ashes. From the crematorium.

Now don't go getting all sentimental on me. Please don't.

I don't think I can stand it. I mean, it's been several days since I had the unpleasant task of having them . . . how do you say it gently? Put down? Put to sleep?

Hey, death happens to all of us, sooner or later. With Carmen and Morgen, it happened later than most pets and I guess we can be grateful for that much.

But it doesn't mean that it's not a tough decision.

These two were indeed a couple of characters. Not that they chose to be, mind you. They just happened to share a household with a breadwinner who is a hopeless hack and who, when all else fails and he can't find a column idea, exploits his personal life in the newspaper.

The two pups took on a life of their own from the beginning 17 years ago. And since they were introduced in these pages, and their youthful exploits were chronicled here, I figured they deserve a decent obituary.

Marilyn and I were newly married, lo, those many years ago when we decided to get a dog. I hadn't had one since I was in the eighth grade, and it died the first year.

I decided on a Schnauzer and I was going to call it Morgen, which is German for "morning."

Well, we fooled around for a couple of weeks and one day the lady who came every Tuesday to clean the house told Marilyn that her dog had had a litter and there were two puppies left, a male and a female, but nobody seemed to want them. We could have our choice.

Long story short, we took them both.

They were not purebred Schnauzers. They were cockapoos – well, sort of. But they were free.

Now, to go from no dogs whatsoever to two at a time is a major transition.

I, of course, took charge of the situation with a firm hand, shouting commands like "heel!" and "stay!", which largely went ignored by the two puppies.

Carmen (she was named by Marilyn) sensed I was a phony, so she did what she pleased most of the time and got away with it.

Morgen embarrassed me when I attempted to discipline him gently in front of company by rolling onto his back, sticking all four legs in the air and assuming a look which pleaded, "Please, master, don't beat me again!"

I mean, this was a male dog whose father was named "Trigger." What a wimp.

They had a good life. We flew them to Jupiter Island, Fla., when they were less than a year old and they stayed with us at Pierre Deziel's place, down the road from George Bush's mother. They went skiing at Shanty Creek, appeared on Channel 2 with Vic Caputo.

The years, naturally, took a toll. At the end, Carmen was deaf and blind and had trouble standing to eat. Morgen had a large tumor in his jaw and had lost weight steadily.

Finally, it fell to the tough guy in the family to take the last ride. The vet, bless him, said they never felt a thing.

Would we do it again? We already have.

He's six months old and he's got brown hair. His name tag says Brady, but I call him Mookie after Mookie Blaylock, the basketball player.

Time will tell if he can measure up to Carmen and Morgen. I'll let you know how it goes, but I've got a feeling that won't be a problem for the Mookmeister.

Kit Gingrich and the B-word

January 6, 1995

All the self-righteous blather about whether or not it was journalistically "ethical" for CBS-TV talking head Connie Chung to coax a crude remark out of Newt Gingrich's mother and then put it on national TV makes me laugh.

And as for the demand by the Republican Speaker of the U.S. House that CBS "apologize" for breeching 68-year-old Kit Gingrich's thinly guarded confidence, well, that makes me roar.

Let's face it. Newt Gingrich heads the most powerful wing of a political party that rose to power primarily on the hot air generated by literally hundreds of electronic media motor mouths whose generic message is, "Anything goes!"

The more outrageous the statements and claims, the bigger the ratings and the more rabble that are roused.

So Newt's mom whispers to Chung that her No. 1 son called First Lady Hillary Rodham Clinton a "bitch" and Chung uses the sound bite to promote her otherwise lackluster show? Big deal. These aren't some punk kids we're talking about here. They're consenting adults – and who knows what they're likely to utter, or even consent to, in public anymore?

Besides, you can see stuff worse than that scrawled on the restroom walls at the local junior high. The only difference is, it's liable to be spelled wrong.

Actually, Newton LeRoy Gingrich has a lot of nerve knocking anybody for using any juicy sound bite to rip the Clintons. This guy and his U.S. Senate counterpart, Strom Thurmond, both have lobbed their share of insults at the White House in recent weeks.

Unable to contain his euphoria after the GOP's November landslide, conservative-guru Gingrich accused President Clinton of being an "enemy of the people," called the First Lady a "Marxist" on one occasion and a "left-wing elitist" on another, and summed up the entire Democratic White House crowd as a bunch of "counterculture McGoverniks."

In some circles, those characterizations make "bitch" look pretty good by comparison.

Said his mother then, when asked for comment on Little Newty's Newtonisms: "He's not thinking when he says stuff " like that. "I mean, c'mon, Newt."

What was Mamma Kit thinking when Chung leaned over confidentially and said, "Why don't you just whisper it to me?" Hard to say. But if I had to guess, I'd venture that she really didn't give a hoot if the remark happened to be splashed all over Page One.

Likewise, Newt apparently didn't think twice about how his remarks would be interpreted early last month when he fired off some wild, unsubstantiated allegations that "25 percent" of Clinton's White House staff are "drug users" and that if Hillary Rodham Clinton really wanted to learn something about how to take care of welfare kids she ought to rent the 1930s movie, "Boys Town."

And Strom Thurmond? You want to talk about talking trash, get a load of this old codger. The ink was still wet on the newly signed GOP "Contract with America" when Thurmond suggested that Commander-in-Chief Clinton would be wise to bring a "bodyguard" if he came to visit any military bases in Thurmond's home state, South Carolina.

Neither Gingrich nor Thurmond, incidentally, ever apologized for their tacky verbal assaults.

Gingrich's alleged use of the B-word on HRC prompted predictable responses from activist women. One said that it typifies a general "anger and hatred" toward any successful female. Another characterized it as a defense mechanism used by men to "trivialize" women.

Intoned former State Sen. Debbie Stabenow, who has spent all of her adult life in politics, arguing that the term "bitch" embodies an insult unique to women: "There is no mean word like this that would be applied to any man in politics across the board."

That statement, of course, is nonsense. If you're really interested, Deb, I can give you a bunch of comparable insults for men that are one-size-fits-all.

New friends all the time

January 22, 1995

It is early morning and Mom is having breakfast in the community dining room with her customary group of friends and acquaintances.

There is Anna who is 97, the youngest of 13 children born to German parents in Cincinnati, who married an Irishman and outlived him by several years. Anna is nearly blind and I ask her if she can see me this day and she tells me I am just a shadow.

That fits.

There is Bill, whose real name is Charles Wilbur Something-or-other but he doesn't like Charles or Wilbur, so he prefers to be called Bill. One of his ears has a piece of the top sliced off cleanly.

He's explained what happened on a couple of occasions, but I think he tailors each story to amuse me. So I listen and we laugh.

Mary arrives a bit late. This day she is wearing those white plastic gloves that the aides use sometimes when they clean the tenants' rooms.

Mary is rail-thin, but erect and observant in her wheelchair. She grew up in Detroit, the daughter of a local judge whose name you wouldn't remember unless you're pushing 100. She went to a very proper Catholic girls' school, never married and worked at Hudson's back in the days when . . . well, when ladies wore white gloves.

She is served breakfast, but she insists that she "never eats breakfast." I have brought fresh coffee cake this day. And seedless grapes.

Mary insists also that she's never eaten grapes, but she accepts them graciously, with thanks, and breaks a piece off the slice of coffee cake and dips it daintily into her coffee cup.

Yvonne has missed her place at table but she doesn't seem to mind being seated elsewhere, away from her usual foursome. I ask if she wants a cup of coffee while she waits for her tray and she answers, "Sure." But then Yvonne tends to respond with "Sure" to everything you say to her.

Nice day, Yvonne. Sure. You feel OK? Sure. Want to go to China?

Sure.

Such an agreeable lady.

Gert, on the other hand, responds "Unh huh." She used to work at Tiger Stadium, probably back when it was Briggs Stadium – for all I know, perhaps when it was Navin Field. In a concession stand, I think. Selling hot dogs and beer.

I think she knows me, but when I tell her my name she only says, "Unh huh." This day, however, I walk past and toss her my usual "Hi, Gert" greeting and I swear she says, "Pete."

Maybe I'm hearing things. It happens, you know.

And then there is Isabelle, well-dressed, hair neatly arranged, sitting over by a window, staring out at the street below. Alone. Her breakfast tray remains covered and she is digging in her purse and she comes up with a crumpled $1 bill, which she straightens and lays flat on the table.

I take her some coffee cake, too, and I see she is crying quietly. I ask why she is not eating.

"I have no money to pay for my food," she answers. "I have no money to get home. All I have is this dollar." I smile and reassure her that there is no charge for the food, that it is included when her rent is paid, that this is where she lives.

Her eyes shift out the window, then back to me. "Is the street car still 8 cents?" she asks.

Ronald Reagan has Alzheimer's disease. I look around at all these warm, friendly faces and wonder how many remember who he is.

Memories of Howard Cosell

April 26, 1995

The first time I had anything to do with Howard Cosell, who died last Sunday in New York, I ended up trying to punch him.

But he was too fast for me and by the time I got close enough . . . and he saw that I was serious . . . he departed with a characteristic flourish, dismissing my anger like the ranting of a petulant child.

It was the early 1960s and the now departed Doc Greene was on one of his frequent, infamous toots and I had been dispatched by The News to Miami Beach to cover the heavyweight title fight between champion Sonny Liston and a brash young challenger named Cassius Marcellus Clay.

I'd been around boxing for quite a while, covering club fights and several of Floyd Patterson's and Liston's bouts, but I'd never had much to do with Howard – mostly by choice, because I thought he was a colossal pain in the tush.

So there I was early one evening, sitting in the press room of some tacky Miami Beach hotel trying to finish a pre-fight column so I could keep a dinner engagement. And from halfway across the room I hear this screeching voice shouting, "Where's that guy from Detroit? Where is he?!"

I look one way. Then I look the other way. And then I realize Cosell is talking about me, so I raise a hand and tell him I'll be with him in a minute.

"You'll be with me now!" Howard shouts. "You're brave enough to write that garbage about me, you should be brave enough to face me!"

Now you have to understand a couple of things here. No. 1, Howard is a Class A jerk. No. 2, I would never, ever write anything about Howard – good or bad – because Howard is a Class A jerk.

He's got me mixed up with somebody else, maybe Joe Falls, who was working for another Detroit paper at the time. And I tell him that, but he won't listen.

"Don't try to weasel out of it!" Cosell screams. "I know you knocked me in your paper! Be a man and . . ."

At that, I began hopping tables to get to the door where he was standing. Howard permitted me to make just enough of a fool of myself . . . and then he departed, leaving me protesting my innocence and looking like, well, a bigger jerk than he was.

In time a mutual friend named Jerry Izenberg brokered a sort of armed truce between us and while I got to know Cosell better, about all I could say for him was, he sure had chutzpah.

One evening, four or five years later, Izenberg invites me to dinner in New York City with him and Howard. We arrive at the restaurant without reservations and are told there's a long wait. Howard surveys the room and strolls over to a table for four where a man and woman are dining alone.

"Hi," he says pleasantly, "I'm Howard Cosell from ABC Sports!" Caught off guard, the man rises politely to shake Howard's hand.

"Listen," Howard says in his best stage whisper, "these dolts have screwed up our reservation and my friends and I don't have a table. Do you mind if we join you?"

Before the man can respond, Howard grabs a waiter and orders three more place-settings and three chairs. The maitre d' bustles over, but Howard dismisses him sternly and we spend the rest of the evening dining shoulder-to-shoulder with the strangers, who Cosell charms and amuses with a gaggle of far-fetched jock stories.

Howard paid the bill, of course. For himself and our "hosts." Izenberg and I tossed a coin for our tab.

Like him or not, they just don't make 'em like Howard any more. And, in retrospect, I'm not really convinced that the sports world is any better off.

What a railroad job

May 8, 1995

Permit me to voice support for some citizens who've been dumped on recently by the almighty, watchdog media and other guardians of the public conscience.

I'm referring here to Michigan Football Coach Gary Moeller, who made a fool of himself in a saloon and lost his job, and to the handful of loyal if somewhat misguided baseball fans who dared to defile the sanctum sanctorum of Tiger Stadium by making fools of themselves on TV on Opening Day and were punished mostly with hangovers.

Bum raps, most of them. One of my colleagues even went so far as to label the baseball exhibitionists "hooligans."

Hooligans? This guy needs to get out of the office more often.

Allow me to take up the cudgel (whatever that is) and attempt to defend these accused, jointly and severally as the lawyers say.

Gary Moeller. What a trashing . . . what a shame . . . what a waste.

What a railroad job.

This is a man who, if my personal knowledge serves me correctly and others who know him are telling the truth, is no garden variety bad drunk. So one night – during the off-season, mind you – he gets a snootfull in a place where they sell liquor to adults only and ends up in the local pokey.

And within days James Duderstadt, the ever-so-righteous University of Michigan president who thinks nothing about an aide spending federal grant money to buy first-class plane tickets to the Rose Bowl, gives Moeller the ziggy and erases 30 years of work.

What kind of world are we living in anyway? One strike and you're out? Guilty until proven innocent? C'mon.

I have known . . . hey, I have been with . . . football and basketball coaches from major Michigan college and professional teams who got blitzed and raised holy hell when they didn't have to show up for work the next day. Occasionally one got nailed and spent the night in the cooler.

But nobody ever broadcast their drunken ravings on local radio and TV or printed the transcripts on Page One. What makes that news? Geraldo? The National Enquirer?

This is hypocrisy in its lowest form.

If every jock . . . or every newspaper, TV or radio reporter or commentator . . . who got drunk and made a jackass out of himself lost his job as punishment, there wouldn't be enough steam grates for them to sleep on.

And, really, the Southfield cops taping Moeller says more about them than about him. They've had their share of problems in the past with citizen mistreatment complaints and law suit losses.

Just doing their job, right? Right.

Along that line, some have suggested that Moeller's 8-4 won-lost records the last two years somehow bore some of the blame for his problem. My, my. Eight losses in 24 games. If George Perles had a record like that he'd be president of Michigan State.

The hooligans? So what's the big deal? Nobody rioted, nobody turned over a car or set fire to anything.

So a bunch of nutsos got beered up and ran on the field. So the bleachers crowd bounced a few beach balls and tossed some stuff from the stands. Like, this is the first time that's happened ?

The way the Tigers have been playing they're lucky they don't have to wear titanium jocks. If anyone's at fault for the Opening Day fiasco (which the Tigers lost, incidentally, in an 11-1 snorer) it's the management for not anticipating some kind of protest demonstration.

Idiots climbing fences and running the bases are part of the game. In fact, after watching some of the TV clips I think the Tigers ought to sign up a couple of those guys. They show more enthusiasm than a lot of the players. And they work cheaper.

Pickpockets in Madrid

July 3, 1995

So I'm wandering around one of Madrid's major Underground intersections the other day, trying to decide which subway to take to which museum I want to visit, when I notice that a well-dressed man keeps turning up nearby each time I alter my course.

His shoes are shined and he's holding an expensive leather briefcase and I figure, hey, these Spanish dudes all look alike and it's probably my imagination.

To the subway regulars, I'm sure, I am your typical pot-bellied, elderly American tourist: Tan safari shorts, white socks, Reebok shoes, loud plaid button-down shirt, gray head topped with a baseball cap, bag slung over one shoulder carrying passport, plane ticket, cash, travelers checks, water bottle, Rolaids, chewing gum and assorted other goodies.

Alone, no less. Studying guidebooks, maps, trying to read the signs and get my bearings.

A subway train arrives with a screech and a hiss. It's half-full and as I step aboard, a bunch of keys and a small coin fall at my feet in the doorway. A man to my right is pointing down and shouting in Spanish.

Instinctively, I step back and get bumped from the left. I turn my head quickly and, when I'm distracted, the man to the right who's yelling goes for my bag.

It's the classic pickpocket move. The "bump" and "dip." The object is to score the mark fast, with the subway door open, grab the goodies and dive off the car as the doors close. Only one problem this time.

I elbow the "bump" to my left, catch him off balance and he stumbles. I jerk away from the "dip" and jump to the other side of the car, shouting a little Dee-troit trash about their mamas. And before the mugger who lost his balance can recover, the subway doors close and there we are, all three of us, locked in and heading for the next stop.

Back to the opposite wall, I search the faces of other passengers and realize no one's going to help me. My mind races. What happens now if they come at me with a weapon? No cops, nobody moves. The pair just stare at me and I realize that, like me, all they want is out.

A minute passes. Seems like an hour. The train's flying through the dark Underground tunnel. Things begin to focus. I take my eyes off the pair long enough to look to my far right.

Guess who? The dude with the shiny shoes and the briefcase. I glance at him, then at them. Bingo.

I point and I count. One, two, three. "You," I say, pointing to Mr. Briefcase, "you followed me, right? You sicked these two ——s on me."

Bright lights. We're at the next subway station. The door flies open and they're gone. Now Mr. Briefcase has a decision to make. Them, I could never pick out of a police lineup and they know it. Him, I can identify.

The door stays open. I stare at him. Just as the warning whistle sounds, Mr. Briefcase bolts and races off after his pals.

Mad? I am burning up. I had nothing to lose. My passport and spare cash are in the hotel safe, I've got $50 in pesetas in my right shoe, a few coins in my pocket and two credit cards in a money belt that is cinched around my ample midsection and tucked into my Jockey shorts.

Anybody who wants them, earns them.

Two days later I'm at the Sunday morning flea market and get almost the same scam. A teen-aged American woman spots the bumper, however, and shouts and pulls me against a wall but he and his pal co-conspirator get nothing. Ten minutes later I'm standing in the doorway of yet another subway – I swear I'm not making this up – when I feel a hand go into my (empty) left rear pocket.

This time it's a woman working with a guy who's on my right, waiting for me to react to her attempt so he can dip me from the other side. I whack her arm while I look him in the eye and he puts his hands in the air like Bill Laimbeer protesting his innocence to a referee. Not me!

I must look like the richest – or the dumbest – gringo in Madrid. We won't vote on which.

J.P. the high priest

August 18, 1995

J.P. That's all you ever have to say and people know exactly who you're talking about.

J.P. on JR in the A.M.

They can take down the signs but the message and the memories will linger for a long, long time. More than any other person, more than Dick Purtan, more than Billy Bonds, more than Ernie Harwell or even Martha Jean the Queen, Joseph Priestly McCarthy was the highest of the high priests of the media in Detroit.

This is a man who could talk to just about anybody . . . and they'd talk to him. Presidents, politicians, movie stars, tour golfers, pro quarterbacks, baseball, football, basketball, hockey, all the players, managers, owners and assorted shooters.

I never saw anything like him. He could have gone into a revolving door behind the Larry Kings and Rush Limbaughs of this world and come out in front of them.

He didn't have to use threats or gimmicks. He was never abusive or condescending. He didn't have to punch anybody or get drunk and make headlines. It always was a privilege to appear on his morning program on WJR-AM. An honor, in fact.

I was as stunned as the next person when I learned of his death Wednesday afternoon. And I had had several hours warning that his death was imminent.

Earlier in the day Hoot McInerney had called to tell me that McCarthy was in intensive care and near death in New York.

"It can come anytime," Hoot had said. "He's on a respirator and his lungs are filling up and it's affecting his kidneys. Say a prayer."

A respirator? Lungs failing? How can this be happening, I asked myself. The guy was working two weeks ago.

Sure, he'd been diagnosed with a rare blood disease. But it wasn't supposed to be something that would kill you right away.

A close friend of mine had been told that he had it, too, only two weeks before J.P.

"They tell me I can live for a long time as long as I take care of myself," that friend said. "I'll just get tired more easily and I've got to watch out that I don't injure myself or need an operation, because the loss of blood then could be fatal."

At dinner one evening last weekend I ran into yet another person who suffered the same illness as J.P.

"Great," Hoot said when I told him that. "Here's an illness that's supposed to affect one in a million and you know three of 'em."

McCarthy was the nearest thing to an icon you'll ever find in the Detroit media. I can't remember a broadcaster ever who could do commercials for rival automobile companies on the same stations, sometimes one after the other, and get away with it like J.P.

About the only medium he never mastered was television. Maybe it was the bulky frame, the rounded shoulders, the bad rug he wore for years and only in recent weeks had begun to go without.

Not that he didn't try on several occasions, with specials on WJBK-TV Channel 2. He just didn't have the same impact, I guess. Years in radio make you a voice with 10,000 faces.

Everyone had their own impression of what he should look like, and when they saw him back in those days, they were disenchanted.

He'll be laid out today at the A.J. Desmond and Sons Funeral Home in Troy and buried at 10 a.m. Saturday after Mass at St. Hugo of the Hills in Bloomfield Hills. The family has asked for relatives and personal friends only.

That covers a lot of territory.

"Funny," said Hoot, his voice cracking, "when I saw him earlier this week we made plans to go to a funeral for someone else this weekend. Now it's his."